OXFORD
UNIVERSITY PRESS

CAMBRIDGE
CHECKPOINT
AND BEYOND

Complete English for Cambridge Secondary 1

Jane Arredondo

ASPIRE
SUCCEED
PROGRESS

8

TEACHER PACK

Oxford excellence for Cambridge Secondary 1

OXFORD

OXFORD
UNIVERSITY PRESS

Great Clarendon Street, Oxford, OX2 6DP, United Kingdom

Oxford University Press is a department of the University of Oxford. It furthers the University's objective of excellence in research, scholarship, and education by publishing worldwide. Oxford is a registered trade mark of Oxford University Press in the UK and in certain other countries

British Library Cataloguing in Publication Data
Data available

978-0-19-836472-6

10 9 8 7 6 5 4

Paper used in the production of this book is a natural, recyclable product made from wood grown in sustainable forests. The manufacturing process conforms to the environmental regulations of the country of origin.

Printed in Great Britain by CPI Group (UK) Ltd., Croydon CR0 4YY

Acknowledgements
The publishers would like to thank the following for permissions to use their photographs:

Cover image: David Newton/Bridgeman Art.

Artwork by Six Red Marbles.

The author and publisher are grateful for permission to reprint from the following copyright material:

Bill Bryson: extract from *Neither Here nor There: Travels in Europe* (Secker & Warburg, 1991, copyright © Bill; Bryson 1991, reproduced by permission of The Random House Group Ltd.

Kevin Crossley-Holland: extract from *Beowulf*, illustrated by Charles Keeping (OUP, 2013), text copyright © Kevin Crossley-Holland 1982, reproduced by permission of Oxford University Press.

Robert Frost: 'The Road Not Taken' from *The Poetry of Robert Frost* Edited by Edward Connery Lathem (Cape, 1971), reproduced by permission of The Random House Group Ltd.

Neil Gaiman: extract from *Coraline* (Bloomsbury, 2007), copyright © Neil Gaiman 2007, reproduced by permission of Bloomsbury Publishing Plc.

Laurie Lee: extract from *As I walked out One Midsummer Morning* (Penguin, 1969), copyright © Laurie Lee 1969, reproduced by permission of Curtis Brown Book Group Ltd, London on behalf of The Estate of Laurie Lee.

Tom Paulin: 'Thistles' from *The Secret Life of Poems; A Poetry Primer* (Faber, 2001), copyright © Tom Paulin 2001, reproduced by permission of Faber & Faber Ltd and Faith Evans Associates on behalf of the author.

Sylvia Plath: 'Mushrooms' from *The Colossus and Other Poems* (Faber, 1967), copyright © Sylvia Plath 1957, 1958, 1959, 1960, 1961, 1962 and 1967, reproduced by permission of the publishers, Faber & Faber Ltd and Alfred A Knopf an imprint of the Knopf Doubleday Publishing Group, a division of Penguin Random House LLC. All rights reserved

Gary Provost: extract from *100 ways to improve your writing* (New American Library, 1985) and on www.garyprovost.com, reproduced by permission of Gail Provost Stockwell.

Wallace Stevens: 'The Snow Man', copyright © Wallace Stevens 1921, first published in *Poetry Magazine*, from *The Collected Poems of Wallace Stevens* (Knopf, 1954/Faber, 2006), copyright © Wallace Stevens 1954, © renewed 1982 by Holly Stevens, reproduced by permission of the publishers, Faber & Faber Ltd and Alfred A Knopf, an imprint of the Knopf Doubleday Publishing Group, a division of Penguin Random House LLC. All rights reserved.

Telegraph: extract from 'How much sugar is in your soft drinks', *The Guardian Food*, 1 May 2015, copyright © Telegraph Media Group 2015, reproduced by permission of TMG Ltd.

J R R Tolkien: extract from *The Hobbit* (HarperCollins, 2012), copyright © The J R R Tolkien Estate Ltd 1937, 1965, reproduced by permission of HarperCollins Publishers Ltd.

Leonard Woolf: extract from *A Village in the Jungle* (Dufour Editions, 2005), first published 1913, reproduced by permission of The University of Sussex and The Society of Authors as the Representative of the Estate of Leonard Woolf.

Contents

Supplementary teaching material can be accessed at www.oxfordsecondary.com/checkpoint-english-resources

Introduction

Oxford's **Complete English for Cambridge Secondary 1** is an enquiry-based course designed to develop students' skills and confidence in English. Recognising the multilingual and multicultural nature of today's world, the approach supports your students in becoming life-long learners who are agile, independent, 21st century thinkers.

Carefully aligned to the latest *Cambridge Secondary 1 English curriculum framework*, you can be assured that Oxford's *Complete English for Cambridge Secondary 1* is meeting your students' learning goals. Arranged under engaging themes, each of the nine units covers topics and skills that facilitate learning across the curriculum as well as providing a firm foundation in preparation for IGCSE® First or Second Language English courses of study.

Student Book and Workbook

The guiding principles for *Student Book 8* and *Workbook 8* are creativity and engagement. Units, which do not have to be followed in a linear fashion, are designed to be accessible to students in any culture and to promote cross-cultural understanding. The course as a whole aims to increase students' awareness and competency in all aspects of English. Students are encouraged to:

- explore the content of texts from or set in countries around the world
- create different types of writing, including poetry and play scripts
- collaborate on grammar tasks and in speaking and listening activities
- engage with new concepts and the writer's craft
- develop evaluation and reflective skills.

All units facilitate Cambridge Secondary 1 Checkpoint learning objectives, building on the Cambridge Primary English curriculum framework and Stage 7. The central learning objectives for each unit are provided at the beginning of each unit in the teacher book. Please note that learning objectives may only be partially covered within a particular unit, with other aspects of the objective covered elsewhere. Some objectives may therefore appear in more than one unit. This holistic approach ensures that, through the nine units of the Student Book, Workbook and Teacher Pack, the curriculum framework is covered fully in an engaging and logical way. Each unit ends with an entertaining but purposeful quiz and an opportunity for students to reflect on their own learning and development in English.

The Workbook is designed as a stand-alone component. As a write-in resource it is connected to but not dependent upon having a copy of the Student Book in hand. The Workbook is ideal for consolidation and extension of concepts and skills that have been covered in a class session using the Student Book.

 Reading

Each unit opens with a 'Thinking time' session in which students examine new ideas and are encouraged to begin exploring the theme of the unit. This leads on to readings from modern and pre-twentieth century non-fiction, media texts, news articles and genre fiction. Reading extracts are accompanied by Word cloud and Glossary boxes. Word clouds can be used to introduce students to new vocabulary, to explore meanings and usage in context. Words that appear in the Word cloud are sometimes a semantic group, sometimes a word-class group, depending upon the extract. Word builder exercises allow students to familiarise themselves with, and utilise, the words in the Word cloud.

Glossary features are also present with some extracts, to help students with words or phrases that may not be found easily in a dictionary because they are uncommon, colloquial, or technical phrases. With the help of the Word builder feature and 'Developing your language' tasks, the writer's craft can be discussed and practised. Within a clearly labelled 'Understanding' section, comprehension skills are consolidated with tasks requiring students to demonstrate their understanding of explicit and implicit meaning and lead from information retrieval to generating new material.

Writing

Students practise writing for different purposes linked to the texts they have read. Stage 8 includes: creating an information leaflet on eating healthily, writing a speech on artificial intelligence, writing a report for a school magazine and an article for a newspaper, writing a story about a superhero. Each task requires students to structure and organise their ideas coherently, using a range of sentences and presentations for particular effects.

All writing tasks are carefully structured, offering step-by-step guidance so that students effectively plan and organise their ideas coherently, using a range of sentence structures and punctuation to create particular effects. Each unit also contains essential grammar and spelling practice to improve technical accuracy.

Speaking and listening

Stage 8 speaking and listening tasks include collaborating on creative tasks such as interviews, giving and listening to short talks, promoting a charity, discussing topical issues to improve active listening and oral skills for debates and presentations at a later stage in students' school careers. Group and pair work tasks enable students to explore complex ideas and feelings in a safe environment, and develop confidence in giving perceptive responses that show an awareness of another person's viewpoint. Activities incorporate a fun element, but there is a serious purpose behind what students are asked to do; it is invaluable preparation for oral assessments in both First and Second Language English exams, and later for group and team work at pre-university level. Being able to conduct a discussion, draw together ideas and promote effective sharing of those ideas is a key life skill.

Formative and summative assessment

Throughout the units, students' work is assessed through teacher, peer assessment and/or self-assessment, with the objective of improving specific competencies and self-confidence. Workbook 8 enables students to practise and expand on what they are doing in lessons individually for homework. Answers and suggested answers can be found within the lesson notes for each unit in this book.

Teacher Pack CD

Here you will find:

- Transcripts of listening tasks as printable word documents
- Audio files for each of the listening tasks shown with this  symbol in the Student Book
- Photocopiable resources

Complete English for Cambridge Secondary 1 offers teachers and students trusted and experienced authors who have crafted an English programme in line with the goals of Cambridge International Examinations whose desire is to develop learners who are:

- Confident
- Innovative
- Responsible
- Engaged.
- Reflective

Acknowledging and celebrating the multilingual classroom, this course supports and stretches both monolingual and bilingual students in their English learning.

Foodies' delight

Learning objectives

In this unit students will:

- Give short presentations and answer questions, maintaining effective organisation of talk. **Pages 2–3** *8SL1*

- Use a range of reading strategies to find relevant information and main points in texts, distinguishing between fact and opinion where appropriate. **Pages 4–5** *8Rx2*

- Explore the range, variety and overall effect of literary, rhetorical and grammatical features used by poets and writers of literary and non-literary texts, considering informal or formal style as well as the choice of words to create character. **Pages 4–5** *8Rw2*

- Demonstrate controlled use of a variety of simple and complex sentences to achieve purpose and contribute to overall effect. **Pages 6–7** *8Wp2*

- Demonstrate understanding of the effects created by features of diaries, magazines and newspaper reports. **Pages 8–9** *8Rv4*

- Demonstrate understanding of the main features of text structure of each genre and text type studied. **Pages 8–9** *8Rv2*

- Spell most words correctly, including some complex polysyllabic words and unfamiliar words. **Pages 10–11** *8Ws1*

- Learn the spelling of difficult and commonly misspelled words and develop strategies for correcting spelling. **Pages 10–11** *8Ws2*

- Adapt speech, non-verbal gesture and movement to meet an increasing range of demands. **Pages 12–13** *8SL2*

- Engage with more demanding material through perceptive responses to other students' talk, showing awareness of the speaker's aims and extended meanings. **Pages 12–13** *8SL5*

- Identify the most appropriate approach to planning their writing in order to explore, connect and shape ideas. **Pages 14–15** *8Wa1*

Setting the scene

The opening of this unit can be used as a way to explore diverse cultural preferences in eating habits and provide students with vocabulary for constructive criticism. Encourage students from different ethnic backgrounds to talk about typical snacks. Go on to compare and contrast the consumption of snacks in your classroom.

As you conduct the class discussion, ask individuals to expand on what they are saying and clarify their points. Use phrases such as 'can you be more precise?' or 'tell us more about…'. Explain to students how these phrases can be used in discussions and when commenting on each other's speaking skills.

Setting the scene

Foodies' delight

Taking about 5–10 minutes, draw out students' views and prior experience in an informal way. Ask students if they have:

- explored ways to encourage young people to eat healthily

- collaborated to devise an advertisement

- created an information sheet about healthy eating

- considered whether a wide choice of products is good or bad for us

- reflected on what makes a certain meal or snack their 'favourite food'.

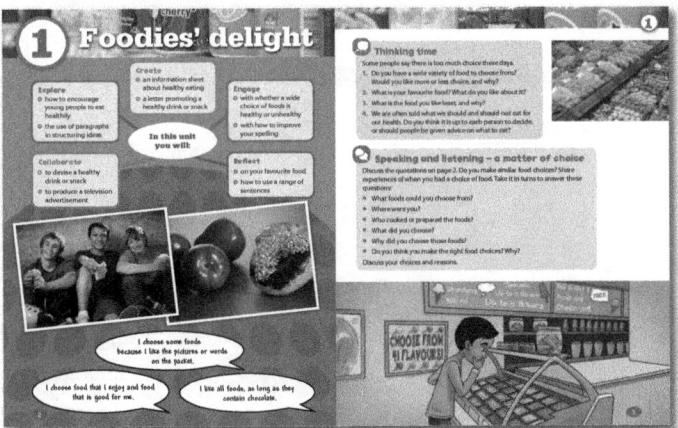

Extension

Communicating effectively

A follow-up activity could be a recorded pair-work 'food history' interview. Students need to think about what they ate as young children and *why* and *how* their tastes have changed. Students then listen to the recording to see how well they explained their thoughts, and whether a listener could appreciate their point of view and preferences adequately.

Extension

Chocolate enquiry

Give students the quotation 'I like all foods as long as they contain chocolate'. Ask them to find out about the history of chocolate. This activity can be adapted, with Activity 1 providing stretch, while Activity 2 is for students who would benefit from improving their use of vocabulary.

1. Stretching students

This can be a small group or pair work activity. Ask students to prepare a chocolate fact booklet for the class. It should include:

The origin of chocolate
Its introduction to Europe and North America
Who grows cacao beans
Different types of chocolate
Data on chocolate consumption in your country

Note: There are numerous sites and articles about chocolate for adults on the Internet; many 'useful facts for kids' sites are specifically for the USA. Students can do a search on their own, but direct them also to information on: http://www.thestoryofchocolate.com

2. Supporting students

This is a pair work activity. Ask students to each find ten facts about chocolate and write them down on a sheet of paper. They should then cut the sheet into ten 'fact slips' and pass them to a partner. Each partner chooses how to order their facts and writes them in continuous writing of between 100–200 words. A suitable order may be chronological or grouped by type of fact, e.g. geographical or statistical. When they have finished, partners show their writing to the original 'fact finders', who check what they have written as a peer-marking exercise.

Reflection

Thinking time

If you have a fairly big class, discuss question 1 with the whole group, then assign questions 2 and 3 to pairs. Arrange pairs into groups of 4 and set a time limit for question 4. Each group should have a leader who reports back to the class.

Assign 'group leader' roles to as many students as possible for Speaking and listening tasks.

Speaking and listening

💬 A matter of choice

Begin by asking the whole class for examples of foods bought because of the packaging. Then ask how much of what we eat is actually good for us. Students could write down their favourite foods and tick those that are healthy. Direct students to the quotations and ask them to talk in pairs or small groups about how and why we try new foods: on the basis of what we have been told about taste; on appearance (wrapping); or on what advertising tells us?

Students then take turns answering the questions in this section of the Student Book. Set a time limit. Students then come together in larger groups to explain their choices and reasons. Listeners may interrogate each speaker's reasons, as in a debate. Remind students to listen attentively and demonstrate they are responding to what someone has said.

Workbook

🧩 My life on a plate – Food interviews

Each of the options asks students to consider food choices and changes of taste or preferences.

A blog about food choices

Prior knowledge

Before you start the reading, ask students to predict how many different types of cereal there are in their local supermarket. If students are not familiar with shopping for food, ask them to guess how many types of chocolate or soft drinks are available in a nearby shop.

In preparation for the reading and subsequent work on making choices, ask students to work in small groups and discuss the names of all the cereals and biscuits they can think of. They should then look at the names of the products and decide how many are a means of describing the product itself, such as 'Crunchie'. Discuss how product names can also act as an advertisement, such as 'Bliss' or 'Raspberry Delight'. A fun activity here is for groups to invent a new product with an appealing name then design eye-catching packaging.

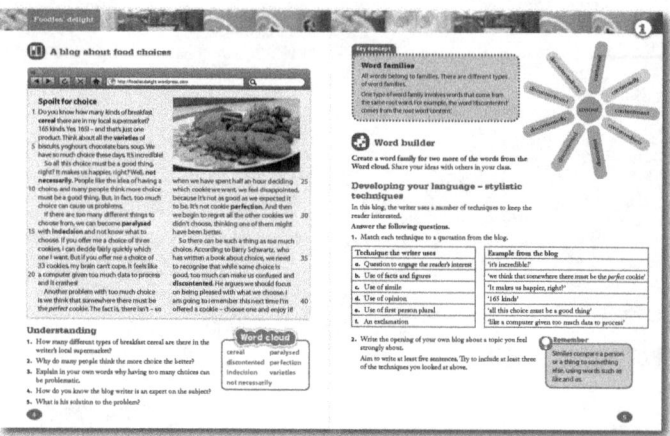

Reading

 ## Spoilt for choice

This reading relates to *choice* more than food itself. For background information on Barry Schwartz's book about choice see: http://www.ted.com/talks/barry_schwartz_on_the_paradox_of_choice/transcript

Schwartz states, 'The secret to happiness is low expectations': the more choice we are offered, the more likely we are going to be disappointed with the choice we make because we are thinking about how something else might have been better.

As this may be challenging for some students take a few minutes to analyse its form and content before they start on the 'Understanding' questions. Ask them to work in pairs and do a brief **'wh–'** analysis. They should try to identify:

What it is about (varieties of food or choice); **who** they think it is written for (target audience); and **where** (the text includes the word 'we', who are 'we'?).

Option 1 of the extension activities stretches students while other students can be asked to write a first-person account of being faced with too many choices in a shop, or when choosing which new mobile phone they would like. Suggest the title 'Which one to choose' and ask students to write 200 words for a blog post aimed at readers of their age.

Student-book answers

Understanding

1. 165

2. People like choice. They think it makes them happier; enables them to find the 'perfect' product (cookie).

3. Students use their own words to say why too many choices can be problematic.

4. He quotes from Barry Schwartz's book on choice.

5. Focus on being pleased with what you have got.

Vocabulary

Model a word family from the Word cloud on the board and direct students' attention to the explanation of root words and words for being 'contented' on page 5 of the Student Book. If you have a largely bilingual group, spend a few moments trying to find direct translations for 'happy' and 'content', and examine the subtle differences.

When taking feedback on this activity, you could add an on-the-spot word field activity to increase and consolidate vocabulary. The objective is to find alternatives to two over-used words: 'sweet' and 'nice'. Ask the class to think of their favourite sweet product (this can include cakes and pastries). They should jot down adjectives to describe the product and the sensation of eating it without using the words 'sweet' or 'nice'.

Finding alternatives for 'sweet' is challenging, but there are many ways to say 'nice'. Offer 'sugary' and 'delicious' as examples. Two students write the adjectives in separate columns on the board. Finish when the class runs out of suggestions. Students can then check their suggestions in a thesaurus. Alternatively, start with the thesaurus then ask for additional adjectives.

The class now works individually with dictionaries to create a word family for two more of the words from the Word cloud. They can then compare their choices in pairs or small groups. If students are unsure about how to start, set them all the same word: 'perfection'.

Stylistic techniques

1. Examples from the blog, matched to technique:
   a. 'It makes us happier, right?'
   b. '165 kinds'
   c. 'like a computer given too much data to process'
   d. 'all this choice must be a good thing'
   e. 'we think that somewhere there must be the *perfect* cookie'
   f. 'it's incredible!'

2. Before students begin this short writing task, clarify with the whole class the form and purpose of a blog post such as this, and why people write them. Students are asked to write an opening on a topic about which they feel strongly. Depending on the size and nature of your class, discuss briefly the following suggestions:
   - Having lots of choice is excellent.
   - School food needs to be improved.
   - What makes me *really* happy.

Alternatively, ask students to work in pairs at the brainstorming ideas stage, but to do the writing individually. When marking, check to see that students have completed at least five sentences and used some or all of the stylistic techniques on page 5 of the Student Book.

Word families

1. Words from root word 'happy' include: happily, happiness, unhappy, unhappiness.

2. From the same word class as 'happy': happier, happiest, unhappier, unhappiest.

3. Synonyms for 'happy': content, cheerful, joyful, jolly, delighted, ecstatic, merry, smiling. Accept synonyms that also relate to happy as in 'happy to do something': pleased, glad, and so on.

Option 1: Stretching more able students

Select sentences and paragraphs from the transcript below on buying jeans (some editing may be necessary) and ask students to read them: http://www.ted.com/talks/ barry_schwartz_ on_the_paradox_of_choice/ transcript. Then ask them to write a script for a radio talk on the choices involved when buying another product they use on a regular basis or would like to own, such as a racing or mountain bike, a mobile phone or trainers, a snowboard or skis. Instruct students to address quality and value for money, as well as the name-brand kudos factor. This extension activity could be carried out in pairs and completed as a whole class listening activity.

Option 2: Similes and clichés

The accompanying CD contains photocopiable material for this unit on the subject of similes and clichés, and can be used to help students improve their vocabulary. Non-native English speakers may find it particularly useful as it increases language awareness.

Sentences and sentence punctuation

Prior knowledge

Before starting the activities on this page, read the explanation of simple, complex, and compound sentences with the class.

Ask students for examples of when they have done some or all of this sentence grammar before, then reactivate dormant knowledge by modelling examples on the board. Be sure to explain that a complex sentence may have only two clauses, but one will be subordinate, so they do not assume all two-clause sentences are compound sentences.

If your students are less familiar with sentence grammar, ask them to copy and label your examples, then write one of their own beneath each. Students should attempt to complete the exercise on page 6 of the Student Book on their own. When they have finished, they may compare their answers with partners and make adjustments before handing work in to be checked for accuracy.

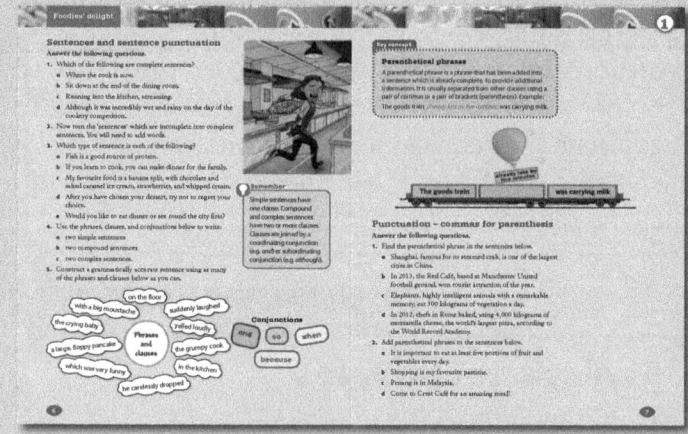

Grammar

Sentences and sentence punctuation

1. 'b Sit down at the end of the dining room.'

2. Students turn unfinished phrases into complete sentences by adding words.

3. a. Simple
    b. Complex (conditional with a main clause and a subordinate clause)
    c. Simple (it is a long sentence but there is only one clause)
    d. Complex
    e. Compound

4. The following are suggested answers. Accept alternatives that use the phrases, clauses, and conjunctions appropriately.

a. i.   The crying baby suddenly laughed.
    ii. The grumpy cook yelled loudly.

b. i.   He carelessly dropped a large, floppy pancake and yelled loudly.
    ii. The grumpy cook yelled loudly and the crying baby suddenly laughed.

c. i.   The grumpy cook yelled loudly and the crying baby suddenly laughed, which was very funny.
    ii. When he carelessly dropped a large, floppy pancake on the floor and yelled loudly the crying baby suddenly laughed, which was very funny.

5. Students' own answers. Suggested example answer: The grumpy cook with a big moustache yelled loudly (when/because) he carelessly dropped a large, floppy pancake on the floor in the kitchen and the crying baby suddenly laughed, which was very funny.

Grammar

Commas for parenthesis

Before completing this exercise, draw students' attention to the Key concept feature about parenthetical phrases, on page 7.

1. a. ,famous for its steamed crab,
    b. ,based at Manchester United football ground,
    c. ,highly intelligent animals with a remarkable memory,
    d. ,using 4,000 kilograms of mozzarella cheese,

2. Suggested parenthetical phrases below. Accept logical alternatives.

    a. It is important to eat at least five portions of fruit and vegetables, preferably freshly bought, every day.
    b. Shopping, which I do every weekend, is my favourite pastime.

c. Penang, a place I have always wanted to visit, is in Malaysia.

d. Come to Crest Café, famous for its syrup pancakes, for an amazing meal!

Workbook

The expanding and shrinking sentence!

To practise identifying and using parenthetical phrases, set the following Workbook task as homework or a silent classroom activity. Students may peer mark subsequently, but it is advisable to check students' answers before moving on.

Suggested answers (accept logical alternatives):

1. a. The *elderly* man, *wearing a green woolly hat*, walked down the street *and stopped at a scruffy yellow door*.

   b. The door opened slowly *and he saw his sister for the first time in thirty years; she had a large parrot on her shoulder*.

   c. The parrot, *which was bright blue and green*, flew away *and his sister screamed loudly at him to catch it*.

2. Suggested answers below; accept logical alternatives. If students repeat the pronoun 'they' more than once in **a.**, ask them how rephrasing these sentences would improve the paragraph. In **b.**, ask students which words they need to change or cut out to avoid repetition.

   a. The children were being chased along the beach by their friend. They ran till they could run no more. They decided to go into the woods. They ran very fast then they hid and waited until it got dark.

   b. Put the butter and sugar into a bowl. Stir well until it's fully mixed. Add the eggs a bit at a time. Beat well and when it's really smooth, stir in the flour until it is all mixed together.

Writing a recipe – using simple sentences and adverbs

A good way to help students who are struggling to understand sentence grammar and/or parts of speech, is to ask them to write out a recipe. Show them a sample recipe and ask them to copy the format, with a list of ingredients followed by the method of preparation and cooking instructions.

When they come to write the method stage, remind them how to construct a simple sentence using one verb only, such as: 'Stir in the flour.' Ask them to use only simple and compound sentences in the method stage, but to include adverbs for *when* and *how*.

As they write, students can identify how we use adverbs of time and manner (when and how) in instructions. For example, 'Before you start'; 'next, beat the eggs'; 'stir in eggs slowly'; 'after it comes to the boil'; 'fry rapidly'.

When students have finished writing out their recipes, ask them to colour all verbs in blue and all adverbs in green. Explain how an adverb describes a verb, so blue (for verbs) mixed with yellow (for adjectives) makes green.

For best results, try to do this activity using real food in the classroom. It could be double-decker sandwiches, or a mixed salad with dressing. *Acting on words*, and identifying how and why we use certain constructions in the process, is much more meaningful for students who struggle with visual aspects of language learning. Tactile or kinaesthetic learners benefit greatly from 'doing and learning'.

An alternative way to demonstrate recipes is to act them out as a television food programme using imaginary ingredients. This can be an individual, pair or small group activity. Ask students to create a running order to show what needs to be done and when, such as mixing the ingredients or putting the food in the oven. Explain programmes of this nature need to be timed exactly and each person needs to know precisely what to say and when. Set a time limit (maximum ten minutes). If possible, show an extract from a popular food programme as an example. Ask students to video theirs so they can discuss their performances as a class or in groups. Individuals should make notes on how clearly they speak and what they can improve. Students should offer constructive criticism to peers.

Are children consuming too much sugar?

Prior knowledge

Ask students if they have ever considered how much sugar they consume in an average day. According to an article in *The Telegraph*, 'How much sugar is in your soft drinks?' (Telegraph Food, 1 May 2015), 'Research last year found that **many smoothies and juices aimed at children contained up to seven teaspoons of sugar** per 200ml, which is one teaspoon more than full fat Coke.' See: http://www.telegraph.co.uk/foodanddrink/foodanddrinknews/11576198/How-much-sugar-is-in-your-soft-drinks.html

This topic may have been covered in Biology or a tutor group session, so before the class starts reading, ask them to predict the content of the article. Do they expect to see a warning, and if so, why? You could then direct them to the Word cloud and ask them what tone the words suggest the article might take if it includes: *concerned, frightening, poison, staggering, threats,* and *worse*.

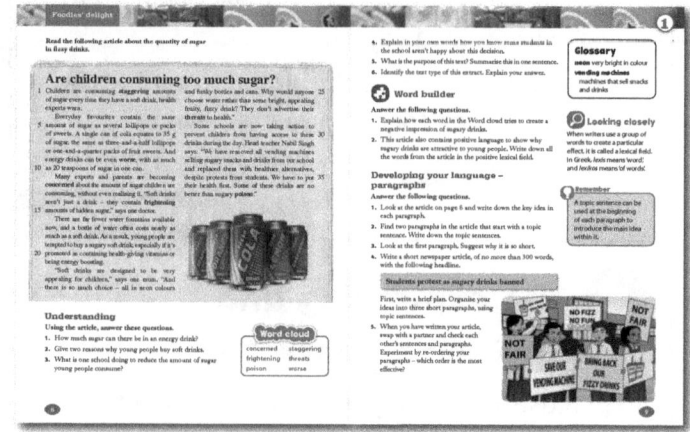

Student-book answers

📖 Understanding

1. 35 g of sugar.
2. Attractive 'funky' bottles and packaging; water is nearly as expensive.
3. Removed vending machines and replaced snacks and drinks with healthier alternatives.
4. Students reword 'despite protests' – accept alternatives such as 'even though students complained', or 'ignoring students' complaints/objections'.
5. The article warns against sugar content in soft drinks.
6. Non-fiction/informative and objective/discursive/neutral register.

Word builder

1. Students should explain how each word in the Word cloud creates a negative impression.
2. Positive lexical field: *health-giving vitamins, energy boosting, bright, appealing, funky.*

Extension

Writing a blog article – 'Sugary poison'

Ask students to write a blog article for teenagers, suggesting ways to reduce sugar in their daily diet. Their articles should include how and why they currently consume too much sugar and suggest ways to reduce sugar intake with appealing alternatives. Remind students to consider carefully their choice of words and lexical field(s). They should make a list of key words to be included and write out their topic sentences for each paragraph before starting.

Students doing this on the computer can include diagrams and/or illustrations and photographs. Remind the class they will need to say where images come from and cite references if they use data or wording from web pages. Take this into consideration when marking the students' work (form and content), and give constructive feedback on use of English and technical accuracy. This writing activity is useful preparation for coursework later in their school careers.

Speaking and listening

Should there be a law against advertising sweets?

In many countries it is now illegal to advertise tobacco on television. Propose to your class that the advertising of sweets and chocolates should also be prohibited. Organise students into groups of 5–8. Each member of the group takes one of the roles below. Name one person in each group to act as leader. Set a time limit. Take feedback from group leaders then take a vote.

Sweet manufacturer

An advertising and marketing professional (from an advertising agency)

A parent   A child

A television programme maker (who needs the income from advertising)

An illustrator looking for a job in advertising

A doctor   A dentist

Paragraphs

1. Key ideas in each paragraph:
   - Paragraph 1: This is technically not a paragraph, but accept 'health experts warn (about staggering amounts of sugar)'.
   - Paragraph 2: 'Everyday favourites contain the same amount of sugar as...'
   - Paragraph 3: 'Many experts and parents are becoming concerned'.
   - Paragraph 4: 'fewer water fountains'/'bottle of water often costs...'
   - Paragraph 5: "Soft drinks are designed to be very appealing..."
   - Paragraph 6: 'Some schools are now taking action...'

2. Paragraph 3: 'Many experts and parents are becoming concerned', and paragraph 5: 'Soft drinks are designed to be very appealing…'

3. Paragraph 1 summarises content and acts as a subheading. It is eye-catching and designed to shock or grab readers' attention.

4. Students may work in pairs to create ideas for the content of their articles, but they should write them out individually. Remind them that media articles: require short paragraphs; incorporate 'witness statements' and/or quote experts; use an appropriate vocabulary for the target reader; and manipulate data. Articles should be a maximum of 300 words. You may allow your class to read sample articles on related topics such as sugar and snacks in online news media, to get a better idea of layout.

5. Students read and edit each other's work, but you as the teacher should mark their writing for both form and content, making suggestions where they need to improve.

When you hand back the articles, ask students to underline their topic sentences. They should then copy out part or all of these topic sentences in a list. From this list they should be able to see how they constructed their essay and how a good essay plan leads to topic sentences.

Lexical fields

Set this page for homework, or ask students to work on their own to develop their thinking skills and take more responsibility for their learning.

1. Are you bored with breakfast? Are you looking for <u>something new</u> to <u>tingle your taste buds</u>? Well, look no further – Raspberry Whiz Crunch is here! It's a <u>brand new</u> cereal made from <u>delicious toasted whole-wheat</u> grain, <u>crunchy clusters</u> of oats and <u>luscious</u> raspberry yoghurt flavoured nuggets. Made from <u>pure organic</u> grain, with <u>real juicy</u> raspberries, this cereal <u>tastes good and does you good</u> too! Look out for this <u>scrumptious</u> new way to start your day – on supermarket shelves now!

2. a. Suggested answer includes: *comfortable, safe, economical, easy to get into/out of, practical, assisted steering*, and so on.

   b. Suggested answer includes: *menace, threat, danger, precaution*, and so on.

   c. Suggested answer includes: *attentive, serious approach, collaborates with peers, willing to make suggestions, good presentation skills*, and so on.

Lexical fields in news media texts

For homework, ask students to choose either print media or radio broadcast news, and select one short item on a current health or welfare issue, such as the sugar article in this unit. They should copy the article or record the news item and write down the lexical field that gives the item its tone, bias, or point of view. Remind them to cite their sources. They should then bring the news item to class. Working in small groups, students take turns to show or play their news item and their peers identify the lexical fields.

More spelling 'rules'

Prior knowledge

Invite students to say words they can never spell properly and write them on the board correctly. Leave them visible for the duration of this exercise. Ask individual students to read the 'rules' aloud, going around the class, and invite students to comment on each. Encourage the class to do the exercise without a dictionary at first. When they have attempted to find an example and/or exception for each rule, they can then use the dictionary to check their suggestions and add more.

Practising your spelling

1. Further examples can include:
   - Rule 1. Examples: queue, quarter, quintet, and so on.
   - Rule 2. Examples: handkerchief, receive. Exception: weird.
   - Rule 3. Example: agency. Exceptions: tepee, settee.
   - Rule 4. Examples: trick, elastic. Exception: drumstick (note the *-ick* ending is usually in compound nouns such as drum+stick and home+sick).
   - Rule 5. Examples: rising, saving.
   - Rule 6. Examples: altogether, welfare, useful. Explain also the spelling of fulfil – using one l.

2. For the 'look, say, cover, write, check' task you can put students in pairs or small groups and do it as a mini spelling bee.

3. Invite students to play around with words and images in pairs or small groups, but set a time limit.

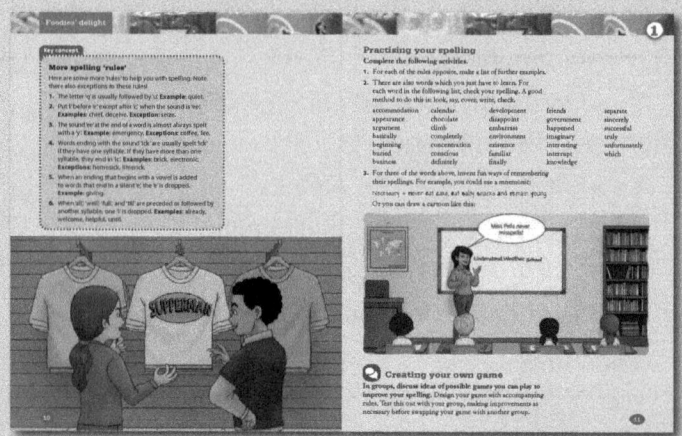

Creating your own game

Organise small groups and assign a leader to each group. Ask students to discuss ideas for games to improve spelling. They may need pencils and paper to design games with accompanying rules. They should test out their ideas in their own groups, then play the game with others in the class. Set a time limit.

Grammar

Spelling activity 1 – Confusing homophones

Explain to students that homophones (or homonyms) are words that sound the same but have different spellings. Write *allowed/aloud* and *knew/new* on the board and ask for further examples.

Now write up the following ten words related to food and ask the class to find their homophones: cereal; flour; pear; piece; waste; scent; currant; dessert, meat, course.

Depending on your class, you can use this to strengthen spelling or to develop vocabulary. To strengthen spelling, students can work in pairs to make a list of more words that sound the same (they do not have to be linked by theme). They then choose five words they frequently confuse and three more they do not often use and write them in sentences to demonstrate their meanings.

To develop vocabulary, ask students to copy the following ten words: stationary; cite; sore; bough; cellar; council; feint; meddle; horde; principle.

They should then:

a. find their meanings in a dictionary

b. find their homophones.

Workbook

Spelling bee

Set this spelling exercise for homework or do it as a silent classroom activity. You can then mark it together in class.

1. a. argument
   b. basically

c. beginning

d. completely

e. disappointed

f. embarrassing

g. environment

h. separate

2. Students identify **five** spellings they need to learn and a way to remember each one. As there are likely to be common words that are difficult for various students, you could do this exercise as a fun feedback activity. Write the words and ideas on the board or on a poster that you can leave visible for a length of time.

can add more words they find tricky when they have finished. (Answers are in brackets.)

Note that musical instruments ending in o need s to make the plural.

- hero (heroes)
- hippo (hippos)
- piano (pianos)
- echo (echoes)
- tomato (tomatoes)
- cello (cellos)
- photo (photos)
- motto (mottoes)
- volcano (volcanoes)
- radio (radios)

Grammar

Spelling activity 2 – Heterophones

Heterophones (or heteronyms) are words that have the same spelling as another word, but a different meaning and different pronunciation. Hetero = different and phone relates to sound. Give examples of some common heterophones such as an object (noun) and to object (verb) and ask the class for further examples. These could include: insult, direct, produce, record, project, research, conduct, progress, present, address, rebel, etc.

Students may work together to create a list that shows the use of the words and whether they are verbs or nouns. To consolidate the activity, individuals should select five pairs of words and write them in sentences to demonstrate how we use them.

Vocabulary

Word game – International cookery

Give students a thesaurus and a dictionary and ask them to look up five words related to cooking. These may include cooking utensils but not ingredients. The Oxford English Thesaurus for schools has a useful 'word web' for cooking on page 141. The object of the game is for students to select less common cookery-related words (verbs or nouns) and mime them in a guessing game. For example, mime the word 'sieve' (show how a sieve sieves flour), demonstrate using a wok or putting on an apron and ask the class to name the item you are using.

When students have chosen their own words they should get into groups of 4–5. One student starts by miming his/her first word, for example 'frying', and the group tries to guess what it is. The first person to say the correct word takes the next turn. The game ends when a student has used up all their words, but set a time limit. Be warned, this can get noisy.

Extension

Tricky spellings – plurals for -o endings

Explain that in English we usually add an s or es to make plurals, such as word/words or box/boxes. However, there are many exceptions to this rule.

- When a word ends in y, we change it to an i and add es, as in baby/babies or pony/ponies.
- When a word ends in o, we sometimes add es, but not always.

Give students these ten awkward words and ask them to work together to make them plural. You

Healthy eating – a radio discussion

Prior knowledge

Before students listen to a discussion on how to promote healthy eating, ask the class to write a few words to define their individual understanding of 'healthy eating', and take feedback. Direct them to the Word cloud and check they understand the word 'field'. Then briefly visit the word family 'nutritious' and the meaning of the verb 'to nourish' and the noun 'nourishment'.

Note: there is a lot to cover in this part of the unit, so you may want to divide your class into groups according to their strengths and needs. Students struggling with language could spend more time on the word-level tasks, while linguistically competent students can go directly to the Developing your language section.

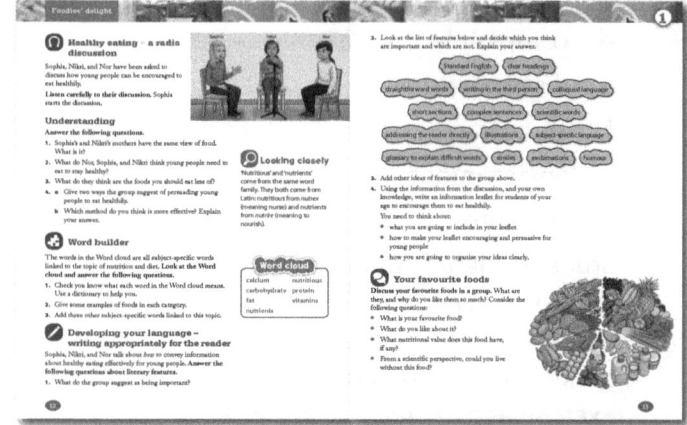

Student-book answers

Understanding

1. They should eat what their mothers prepare/ give them/put on their plates.

2. Protein, vitamins, nutrients, some fat, calcium.

3. Sugar and salt.

4. a. By making healthy food sound interesting and appealing, and using an appropriate style of language/words they understand.

    b. Accept either answer from 4a. that shows sound reasoning.

Word builder

Students can work together on this exercise, but they should make notes individually.

1. Students will need a dictionary for this task.

2. Accept examples of foods for each category, but query and ask students to justify their choices orally if they look dubious. Peers can correct as required.

3. Suggested words include: balanced (diet), minerals, amino-acids, energy.

Developing your language

Writing appropriately for the reader

1. Not too formal, but not childish.

2. Students' answers should contain sound reasoning for their choices.

3. Other ideas might include: font; layout; use of *we* not *they*; first person and second person (*we* or *you*); mnemonics, rhymes, or jingles.

4. For this part of the exercise, students can work in small groups. Finished leaflets can be taken to tutor groups or to Biology lessons, or left in the school dining hall.

Speaking and listening

Your favourite foods

Organise the class into groups of four or five with a group leader. Ask them to discuss their favourite foods using the questions suggested. Set a time limit. While students are speaking, circulate to ensure that there is turn-taking and quieter students are having their say. At the end of the session, ask leaders to summarise their groups' preferences and ideas then open the topic of what we could and *should* live without for general discussion.

Punctuation of sentences

Students are asked to mark the beginning and end of each sentence then insert capital letters and end-of-sentence punctuation. The corrected paragraphs are given below.

Cooking for Kids and Teens was started in 2013 by two mums who wanted their kids to learn how to cook and knew they couldn't do it alone. It started with two mums and three kids in Laila's kitchen. Now Cooking for Kids and Teens runs classes across the country. Click here to find a class near you. We want kids and young people to learn how to make simple, wholesome food and understand that FOOD IS FUN!

Our classes for juniors aged 6 to 11 include after school clubs, weekend workshops, preschool 'fun with food' sessions and the very popular day camps for primary kids. Cooking with new ingredients and flavours will encourage your child to try new foods and expand their diet. They will go from cooking simple individual dishes to making a whole meal from scratch.

We have created special sessions for teens and young adults aged 12 to 16 where they can have fun with friends and learn how to cook well for themselves when they go off to college. Our classes include guidance on nutrition and hygiene as well as the opportunity to invite friends and family to sample their cooking and admire their skills.

Survey – Food for life

In this interactive writing activity students will design a very brief survey and write a report for their class. The objective is to find out which foods members of the class believe they need on a daily basis, and which they could not live without. Each student needs to formulate the appropriate questions and decide who to ask. Explain how surveys use a cross-section of the public and tell students they need to consider which people to ask in their class to get as wide a selection of opinions as possible. After finding the results to their questions, students then write a brief report on their findings. They may include

their personal opinions on the results but they should write in a formal register.

Stage 1: Ask students to design two questions which will provide them with information on: a. what foods their peers think are necessary for their well-being; and b. what foods they could not live without.

Stage 2: Each student approaches a given number of students in the class (minimum five, maximum ten depending on the size of your group). They should make anonymous notes on the replies to their questions, or they may record answers. They should not write down anybody's name.

Stage 3: Students analyse their results and make notes for their reports.

Stage 4: Students write up their notes using two subheadings of their own choosing: a. for foods their peers think are important to eat every day; and b. foods they would not want to live without.

Stage 5: Students read their reports in groups and compare their results. If you have a small class this can be done as a whole-class activity.

Encourage your class to write out at least two drafts before they complete their final report. Collect the final drafts to mark for writing skills and technical accuracy.

Speaking and listening – Choosing a charity

Ask students to select a charity they consider worthy and feel strongly about. They should make notes on what it does and why people should support it. These notes are to be used for a 3-minute persuasive speech for the whole class. Students may use visual aids to demonstrate aspects of the charity but they may not read a script. At the end of the session, after everyone has spoken, ask the class to say or vote on which charities they would support and who were the most persuasive speakers.

Promoting healthy eating

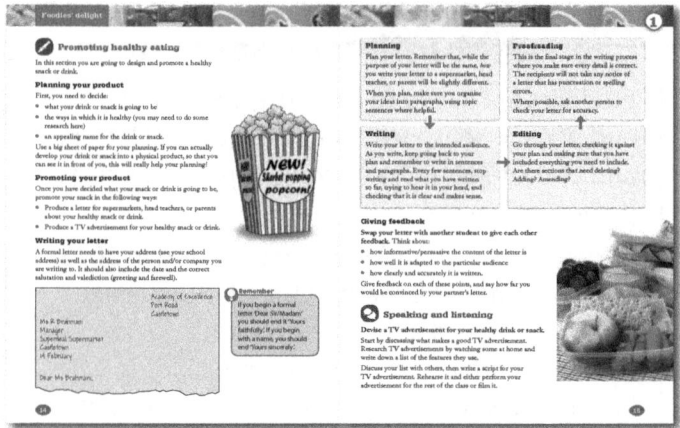

Setting the scene

Planning your product

Tell students they are going to design and promote a healthy snack or drink, and they need to plan their product and an advertising campaign. This activity involves writing, so at this stage it is best undertaken individually, although students can help each other out with ideas and editing. Provide each student with a large piece of paper (A3) and direct their attention to 'Planning your product' on page 14 of the Student Book. Allow time for students to research products and ingredients, and to design their product and its packaging.

Promoting your product

The letter and advertisement-writing tasks for this activity are outlined under the Writing and Speaking and listening headings on the next page. Set the planning stage of 'Writing a letter' for homework if time is limited in class.

Writing

Writing to persuade

Remind students that when they are writing to persuade they are 'arguing a case' so they need to develop each point logically and convincingly. This means not making exaggerated claims that

no one will believe. The first paragraph acts as an introduction to their argument or point of view. It should tell the reader about the topic, the need for a change, or the benefits of a new product. Subsequent paragraphs should then develop one idea or one point at a time. In this style of writing it can be effective to start each paragraph with the topic sentence and expand on that. For example: *Eating less sugar will mean that students are fitter and healthier. Healthier students who eat wisely and take regular exercise are more attentive in lessons.* This rest of this paragraph would then show how and why, using facts and statistics to support the claim.

Persuasive writing can also include personal anecdotes and experience. The final paragraph, before the conclusion, can contrast how things are now with how they should or could be in the future, including the benefits to those involved. An effective conclusion should refer back to the introduction and briefly summarise the arguments made.

Before you set the formal letter writing task on page 14, review on the board aspects of persuasive writing. Suggest students:

write a clear, reasoned introduction; build their argument (using examples, data or statistics if possible); compare the benefits of their new product with less healthy options; summarise their argument and end on a positive note.

Remind them that typical persuasive techniques use: short sentences, rhetorical questions, tripling (three words or phrases to emphasize a point), and emotive vocabulary.

Writing your letter

When you come to the writing stage for this topic, take a few minutes to review tone and register, and set the formal letter task as an individual assignment. When students have completed a first draft, they may share with a partner for peer editing, then again for final editing and proofreading, but each student should produce a formal letter. This is excellent practice for Checkpoint and further exams; it is also a very useful real-life skill. At the end of the task, collect all the letters then hand them out randomly (not to partners or known friends), for students to read and comment on. Take feedback.

Devise a TV advertisement for your healthy drink or snack

If possible, show a selection of advertisements and discuss target audiences, presentation, and persuasive features.

Ask students to watch and make notes on other advertisements at home, and take feedback the next day as a class.

For the Speaking and listening task, depending on time, you could arrange your class into groups for similar products such as fizzy drinks, salty snacks, and dried fruits, and ask them to create their television scripts then rehearse and perform them together. Whether they are undertaken individually or in groups, set time aside to watch all the finished advertisements. Encourage students to discuss their persuasive features and use of language in general.

Keeping in touch with friends and family

1. Students write a short email invitation to a friend. Mark for style and content.

2. Students should write a carefully worded letter that shows what they have been given and expresses their thanks politely, regardless of whether they like the gift or not.

Editing a formal letter

Give students a copy of the short letter below, or write one similar. Include numerous spelling and grammar mistakes and use an inappropriate register. Ask students to edit and/or rewrite it. This letter is to the head of a school, proposing a new way of providing snacks at morning break.

Dear Head,

Me and my mates want to start a shop for us kids during morning brake. We'll get bottles of minreal water and stuff from the local supermarket and sell it at a bit of proffit. That extra bit of money can go to the school sport's fund or whatever else you think's a good idea. We won't get cola's nor anything too sugarry because parent's are always complaning about the cost of dentist's. But we want crisp's – everyone wants crisp's because they've got salt in them and we mostly like salty stuff.

We'll set the shop up in the dinning hall that way kids can drop their enpty bottles and pakets in the bin their.

Hope you like out idea.

Jose (with Noor, Dima, Anton, Yasmin, Barbie, Hassan and Carla (in mr Watts class)

Progress check

Student Book progress checks are designed to help students revisit what they have learned in a relatively informal manner. They should be completed in class if possible, and in silence. But do not impose exam conditions. You may want to allow students to refer to both their Student Book and Workbook as need be. When they have finished, read the answers aloud and let students mark their own or a partner's. Collect their answers in later to see what progress students are making and what areas need repeating or practising.

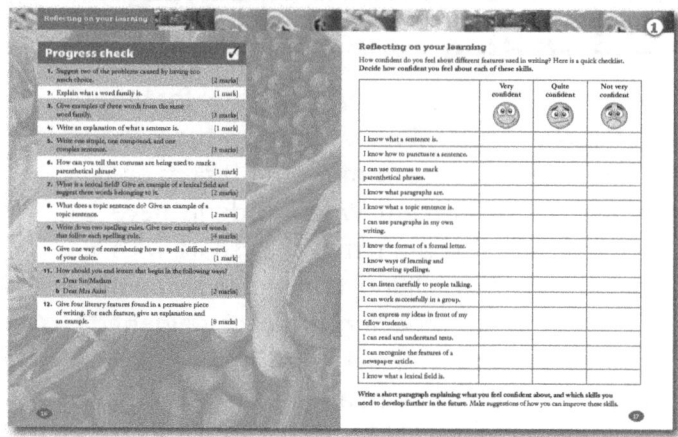

Student-book answers

End of unit test

1. 'Paralysis' (inability to choose) and disappointment. [2]

2. Words that come from the same 'root word'. [1]

3. Accept any three words from the same word family. [3]

4. Explanations may include mention of punctuation and clauses or verbs. Do not accept answers such as: 'they start with a capital letter and end with a full stop'. [1]

5. Students write one simple, one compound, and one complex sentence. [3]

6. The sentence contains extra or inessential information that can be deleted. [1]

7. A group of words to create a particular effect. Students give a suitable example of a lexical field and three words belonging to it. [2]

8. Demonstrates or indicates content of paragraph. Students give an example of a topic sentence. [2]

9. Accept any two spelling rules. Students should include examples of words that follow each identified spelling rule. [4]

10. Accept one way of spelling a difficult word of the student's choice. [1]

11. a. Yours faithfully
    b. Yours sincerely. [2]

12. Accept any four persuasive features with explanations, such as: tone, register and colloquial language; use of second person 'you' or first person 'we'; positive lexical field, and so on. [8]

Reflection

Ask students to do the Progress check in silence, then open the topic for feedback and discussion. Ask students to say which areas they would like to review or revisit before moving on to the next unit. If you are doing this early in the school year, before students are fully comfortable with each other, they could write their paragraphs on slips of paper and hand them in at the end of the lesson. Spend a few minutes discussing with the class how they will use the different persuasive techniques covered in this unit as they proceed through school and further education, then in their working life. Discuss why learning how an advertisement is created and how it affects people is useful knowledge, then go on to discuss the different ways they may one day have to write a letter in a formal register.

Once the class has completed the Reflection section, return to the quotations in the Student Book. Ask students if they now see any of the quotations in a new way after examining healthy eating in this unit. Take feedback on what students have enjoyed doing in the unit, such as inventing new snacks, and make a list on the board of topics and language tasks they would like to revisit.

Workbook

🧩 Foodies' delight quiz

1. Accept any three synonyms for the word 'scared' such as: *frightened, afraid, terrified*.

2 a. Accept any sentence with a coordinating conjunction such as: *and, but, or*.

   b. Accept sentences with subordinating conjunctions such as: *although, however*.

3. Accept three different ways to expand the simple sentence: 'The mouse ran into a hole.'

4. Accept three techniques writers use to keep the reader interested, with examples, such as: use of rhetorical questions, dramatic or shocking statements, similes, data, use of powerful words and vocabulary for target audience, and so on.

5 a. Start with 'Dear Uncle…', and end with 'Love' or 'Best wishes'.

   b. End with 'Yours sincerely' (if starting with 'Dear Mr/Mrs/Ms…') or 'Yours faithfully' (if starting with 'Dear Sir/Madam').

Vocabulary

The buying game

A fun round-up activity for this unit and a good way of practising a bit of brain gym is to play this memory game. Seat the class in a circle where they can all see each other and tell them they are going to play an alphabet memory game. Give them the opening line: *I went to the hypermarket* (or the market or mall, or name a specific type of store) *and I bought an anorak* (or any appropriate item beginning with 'a'). The next person has to repeat what you have said then add an item beginning with the next letter, 'b': *I went to the hypermarket and I bought an anorak and a pair of boots*. The third person has to repeat what you have both said then add an item beginning with 'c', and so it goes on for the 26 letters of the alphabet.

To prevent the game becoming tedious, keep the pace moving. Explain that each student has a maximum of 30 seconds to think of an item for their letter of the alphabet. Students are eliminated when they can't think of an item or when they cannot remember what has gone before. Turn a blind eye to visual clues, for example, the 'b' student waggling their feet for 'boots', but do not allow any other form of helping.

This game can be played as a warm-up activity for many topics such as animals at the zoo or walking down a street by simply changing the wording to, for example, *I went to the zoo and I saw* or *I walked down the street and I saw*. Allow students to be fairly inventive with difficult letters, for example, accept 'yellow scarf' for 'y'.

Listening

A printable version of the full transcript for this unit is available on the CD.

Amazing arts

Setting the scene

Amazing arts

This unit provides students with an opportunity to engage with more demanding pieces of classic literature than they may have encountered up to now. Some activities require good reading skills and critical thinking but, where possible, give your class time to think about what they are reading and discussing, and encourage them to risk offering original interpretations supported by evidence from the texts before explaining content. Most activities may be carried out in pairs or small groups, but students should also be given the opportunity to work on their own, this being excellent practice for Checkpoint assessments and exams in later secondary.

The quotations on page 18 of the Student Book relate to classics of English language literature. Shakespeare's romantic drama *The Tempest*, which opens with the main characters being cast upon a lonely island, was first performed for King James I at court in 1611. Benjamin Franklin (1706–1790) was an American statesman, author and scientist. Charles Dickens (1812–1870) was a prolific Victorian novelist and social commentator.

Take a few minutes to discuss what makes a literary classic: memorable plot and characters and enduring (universal) theme(s). If you have a multinational or bilingual class, draw out titles of classics in students' other languages and discuss briefly why they are considered 'classics'. Ask whether anyone can name famous works of English-language literature. Then ask if students have:

- explored the strange world of a Dickens novel
- collaborated in a problem-solving exercise
- created a drama script
- engaged with reading pre-20th century literature
- reflected on how writers from the past are still relevant today.

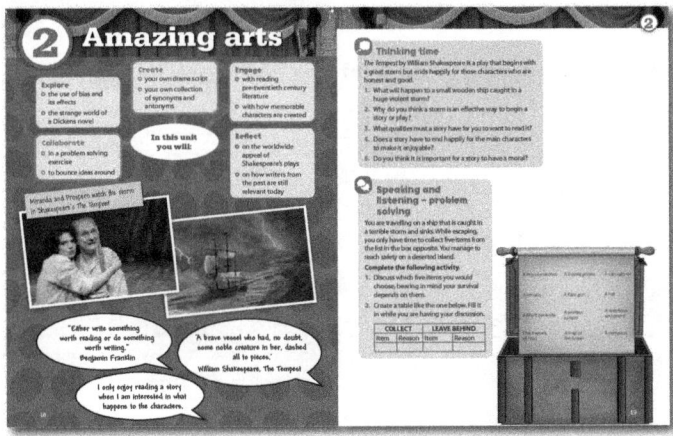

Amazing arts

You could set this Workbook activity on Shakespeare and Dickens for homework. Alternatively, you could use it as a short research task in class or the library. If students look for information online, warn about the dangers of Wikipedia (and the way some so-called educational sites can oversimplify texts).

1. **Shakespeare:** Born in Stratford-Upon-Avon in 1564; a playwright and poet; died in 1616; part-owned The Globe Theatre; not much is known about his personal life; wrote 37 plays; married Anne Hathaway.

   Charles Dickens: Born in Portsmouth in 1812; wrote *Great Expectations*; had a lifelong fear of being poor; a novelist; died in 1870; lived in the Victorian era; many of his novels are about social inequality.

2. Plays by William Shakespeare – accept any five, for example: *King Lear, Hamlet, Romeo and Juliet, A Midsummer Night's Dream, Twelfth Night, Macbeth, Richard III, Henry IV (parts 1 & 2), All's Well That Ends Well, Antony and Cleopatra, Measure for Measure, The Tempest, Othello*.

   Novels by Charles Dickens – accept any five, for example: *Oliver Twist, David Copperfield, Bleak House, Nicholas Nickleby, Dombey and Son, Our Mutual Friend, Little Dorrit, Great Expectations*.

Thinking time

Briefly introduce the class to *The Tempest* by William Shakespeare. Explain that it is a famous play that opens with a great storm and ends happily for the good characters. If possible, do questions 1–3 as a whole class activity.

1. Students should bear in mind when the play was written and what a ship of the time would have been like.

2. This is an effective way to start a play/film/story because characters are thrown together in strange circumstances. It is also very engaging and dramatic.

3. Draw out and focus on aspects relating to plot and character.

Then organise pairs or groups of three to discuss questions 4 and 5. Allow students time to make notes here, which can be used later in the unit. Take feedback and open the question of literature containing a message or moral for further class discussion.

Talking about a famous novel or play

Ask your class to choose one famous novel or play. It can be in English or another language, pre-20th century or more modern. Ask them to make notes on when it was written, who wrote it, and why they think it became famous and a 'classic'. Using their notes, students give a very short (three-minute) presentation to the class or in groups. No visual aids are necessary. The talk should be given 'off the cuff' – do not allow students to read their notes. The objective is to broaden students' general knowledge of literature and what constitutes a classic.

Problem solving

Read through the rubric on page 19 of the Student Book and write 'Five items only' on the board. Remind students that this is an uninhabited desert island. Arrange groups and assign a leader to give feedback and control discussion, but insist that all students keep a grid as instructed and complete it during the conversation. Set a time limit. When you take feedback, write the useful items on the board then reduce again to five if necessary, with some class discussion.

The world's most famous play

Prior knowledge – *Hamlet*

Take a few minutes to discuss Shakespeare and contemporary classics in other languages (for example, Cervantes), reviewing prior discussion of classics. *Hamlet*, a tragedy about a young man who feigns madness in order to avenge his father's murder, was written in about 1599 and first performed during the next two years. Explain that there are different types of theatrical tragedies but they basically trace the life and downfall of an individual through human weaknesses, such as ambition, greed, or desire for revenge. *Hamlet* conforms to the category of 'revenge tragedy', where a quest for vengeance ultimately leads to loss of life in a bloodthirsty climax. Following on from work covered in the first part of this unit, draw out students' familiarity and understanding of this type of theatre and move on to the reading.

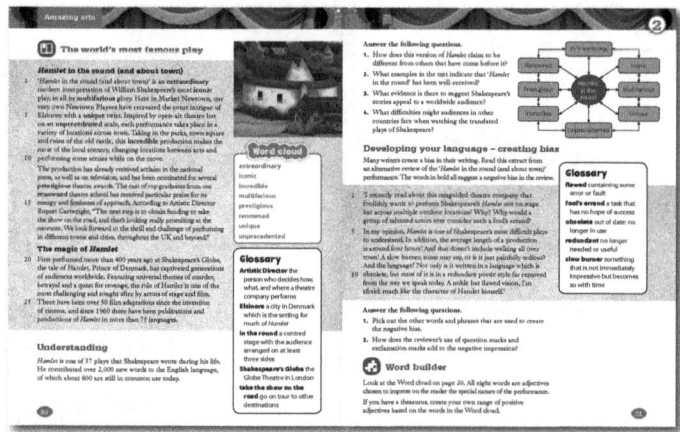

Student Book pages 20–21

Writing

 Hamlet in the round (and about town)

The 'Hamlet in the round' article on page 20 of the Student Book contains vocabulary some students may find challenging. Read it with them as a class, explaining new words and those in the Word cloud as you go. Then ask them to read it again in silence before starting the questions.

To give students good practice in reading comprehension, ask them to work individually and answer in full sentences, quoting from the text to support their ideas. They may then discuss answers with partners and make adjustments before handing in their work. When marking, comment on how clearly each student expresses himself/herself and uses the text for evidence.

Student-book answers

 **Understanding**

1. It claims to be 'modern' and 'unique', using a variety of outdoor locations and performing scenes 'on the move'.

2. The production has received media acclaim, award nominations, praise for the cast, and there is potential funding for a tour.

3. Hamlet has been translated into more than 75 languages. Students may also comment on the play's longevity, 'universal themes', popularity with actors, and many film adaptations.

4. Language and setting. Accept answers that comment on 'old-fashioned' values and costumes.

Vocabulary

 Word builder

Using a thesaurus for words in the Word cloud on page 20, students create their own range of positive adjectives based on the words in the Word cloud. Warn students that 'unique' is frequently misused but can mean 'special' or 'unusual'. Accept any of the following and valid alternatives:

- **extraordinary** and **incredible**: amazing, astonishing, astounding, phenomenal, sensational, marvellous, unbelievable, etc.

- **iconic**: famous, admirable

- **multifarious**: very varied

- **prestigious** and **renowned**: reputable, highly regarded, well known, celebrated

- **unique**: one of a kind, but sometimes also distinctive, different, special

- **unprecedented**: has never been done before.

Developing your language

Creating bias

Briefly discuss the meaning of 'bias' as 'leaning' one way or another, and show how the previous reading contains a positive bias. Ask students to read the page 21 extract on the 'Hamlet in the round' production, noting how the words in bold that are also listed in the Glossary box all suggest a negative bias. Discuss the words in the Glossary box and set the questions, to be completed in pairs.

1. Other words and phrases that are used to create the negative bias include: misguided theatre company; foolishly; one of Shakespeare's most difficult plays to understand; four hours!; slow burner; painfully tedious; redundant poetic style.

2. Rhetorical questions invite the reader to share in the negative opinion. Exclamation marks reinforce the idea of tedium in 'four hours!'

Positive bias	Negative bias
fascinating and complex	dull and boring
a 'must-see' event	rarely encountered worse
completely absorbing	weak and insipid
thought-provoking	endlessly tiresome
a magical experience	completely irrelevant
surprisingly engaging	a new low point

Workbook

 ### Bias – being assertive

Summarise the plot of *Romeo and Juliet* and ask the class what else they know about the play. Then set this task to be completed individually in class or as homework. Students can peer mark and/or you can review their alternative vocabulary with the whole class.

1. Accept suggested changes to wording below, or valid alternatives to make the comments positive.

   'I love/thoroughly enjoy *Romeo and Juliet*. Even the fighting is exciting and makes me sympathise with both sides/makes me feel sorry for Romeo. The ending is so sad. I can perfectly understand the appeal of such a wonderful story.'

2. Assertions that create bias should be placed in the most appropriate box:

Extension

Students in need of support – critical vocabulary

Ask students to work in pairs. Together they make a longer list of negative critical words and expressions used to comment on a play, novel, poem, or a character in a film or book: words such as 'dull', 'boring', 'rubbish'; expressions such as 'a total waste of time', and so on. They should then decide which words and expressions can be used politely, and which are more colloquial and only appropriate for use in conversation with their friends and peers. Bring the class together and ask for feedback. Discuss how and why some expressions are polite and valid and why others are not.

As a means of practising polite negative vocabulary ask students to write a film or book review for something they did not enjoy. Their comments may be very critical but they must remain polite at all times and keep to a formal style. Reviews should include a paragraph for some or all of the following:

plot or storyline

characters and/or actors playing those characters

opening scenes

ending

any personal reasons for not enjoying the book or film

When they have finished, ask them to show their review to a partner and to compare their choice of language. Pairs can then share their reviews in groups. Groups vote for the best review, that being the one that says the meanest things in the nicest ways.

Synonyms and antonyms

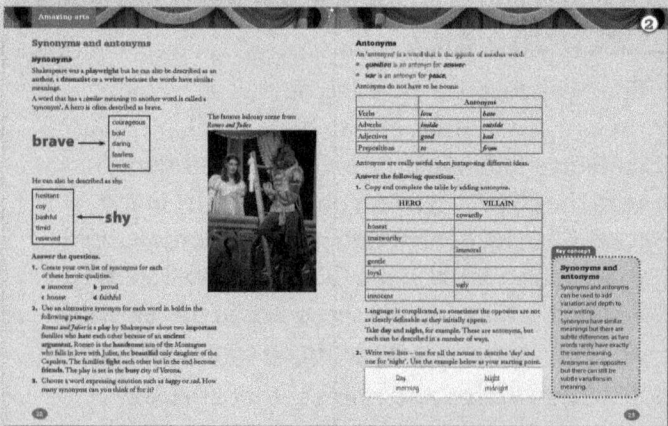

Grammar

Synonyms

As a way of introducing the idea of context and the subtleties in choosing synonyms, ask if someone who's 'timid' (as in shy), is afraid or a coward. Direct students to question 1: they may work individually or in pairs with a thesaurus to create a list of synonyms for heroic qualities. Students may also need a dictionary to check the meaning of any words that are new to them. Accept any valid alternatives to the following:

1. **a.** innocent = virtuous, naive, artless

    b. proud = arrogant, conceited, vain, haughty, superior

    c. honest = good, moral, virtuous, law-abiding, decent, honourable

    d. faithful = true, loyal, constant, dependable

2. Students should now find an alternative synonym for each word in bold. Those with less familiarity with English should be paired with more articulate partners. Remind students to use context clues before choosing a synonym.

    Accept any valid alternatives to the following: play = drama; important = influential/ high-ranking; hate = loathe; ancient argument = old feud; handsome = good-looking; beautiful = pretty/charming; fight = battle (with)/oppose; friends = allies; busy = bustling.

3. Students can do this task individually, and then peer mark. They choose a word expressing emotion such as *happy* or *sad* and find synonyms using a thesaurus. Take feedback from the class and put less commonly used words on the board. Review contexts and how to use selected words appropriately.

Grammar

Antonyms

A fun way to introduce this exercise is to have a pair-work 'Yes-versus-No' session. Ask partners to face each other. One may only say 'yes', the other may only say 'no'. Set a two-minute time limit and ask them to see how many ways they can pronounce or use their single word to persuade or convince, argue or disagree. (Warning: this can get noisy!)

Explain that antonyms do not have to be nouns, as with 'yes/no' (adverbs), and review the parts of speech on page 23 of the Student Book.

1. Set the comparison task to be completed individually and then peer marked, then review answers with the class. You could suggest a pair of opposing characters from a book, play, or film your class knows.

    Accept any valid alternatives to the suggestions in bold below.

HERO	VILLAIN
brave	cowardly
honest	**dishonest**
trustworthy	**untrustworthy**
moral	immoral
gentle	**cruel/rough**
loyal	**unfaithful/disloyal**
pretty/beautiful	ugly
innocent	**guilty/wicked**

2. This task can be completed in pairs. Students find ways to describe 'day' and 'night'. Accept any valid alternatives to the suggestions below. When taking feedback, encourage students to explain their choices. Depending on your location (country and culture), qualify that 'midday' in English means 12:00 or 'twelve noon'.

DAY	NIGHT
noon/midday	midnight
early morning	late evening
sunlight	starlight/moonlight
morning	evening
early hours	after midnight
dawn/daybreak	dusk
afternoon	

Ask students why they think there might be more nouns to describe day than night and whether the same is true of other languages they know.

Workbook

 Synonyms and antonyms

Before setting this task for homework or as an individual language consolidation exercise in class, remind students how synonyms and antonyms function. This exercise will help students who require support, but you may want to modify it to stretch others.

1. Suggest students find alternatives to their usual vocabulary when they complete the grid below. They then test a partner by saying a word and asking where it goes. For example, 'despise' for hate or 'snag' for difficulty.

Original word	Synonym	Antonym
question	query	answer
answer	response	**question**
strong	**fortified**	weak
enemy	**foe**	friend
begin	**start**	**end/finish/ complete**
difficult	**tricky**	easy
angry	**irate**	calm
hate	**loathe**	love
child	**juvenile**	adult
lose	**mislay**	**find/encounter**

2. a. never
   b. fascinating
   c. passed (note spelling of verb); well
   d. most
   e. unsuitable

Extension

Synonyms and antonyms – Extending vocabulary

Provide students with an A4 sheet of paper with three columns (as for the synonym/antonym activity on page 12 of the Workbook), plus a thesaurus and a dictionary. Ask them to write down the following ten common words in the 'original word' column: *absent, accept, huge, famous, clean, hide, numerous, private, fast, rich.*

Set a time limit and tell students they need to find a synonym and an antonym for each word and put it in the appropriate column.

Suggested answers: *absent, missing, present; accept, take, reject; huge, immense, tiny; famous, well-known, unknown; clean, spotless, dirty; hide, conceal, reveal; numerous, many, few; private, personal, public; fast, rapid, slow; rich, wealthy, poor.*

This can be developed as a pair-work vocabulary activity for more able students. Ask each student to fill in a three-column grid as above, choosing ten less common words or unusual words, such as *temporary, prosperity, fertile* etc. They should fill in the first column then read their ten original words to a partner, who has to find the synonyms and antonyms for those words. Students then exchange papers and compare their word choices.

Great Expectations

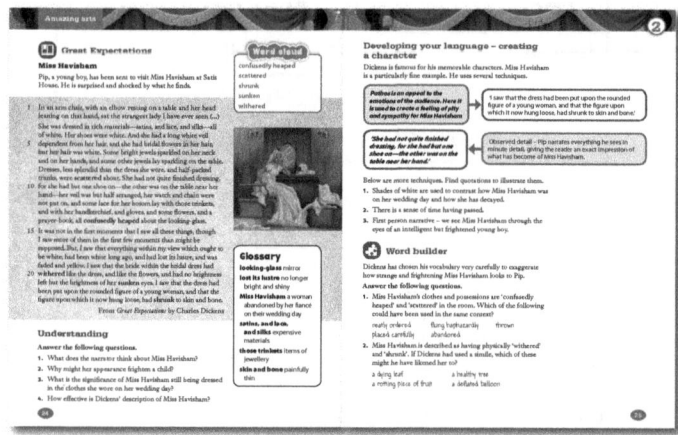

 ## Miss Havisham

Read the text to the class then go through it, asking for impressions of Miss Havisham and her room. Try to let them work out 'jilted bride' without prompting, but direct their attention to the Glossary box if necessary.

Review the adjectives in the Word cloud and ask what they contribute to the text. Go through the Glossary box to ensure understanding before students start the questions on their own. Tell them to answer in full sentences and provide evidence from the text to support their answers.

 ## Understanding

1. Pip thinks Miss Havisham is 'the strangest lady' he has ever seen.

2. Accept answers suggesting grotesque and/or cadaverous appearance/half-dressed/sense of abandonment. Suggestions of 'madness' must be reasoned and justified.

3. Accept valid alternatives or different wording to Miss Havisham being a jilted bride unable to forget her cancelled wedding.

4. Answers are personal responses, but students should mention Dickens's descriptive detail. Very good answers will acknowledge Pip's point of view (the reader is shocked/surprised/feels pity – like Pip).

Creating a character

Dickens's descriptive techniques are: pathos to create a feeling of pity and sympathy; and minute detail, giving the reader an exact impression of what has become of Miss Havisham. Explain the techniques as necessary then ask students to work in pairs to find quotations illustrating them. They should each write answers in their 'Understanding' responses.

- Shades of white are used to contrast how Miss Havisham was on her wedding day and how she has decayed. Observed detail: 'everything within my view which ought to be white, had been white long ago, and had lost its lustre, and was faded and yellow'.

- A sense of time having passed; pathos: 'I saw that the bride within the bridal dress had withered like the dress, and like the flowers, and had no brightness left but the brightness of her sunken eyes'.

- First-person narrative. We see her through the eyes of an intelligent but frightened young boy; point of view: 'the strangest lady I have ever seen, or ever shall see'/'It was not in the first few moments that I saw these things, though I saw more of them in the first few moments than might be supposed'.

Students work on this task individually then swap papers to peer mark and discuss choices and reasons.

1. 'confusedly heaped' and 'scattered' = flung haphazardly/thrown

2. 'withered' and 'shrunk' = a dying leaf

Extension

Stretching students – Writing a description of a place

Read the following extract from Woolf's *The Village in the Jungle* (1913), and show students the text.

All jungles are evil, but no jungle is more evil than that which lay about the village of Beddagama. If you climb one of the bare rocks that jut up out of it, you will see the jungle stretched out below you for mile upon mile on all sides. It looks like a great sea, over which the pitiless hot wind perpetually sends waves unbroken, except where the bare rocks, rising above it, show like dark smudges against the grey-green of the leaves. For ten months of the year the sun beats down and scorches it; and the hot wind in a whirl of dust tears over it, tossing the branches and scattering the leaves. The trees are stunted and twisted by the drought, by the thin and sandy soil, by the dry wind. They are scabrous, thorny trees, with grey leaves whitened by the clouds of dust which the wind perpetually sweeps over them: their trunks are grey with hanging, stringy lichen. And there are enormous cactuses, evil-looking and obscene, with their great fleshy green slabs, which put out immense needle-like spines. More evil-looking still are the great leafless trees, which look like a tangle of gigantic spiders' legs—smooth, bright green, jointed together—from which, when they are broken, oozes out a milky viscous fluid.

From: *The Village in the Jungle* by Leonard Woolf (1913)

Discuss how the author describes an unpleasant place using the five senses and ask students to think about what life must be like in a village in a jungle. Then ask them to think about the unpleasant side of a place they know or have visited. Ask them to write a description of this place using the five senses. They should try to use similes and metaphors to help create the atmosphere. Mark for original use of English and imagery, and give feedback on technical accuracy.

Creating a caricature

You may prefer to set this task as a class activity with students working in pairs or small groups, or as individual homework.

1. Adjectives to describe Miss Havisham. Accept any valid alternatives to the following suggestions: abandoned; stay-at-home; reclusive; man-hater; unhealthy; decrepit; uncaring.

2. Students should make notes then write a caricature description of a grumpy old lady, an angry young man, or a spoilt child. When marking, credit interesting use of English. Students may read their description in groups or to the class.

Extension

Supporting students – Using adjectives in context

An effective way to consolidate use of descriptive language is for students to see how some words can be applied to people, some to places or buildings, and some to objects. For example, we can say 'an old chair or an old man'; you can have an 'antique chair', but not an 'antique man'.

Working with a thesaurus and dictionary, students should find different ways to say 'old' and put them in the following categories: people, places or buildings, objects. Students may work in pairs for this task.

Provide the following words to get started: archaic, vintage, historical, shabby.

(Note: The *Oxford English Thesaurus for Schools* has a section on 'old' and 'old-fashioned' as over-used words; see pp. 391, 392.)

When students have finished, review word lists with the class, explaining subtle differences where necessary. Students should add any extra or new words to their lists.

Semi-colons

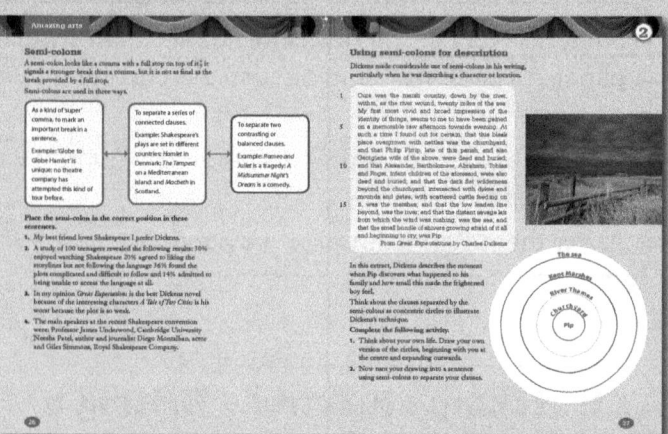

Student-book answers

1. My best friend loves Shakespeare; I prefer Dickens.

2. A study of 100 teenagers revealed the following results: 30% enjoyed watching Shakespeare; 20% agreed to liking the storylines but not following the language; 36% found the plots complicated and difficult to follow; and 14% admitted to being unable to access the language at all.

3. In my opinion *Great Expectations* is the best Dickens novel because of the interesting characters; *A Tale of Two Cities* is his worst because the plot is so weak.

4. The main speakers at the recent Shakespeare convention were: Professor James Underwood, Cambridge University; Neesha Patel, author and journalist; Diego Montalban, actor; and Giles Simmons, Royal Shakespeare Company.

Grammar

📖 Using semi-colons for description

Read through the extract from *Great Expectations* with the class, explaining the purpose of the semi-colons where Dickens describes Pip and the location. Emphasise how details of the churchyard and landscape make Pip appear small and vulnerable for later tasks.

Working together, students then go through the text again, identifying where and why semi-colons have been used. Ask them to think about the clauses separated by the semi-colons as concentric circles to illustrate Dickens' technique of showing Pip as frightened centrepiece. Then they should go to the end of the text and, working backwards, find references to: the sea; Kent Marshes; River Thames; churchyard; Pip.

1. Students draw their own version of the concentric circles. They should think of their own lives, then beginning with themselves at the centre, expand outwards by adding the key elements of their lives.

2. Students turn their circles into a sentence, using semi-colons to separate the clauses.

their partner's choice of punctuation is correct because there are numerous instances where a comma is now more commonly used than a semi-colon.

 ## Semi-colons

As this exercise clarifies use of the semi-colon, set it as a consolidation exercise to be completed individually as homework or silently in class. Review answers with the whole class, with each student marking their own work. This will enable them to ask for explanations where they have not placed semi-colons correctly.

1. **a.** Reason 3

   b. Reason 2

   c. Reason 1

   d. Reason 2

2. Students write three sentences, each showing a different use of semi-colons. These can be peer marked and/or collected in, to check for accuracy and variation.

Supporting students – Creating sentences

Provide students with A4-sized sheets of coloured card and scissors. Write punctuation points on the board, separating the opening and closing of speech marks. Ask students to copy them in thick felt tips across the top of their card. They then cut the punctuation marks out. On the rest of the card they write out random clauses, nouns, subjects, connectives and verbs then cut them out. Having done this individually, students form pairs, jumble all their words and punctuation together and have fun making sentences across the desk, arranging word order and putting in the correct punctuation. They may make extra words or punctuation marks on more card as need be.

Punctuation practice worksheet

To practise using commas and semi-colons give students the photocopiable sheet on punctuation for this unit: **Comma or semi-colon?** When they have finished they can invent ten sentences of their own then copy them out without punctuation to give to a partner. Allow students to argue about whether they think

Consolidating use of punctuation

Ask students to select a paragraph or short section of a novel that contains different forms of punctuation, including at least one semi-colon. Ask them to copy the paragraph by hand. (This provides good practice in selecting and using an author's words, a skill they will require for later assessments and English exams.) They should then highlight all the different punctuation marks and label them. Working in pairs, students then explain to their partners how and why authors have punctuated their sentences.

Practising punctuation

Read the following sentences to students as dictation. Tell students to write down what they hear and put in the punctuation. All but one contain at least one semi-colon and some also have a colon.

1. Hens are incapable of flying very far; their wings are too small.

2. There are a few things I want you to do before you go to bed: tidy away your school books; prepare your bag for tomorrow; and make sure the doors are locked.

3. Fine rain fell gently, watering the flowers and bringing the grass back to life.

4. I looked up and saw a female bear. Her fur was covered in leaves; her claws were long and very sharp; she was enormous.

5. The motorcycle skidded round the corner; no one was surprised by the accident.

'Great Expectations – The Play'

Prior knowledge

Take a few minutes to review what the class now knows about the novel *Great Expectations*. Go on to discuss why there are different TV or film versions of the novel. If students are using computers, they can do a quick search and count how many times it has been made into a film, and in what years.

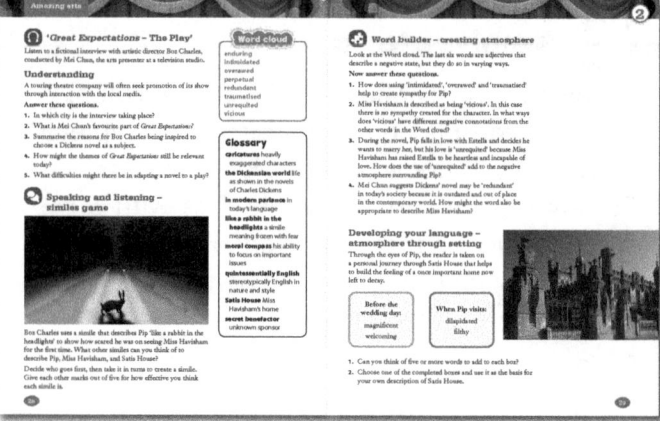

Speaking and listening

 ## 'Great Expectations – The Play'

The vocabulary and use of English in this recording are formal and may be challenging for some students. Nevertheless, while some students may not grasp the meaning of all words or expressions, they should be able to follow the gist of the conversation and use the Glossary box. Allow the class to hear the recording once before going through the Word cloud, which they should copy out and supplement with more common or colloquial vocabulary.

Suggested alternatives for the Word cloud, in the context of the interview are:

enduring = long-lasting

intimidated = frightened

overawed = in awe and afraid

perpetual = continual

traumatised = shocked by her distressing experience

unrequited = unreturned

vicious = mean and nasty

Student-book answers

 ## Understanding

1. Hong Kong.
2. When Pip meets Miss Havisham for the first time.
3. Boz is a 'massive admirer'; he loves: Dickens's ability to weave desolation and vivid characterisation into narrative; the way Dickens highlights social injustice; the 'rich

texture' of his writing – comedy and cruelty, inequality and caricature; the 'enduring quality' of this novel; the way Dickens enables an audience to empathise and sympathise.

4. It is 'a morality tale that still has value today', similar to a boy winning the lottery and squandering his money, plus the universal theme of unrequited love.

5. Personal responses may include reference to: character, setting and costumes; outmoded/ Victorian ideas and/or vocabulary.

Speaking and listening

 ## Similes game

You may choose to do this activity after the Word builder activity opposite, so that students have a thorough idea about the content of both Dickens' novel and the interview.

Organise the class into groups of three. Explain how Boz Charles uses the simile 'like a rabbit in the headlights' to show how scared Pip was on seeing Miss Havisham for the first time. (Rabbits sometimes become paralysed with fear when caught in car headlights.) Students take turns to think up new similes for Pip, Miss Havisham, and Satis House. Suggest they use the illustrations and images on pages 24 and 29 of the Student Book. Students mark each other out of five for how effective their similes are. Set a time limit. Take feedback and ask groups to share their best examples with the class.

Word builder

Creating atmosphere

Return to the Word cloud and discuss how six of the seven words are adjectives describing a negative state in varying ways. Students may work in pairs for this task, or it could be done with the whole class as an oral activity.

1. The words tell the listener just how vulnerable and small Pip is in regard to the situation in Satis House.

2. 'Vicious' suggests aggressive, angry, ready to 'snap' at Pip. 'Vicious' is a powerful word, suggesting Miss Havisham's effect or power over Pip. The other words demonstrate Pip's passive condition.

3. Explain that in the novel Pip falls in love with Estella, who is an orphan and Miss Havisham's ward. Estella has been raised to be heartless and incapable of love. Students should use a dictionary to find the full meaning of 'unrequited' and match it to this information. It suggests Pip will never be loved in return.

4. 'Redundant' can be applied to Miss Havisham, because she lives in the past and contributes nothing to the present or the people around her.

Developing your language

Atmosphere through setting

Ask students to look at the image of Satis House on page 29. Ask them to suggest words for what the house may once have been like. Write words on the board and ask for alternatives to describe its dilapidated state. Students should then complete the activity on their own, and compare their choice of vocabulary with a partner when they have finished. Accept suggestions here and valid alternatives.

1. Before the wedding day: splendid, imposing, beautiful, grand, tidy, glorious, well-tended, well-cared for, etc.

   When Pip visits: ruined, unloved, broken-down, untidy, unkempt, a ruin, shambles, shabby, tumble-down, etc.

2. Working individually, students now choose one of the completed boxes and use it as the basis for their own description of Satis House. Collect finished descriptions and mark for use of

vocabulary, use of figurative language such as similes, and correct use of punctuation. Students may read their descriptions to the class later.

Workbook

Creating atmosphere in your writing

Students read a short extract from *Bleak House* about fog on the River Thames. Warn students that there may be a number of words we do not use today, but they should try to work out the content of the piece from what they understand. The point is to focus on the way Dickens creates atmosphere, the notion of fog here being that nothing is clear (in the novel); everything is obscured by the miasma of the London fog.

Set the activity for homework or ask students to work on their own in silence in class. Review the text with them after they have completed the questions.

1. Eleven times.

2. Students give three locations and three people the fog encounters.

   Locations: river; green meadows; docks (shipping); city; Essex marshes; Kentish heights; Greenwich; boats; bridges.

   People: Greenwich pensioners; skipper of boat; apprentice boy; random people on the bridges.

3. Students now choose one of the types of day (rainy, windy, snowy, or sunny) and make notes on their thoughts and feelings about the weather. They then write two sentences of description, concentrating on creating atmosphere.

Extension

Collaborative description

When students have completed the Workbook activity, ask them to make groups for the four different types of weather and assign group leaders—for example, all sunny day students come together. Working as a group, they write a longer piece of collaborative description. Set a time limit. Take feedback on the problems encountered in writing together, then ask one student from each group to read the final pieces.

Writing a dramatic scene

Prior knowledge

Take a few minutes to ask students to think about memorable characters and actors from films they have seen. Ask them how good actors make the roles they play so convincing. Bring the discussion round to how an actor prepares for a role. You could mention the Stanislavski method of 'living' the character for a period of time before playing the part on screen or stage. Go on to ask when the class has written a play script before and remind them of drama writing conventions. At this stage, you may want to turn to page 16 of the Workbook and read through the bulleted items under 'Writing a script – adapting a story', before moving on to the writing activity in the Student Book.

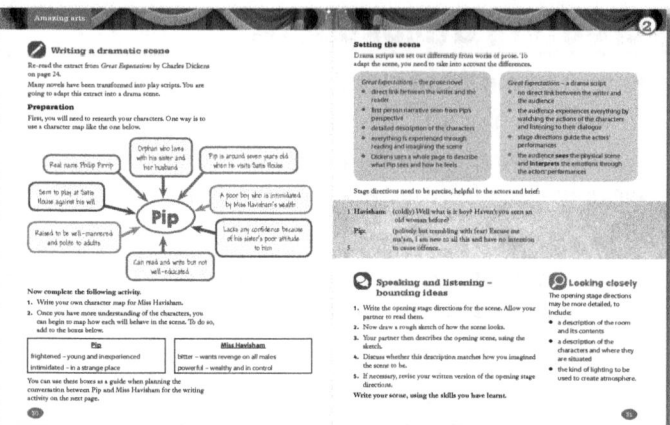

Writing

 ## A character map

Before students re-read the extract from *Great Expectations* that appears earlier in this unit (where Pip first meets Miss Havisham, on page 24), model the character map, as suggested, on the board. Add useful information about Pip's background as you go. He is small, and terrified of his sister – who bullies both him and his brother-in-law (her husband Joe). Run through the details about Pip on pages 24 and 27 of the Student Book. Ask students to complete question 1, the character map for Miss Havisham, using information from the scene with Miss Havisham on page 24 of the Student Book.

For question 2, ask students to plan the interaction between Pip and Miss Havisham. This can be done in pairs or very small groups. Students start by adding information to the boxes for Pip and Miss Havisham, which they will use as a guide when writing the drama script.

Before students start to write the script, you can direct their attention to the sample dialogue in 'Setting the scene' on page 31. Go through the differences between prose and drama with the class, discussing how novels have been transformed into plays or film scripts. Include the need to portray characters as written in the novels and not change the plot (too much).

Setting the scene

Novels and drama scripts

Direct students' attention to the Looking closely feature and read it through with them. This is a good moment to discuss, compare and contrast how fiction authors and theatre and film directors use setting and scenery to show a character's situation and/or personality. Turn back to the reading on page 24 and ask students to make notes on what stage properties they would need to include if they were doing this scene on a stage, or read it through with them and draw attention to how what is in the room shows Miss Havisham's social class and personality. Items include: jewels on a table; there are dresses scattered about and half-packed into open trunks; her watch, handkerchief and prayer book are 'heaped' around a looking glass (perhaps on a dressing table). Ask students what colour they would paint the scenery walls (ochre yellow to show decay). Now ask them to think about how an audience might interpret the atmosphere of the scene from this colour and the state of the room. When you have covered these aspects with the class, ask them to make notes individually for the costume designer and the actress playing Miss Havisham, saying how she should look. We are told she is wearing silks, lace and satins, but everything that was once white is now a dingy yellow; she has one shoe on only; she is wearing some jewels but it is evident she has not finished dressing for her wedding day. The wedding dress should look too big as Miss Havisham's figure has 'shrunk to skin and bone'.

Students may also use these notes during the Speaking and listening activity. As an additional task either now or later, you can develop question 2 of the Speaking and listening task to create wall posters with the accompanying extract from Dickens' novel.

Explain to the class that the stage directions at the beginning of a scene are for:

- stage managers, who direct stage hands (the people who move furniture, scenery, and props)
- costume designers
- directors (who tell actors where to move on the stage in the course of a performance and decide on lighting).

The stage directions need to be thorough but brief. For this reason, students' scenes should contain details about: Miss Havisham and her room; its contents; the type of lighting for Miss Havisham; where characters should sit or stand, etc. As there is a lot to think about, arrange the class in pairs or groups of three for the following Speaking and listening activity.

Bouncing ideas

During their discussion, students should each make notes and draw sketches as requested in the activity. They may then use their stage directions for the scenes they are asked to write.

Given that students have had a good deal of help by now and have worked together collaboratively, set this writing task to be completed individually, preferably in class, where you can supervise as necessary. Mark finished scenes for dialogue (style and content), stage directions, and overall effect (atmosphere).

If some students struggle with this task, set the Workbook activity before they do this writing task in class.

Select the most effective scripts and ask students to perform the scenes in front of the class. Through their effective use of speech, gesture and movement, students should be able to demonstrate their understanding of character. Ask the students to carry out peer reviews, giving each other feedback on how well they have empathised with the characters in their performance.

Writing a script – adapting a story

Students are asked to convert the narrative dialogue from the scene with Miss Havisham into a play script. They should use the dialogue appropriately and set it out as a script, using the opening lines provided and including stage directions. This activity can be peer marked in class.

Script to fiction narrative

Choose a scene from a play, preferably one your students know, and ask them to write it out as prose with dialogue for a novel. Mark for how well students create the characters and atmosphere of the scene. Remind them that in a novel, you start a new line and indent for each new person speaking (like a paragraph). Mark for correct use of English, form, and content.

Progress check

Student Book progress checks are designed to help students revisit what they have learned in a relatively informal manner. They should be completed in class if possible, and in silence, but it is not necessary to impose exam conditions. You may want to allow students to refer to both their Student Book and Workbook as required. When they have finished, read the answers aloud and let students mark their own or a partner's. Collect their answers in later to see what progress students are making and what areas need repeating or practising.

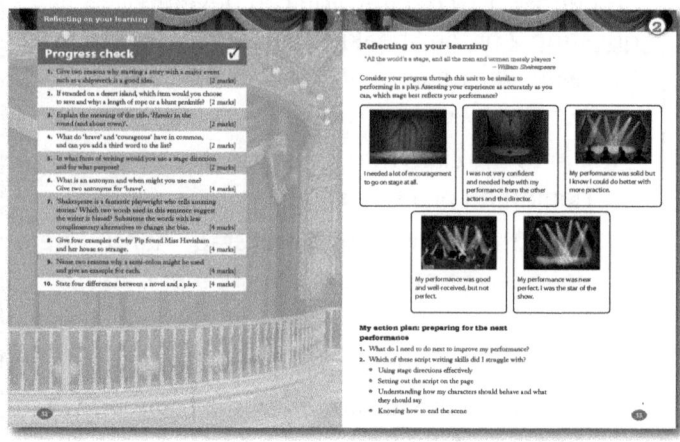

Student-book answers

End-of-unit assessment

1. Accept valid alternatives or other ways of saying any two of the following: dramatic; exciting; straight into the action; throws characters together. [2]

2. Either item is useful – students should justify choice adequately. [2]

3. Performed with audiences on at least three sides, at a variety of outdoor venues. [2]

4. Synonyms: accept alternatives to *bold, heroic, valiant*, and so on. [2]

5. Stage directions give actors, directors, and so on information about a scene to be played on stage or a film set. [2]

6. An opposite word that might be used for juxtaposing different ideas in one's writing. Accept any two words that are suitable antonyms for 'brave', e.g. cowardly, timid, frightened, scared, etc. [4]

7. 'Fantastic' – boring; 'amazing' – dull. Accept any valid antonyms for fantastic and amazing. [4]

8. Pip found Miss Havisham and her house so strange because of: his age/his previous experience; Miss Havisham's illogical behaviour; her appearance; the conditions in the room and the state of the house. Accept any four answers and valid alternatives. [4]

9. As a 'super comma'; to separate items in a list; to present a balanced argument in a sentence. Accept any two suitable examples showing correct use of the semi-colon as stated. [4]

10. Accept any four or valid alternatives to: format, layout, script, prose, paragraphs, naming characters (in margin) or 'he said', length, time sequence, description or stage directions, and so on. [4]

Workbook

🧩 Amazing arts quiz

1. William Shakespeare.

2. 'An amazing novel' and 'entertained for hours' show positive bias.

3. A synonym is a word similar in meaning; an antonym is an opposite.

4. Exaggerated features (and setting).

5. As a 'super comma'; to separate items in a list; to present a balanced argument in a sentence.

6. Repetition, use of semi-colons to create one long complex sentence; detail that focuses on exactly how fog behaves.

7. 'Creeping', 'lying', 'hovering', 'drooping'.

8. Any four suggestions from: format or layout; stage directions; script (dialogue); no description; no paragraphs; names of characters in margins, and so on. Also accept valid alternatives to the suggestions given here.

2

Reflection

My action plan: preparing for the next performance

Spend a few minutes discussing with the class how their progress through this unit can be seen as similar to performing in a play. Explain as necessary the metaphors regarding stage fright, being lonely on stage, and how their performance was received. Encourage students to discuss how their learning affects other people (their audience) such as parents, teachers and peers, and whether they consciously want to be 'the star of the show' or just a member of the cast. This could be done with a partner if you have a large class, but if possible encourage students to complete all aspects of the assessments and reflection on their own first. Give them time to write out their personal action plans individually then collect in their thoughts to monitor their self-assessments.

Once the class has completed the reflection section, return to the quotations in the Student Book. Ask students if they now see the quotation about being interested in what happens to characters differently, having studied how authors and directors influence a reader or audience to see a character in a certain way. Take feedback on what students have enjoyed doing in the unit and make a list on the board of topics and language tasks they would like to revisit.

To round off this unit you might like to read the following extract from Shakespeare's *As You Like It*. The extract is readily available on the internet.

As You Like It

Act 2, Scene VII

(Jaques to Duke Senior)

All the world's a stage,
And all the men and women merely players;
They have their exits and their entrances,
And one man in his time plays many parts,
His acts being seven ages. At first, the infant,
Mewling and puking in the nurse's arms.
Then the whining schoolboy, with his satchel
And shining morning face, creeping like snail
Unwillingly to school. And then the lover,
Sighing like furnace, with a woeful ballad

Made to his mistress' eyebrow. Then a soldier,
Full of strange oaths and bearded like the pard,
Jealous in honor, sudden and quick in quarrel,
Seeking the bubble reputation
Even in the cannon's mouth. And then the justice,
In fair round belly with good capon lined,
With eyes severe and beard of formal cut,
Full of wise saws and modern instances;
And so he plays his part. The sixth age shifts
Into the lean and slippered pantaloon,
With spectacles on nose and pouch on side;
His youthful hose, well saved, a world too wide
For his shrunk shank, and his big manly voice,
Turning again toward childish treble, pipes
And whistles in his sound. Last scene of all,
That ends this strange eventful history,
Is second childishness and mere oblivion,
Sans teeth, sans eyes, sans taste, sans everything.

Listening

A printable version of the full transcript for this unit is available on the CD.

3 Terrific technology

Setting the scene

Terrific technology

Spend about 5–10 minutes with students, drawing out their views and prior experiences in an informal way. Ask them whether they have previously:

- explored the debate about the value of genetically modified crops in their country and/or worldwide

- collaborated in a hot seating exercise and defended their opinion

- created rhetorical questions with a particular effect in mind (for example, to alert, warn or persuade)

- engaged with the arguments for and against artificial intelligence (A.I.)

- reflected on how people react to major advances in technology.

Reflection

Thinking time

With the whole class, ask students to consider how well we take notice of what we hear in the news or television documentaries. Lead into how well they accept new technological developments and why.

Round up this discussion about how their (generally) positive attitude to scientific progress may mean that they accept too much without discussion. Relate this to not listening properly and why it is important to actively listen to the news, etc.

Ask for examples of people who 'speak a thousand words' without saying very much at all – and why they do this.

Ask students to think about why older people may panic when confronted with something very technical and modern, such as an iPhone or wireless router.

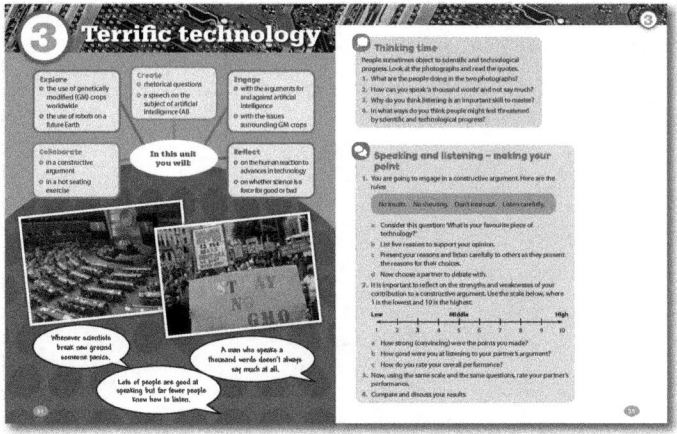

3

Technology for us all

Students now work individually to complete the activity on Workbook page 18.

The short summary task (question 1) is good practice for more challenging summaries in Checkpoint assessments and at IGCSE level. When marking, point out any grammar and spelling weaknesses that students should be able to correct themselves. They should be using a variety of sentence structures.

The answer to question 3 should include sound reasons based on their bulleted points in question 2.

Pair work listening and speaking activity

Challenge individuals to give an off-the-cuff, one-minute speech with no preparation on a piece of modern technology they couldn't live without. They may only focus on positive aspects of the device and they may not use any negative words or phrases.

Partners respond to the challenge of speaking for one minute without any preparation by presenting only the negative aspects of this device.

Depending on time, students then have a second go, with the 'opposer' presenting a 'must-have' device as above.

This activity tests students' memory and speaking skills.

Speaking and listening

Making your point

In groups or pairs, students discuss the implications of the statement, 'It is the nature of humans to argue and disagree, but out of this is born reason and understanding.' They then examine why 'it is fine to disagree with another person's perspective, but the way you articulate your viewpoint is important.'

1. If this exercise is completed as a group activity, make one person in each group a referee or arbiter to ensure the rules are observed.

2. Students should reflect on their individual performance, acknowledging weak areas and where they need to improve.

3. Students should then rate their partner's performance and compare and discuss results.

4. Finally, students make a note of their performance; they can revisit this as they progress through the year.

The Robots of Dawn

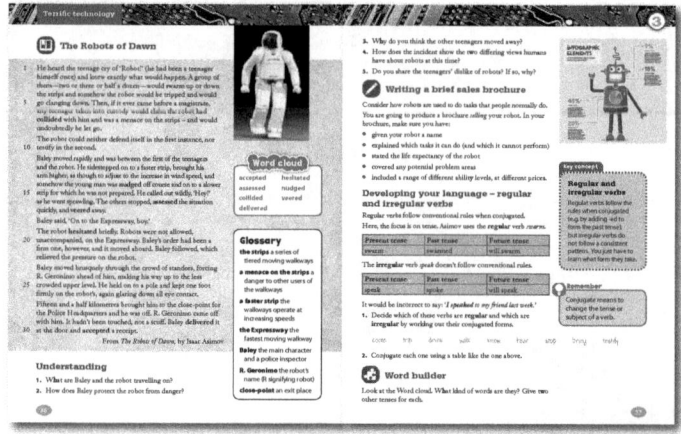

Understanding

1. Baley and the robot are on a moving walkway 'strip'.

2. Baley manoeuvres the first teenager off the strip and sends the robot onto the Expressway.

3. The other teenagers see Baley and realise they cannot get away with their mean/ prejudiced tactics.

4. Baley treats the robot with respect/concern but as a piece of equipment for which he is given a receipt; the teenagers treat the robot as an inferior 'creature'.

5. Accept any reasoned answer; students must explain their points of view.

✏️ Writing a brief sales brochure

This is a useful speaking and listening activity which can be used to help students think about what they need to include in their written sales brochures for the writing task in the Student Book. It also demonstrates how 'thinking time' is a necessary part of any writing activity. Ask students to work in pairs and list all the things they would like a robot to do for them in a given situation, at home or at school. They then review their list and decide which tasks are practical and possible. For example, will a robot really be able do their homework and/or forge their handwriting? Set a time limit, take feedback then direct the class to the sales brochure writing task.

This is a light-hearted activity that is designed to consolidate the ideas and language points covered earlier. Students' brochures can be handwritten, illustrated triptychs, or you could allow them more time to create professional-looking brochures; they should keep these for later use. You could refer them to the www.robocup2014.org video, as described to the left.

When students have completed their brochures they can share them with the class. When marking students' work, credit content, layout and appropriate use of language for the task.

Regular and irregular verbs

More able students may race through this activity and the following Word builder, but both are useful revision.

Suggested answers:

1. Regular = trip, walk, stop, testify (review spelling)

Irregular = come, drink, know, hear, bring

Developing your language

2.

Present tense	Past tense	Future tense
come	came	will come
trip	tripped	will trip
drink	drank	will drink
walk	walked	will walk
know	knew	will know
hear	heard	will hear
stop	stopped	will stop
bring	brought	will bring
testify	testified	will testify

Word builder

 Word builder

The Word cloud contains verbs in the simple past to be conjugated as regular verbs.

Workbook

 Regular and irregular verbs

Mark this activity also for correct spelling.

Present tense	Past tense	Future tense	Regular/ irregular
take	took	will take	irregular
swarm	swarmed	will swarm	regular
copy	copied	will copy	regular
drink	drank	will drink	irregular
write	wrote	will write	irregular
bring	brought	will bring	irregular
teach	taught	will teach	irregular
study	studied	will study	regular
stare	stared	will stare	regular
complete	completed	will complete	regular
break	broke	will break	irregular

Extension

Supporting students – Regular and irregular verb spellings

This activity provides students with further practice of regular and irregular verb forms. They should change the following verbs to the past tense and put each one in a short sentence.

1. catch
2. cough
3. think
4. buy
5. seek
6. laugh

Example: 1. Catch – caught. I caught the ball.

Extension

Stretching students – New verbs for old

Provide all students with a dictionary and assign them letters. Using a thesaurus and working individually, students find less-used or unusual verbs to replace those in the regular and irregular verb task: *come trip drink walk know hear stop bring*. They then write down the correct simple past tense for each new verb.

This activity can be extended by assigning letters or groups of letters to students (A/B/C; J and K; or O, P, Q) and asking them to find ten unusual verbs. They should make a list of the ten infinitives then swap lists with a partner, who has to guess the meanings. They may put the words in a sentence orally and/or write down the simple past tenses. Students can take turns and do this together, or work individually, writing the new words into sentences in the past tense and hand back their answers for partners to check.

Here are examples for letters 'A' and 'S'.

'Alight': a partner would have to decide what 'alight' means and whether it becomes 'alit' or 'alighted', *I alighted the bus when it stopped* is correct;

'Smite': *he smote the door with his hand* (correct).

Questions

Phrasing a question

1. Closed questions:
    a. *Do you* like robots?
    b. *What* is its name?
    c. *Can you* afford a robot?
    d. *Are you* satisfied with your robot?
    e. *Where/when* did you first see the robot?
    f. *Who* is in charge?
    g. *When* will it be ready to collect?
    h. *Did you/can you* find the 'on' button?
    i. *Would you* buy that robot?

2. Open questions:
    a. *How* can robots benefit society?
    b. *Why* might robots be considered a threat to humans?
    c. *What* could happen if robots become too intelligent in the future?
    d. *What* potential advances are there likely to be in the field of robotics in the next ten years?

To extend this work, students can work in pairs, taking on the roles of robot and owner. The owner starts the dialogue by asking a closed question, and follows this with an open one. Robots respond with actions and may speak, but they can only tell the truth. After a few minutes, students swap roles.

Leading questions

Ask students to identify the 'loaded word' in the example ('bad') and discuss how this will influence responses.

Rhetorical questions

Direct students to find the meaning of 'rhetoric' then ask how rhetorical questions can be effective in speeches and why they are not appropriate in serious essays. A rhetorical question is employed for dramatic effect and does not require a straight answer.

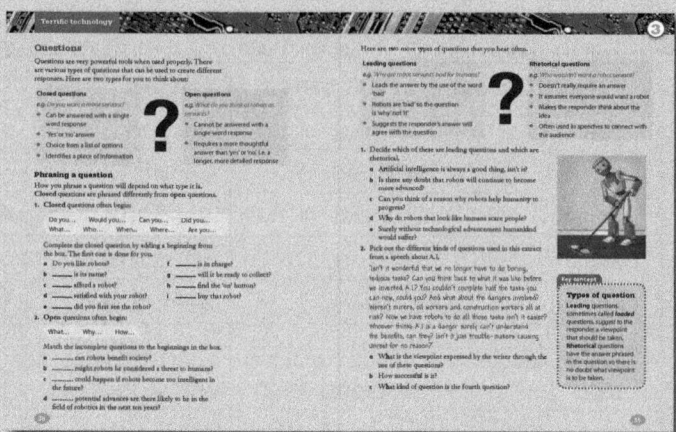

1. a. leading
    b. rhetorical
    c. leading
    d. leading
    e. rhetorical

2. Students should read through the text independently. They may then work with a partner to identify the different kinds of questions.

- Isn't it wonderful that we no longer have to do boring, tedious tasks? (*Rhetorical*)
- Can you think back to what it was like before we invented A.I.? (*Closed*)
- You couldn't complete half the tasks you can now, could you? (*Leading*)
- And what about the dangers involved? (*Rhetorical*)
- Weren't miners, oil workers and construction workers all at risk? (*Leading*)
- Now we have robots to do all those tasks isn't it easier? (*Closed*)
- Whoever thinks A.I. is a danger surely can't understand the benefits, can they? (*Leading*)
- Isn't it just trouble-makers causing unrest for no reason? (*Leading*)
    a. Viewpoint is positive in favour of A.I./robots.
    b. Students' answers will vary, but the questions lead to a positive response.
    c. Rhetorical.

🧩 Questions and answers

Introduce students to some different types of answers:

- **Partial answer** – the response is only a part answer and is selective in its content
- **No response** – not really an answer at all: when someone refuses to respond or is silent
- **Avoidance** – a response designed to avoid the question because it is too difficult to answer or the responder is stalling for time
- **Direct response** – answers the question in a straightforward, honest way as fully as possible
- **Misdirection** – an answer that leads the questioner away from the intended topic
- **Lie** – a deliberate untruth to mislead the questioner

As some students may find this task challenging on their own, you could ask them to do it in class. When they have finished the Workbook task, review how open and closed questions function, drawing their attention to how we use our voices for different types of question, by raising or lowering the tone. Ask students to practise saying leading or loaded questions to suggest the response they want. They should then create a rhetorical question so there is no doubt about the right answer and try it out on a partner. To consolidate the Workbook activity, ask students to work in pairs and practise saying the questions and giving the responses.

1. **a.** Direct response
   b. Misdirection
   c. Avoidance
   d. Direct response
   e. Partial answer
   f. Avoidance
   g. Misdirection

2. A robot can give direct answers and no response. It cannot tell a lie, avoid or misdirect questions.

3. **a.** Closed
   b. Rhetorical
   c. Leading
   d. Open

Language support – 'Can I help you?'

This is a class pair-work game designed to practise framing questions. The objective is to turn every answer into another question. Ask students to choose one of the following situations: in a shop with a shop assistant and a customer; in a cafe with a waitress and a customer; or out in the countryside with a traveller asking for directions. The winners are the pair who can keep the questions going for longest.

Model this opening gambit to get them started:

Shop assistant: Can I help you?

Customer: Yes, please. Do you sell hats?

Shop assistant: Yes, what colour would you like?

Customer: I was thinking of blue. What colours do you have?

Shop assistant: Most colours. What shade of blue would you prefer?

Extension

Students read the PCM 'The Kitchen Robot' on the Teacher's Book CD.

This one-act play is designed to help students practise different question forms. The script requires three characters. They may use props and act it out in class, but they need to finish the script first.

Encourage students to record their play readings and listen to the way they speak. At this stage all students should be becoming more aware of their personal language acquisition and learning how to improve their speaking skills. Demonstrate how peers can criticise constructively with polite suggestions because later in their school careers students may be asked to comment on their peers' performance in speaking and listening activities.

A balanced argument

Prior knowledge

'The impact of biotechnology' is a challenging text, so familiarise students with the glossary and go over any words they do not know. Ask if they have discussed GM foods and sustainable cultivation in Science or Geography lessons. If so, do they have positive or negative ideas about the value and use of GM crops? Are they aware of any GM crops they eat on a regular basis? Try to draw out opposing views on GM foods then ask students to look at how the article on page 40 of the Student Book presents a balanced argument. They should find examples from the text to show it is written in a formal style. Explain why formal writing is necessary here. Draw attention to the absence of rhetorical features.

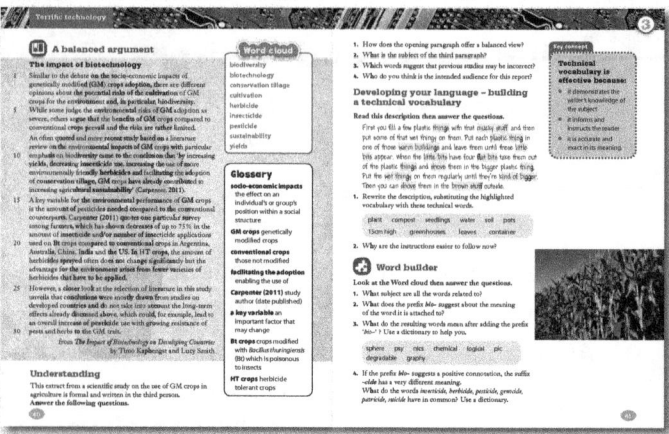

Student-book answers

📖 Understanding

1. It acknowledges both sides of the argument.
2. Pesticides/insecticides.
3. Key phrases are: 'a closer look (at the selection of literature)'; 'conclusions were mostly drawn'; 'do not take into account'.
4. Agricultural engineers, scientists, government advisers; also accept 'modern farmers'.

Vocabulary

Word game to improve vocabulary

If you have a relatively small class, this game can be played as a whole-class activity. Otherwise, ask students to work in pairs or groups of three. Direct them to the reading 'A balanced argument' on page 40 in the Student Book and ask them to find a long word from the text such as 'sustainability' or 'biotechnology'. They each write out the word they have chosen across the top of a blank sheet of paper in capital letters. It is then a race to see who can make the most new words using the letters of their chosen word. No

letter may be repeated (unless it is repeated in the word itself, for example, the letters 's' and 'i' in *sustainability*). There are two winners in this game: the person who can form the most new words and the person who can form the longest word. Set a time limit. At the end of that time ask students to count and check each other's words.

Developing your language

Building a technical vocabulary

1. First you fill a few plastic <u>pots</u> with <u>compost</u> and then put <u>water</u> on them. Put each <u>pot</u> in one of those <u>greenhouses</u> and leave them until <u>seedlings</u> appear. When the <u>seedlings</u> have four <u>leaves</u>, take them out of the plastic <u>pots</u> and <u>plant</u> them in the bigger plastic <u>container</u>. Put <u>water</u> on them regularly until they're <u>15cm high</u>. Then you can <u>plant</u> them in the <u>soil outside</u>.

2. The instructions are now more specific/clearer.

Word builder

1. Farming/agriculture.

2. Prefix *bio–*, from Greek *bios* = life.

3. Biosphere = all parts of the Earth containing living creatures, organisms and plants.

   Biopsy = tissue taken from a living body for examination.

   Bionics = a part operated by electronic devices.

   Biochemical = the chemical composition of living things.

   Biological = to do with biology/nature.

   Biopic = a film about a person's life.

   Biodegradable = can be broken down by bacteria/ the environment.

   Biography = a person's life story.

4. All words relate to death/killing, from Latin *cidium* = killing, or *caedere* = to kill.

Using subject-specific words

1. Roboticists within the robotics field of science have disagreed over the moral question of artificial intelligence for decades. Some have argued the neural pathways in the positronic brain make robots much more dependable because they aren't capable of lying. Others have countered that, by using 264-bit binary code programming, the neurons in the artificial neural network can be taught to make the robot autonomous.

2. Neural.

3. The extract is about robot 'brains'.

4. Set a time limit in class or set as homework. Do a feedback session and organise peer marking. Partners decide what the topic is and whether all words are technical. If students have access to computers, discourage the use of Wikipedia or popular 'simplified' school subject sites.

Extension

Grow your own list of technical terms

Challenge students to match the technical names to their meaning (as shown below) then add five more terms related to agriculture.

Conservation tillage = not damaging the environment.

Cultivation = the preparation and farming of land.

Sustainability = leaving some of the seeds in the ground when ploughing.

Yield = the amount of crops grown.

Extension

Practising formal writing

To enable students to practise using technical words and a formal register, develop Workbook question 4 on page 21 into a writing task. Students choose a topic of interest to them in physics, chemistry, biology or computing, then write a paragraph for a school encyclopaedia.

Explain that writing in a formal, accurate style is a valuable skill that applies to all school subjects; it will be very useful when students come to do coursework and formal exams at IGCSE and beyond.

Sentences

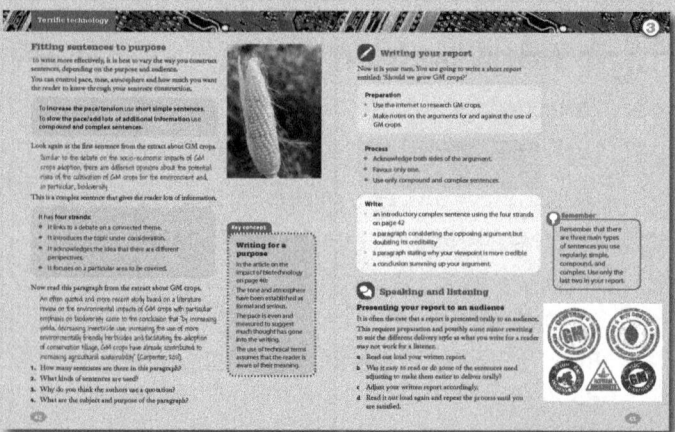

✏ Writing your report

This work should be carried out independently, as far as possible. Draw students' attention to how the question forms the title, meaning they must include both sides of the argument but also demonstrate why their opinion is of more value.

Students may only use compound and complex sentences. Explain why rhetorical questions are inappropriate. You could model a poor opening paragraph, starting with a rhetorical question or a simple sentence (e.g. 'GM foods are destroying the environment. What good are they to us if they destroy the very soil we depend on?'), and show how this takes the report into persuasive writing. Remind students that this kind of writing is more appropriate to a speech or an article. Discuss why this writing style is not right for a formal report or a balanced argument.

In marking, look for how argument has been examined and how the student establishes his or her views. Look for sound reasoning leading to a clear conclusion. (Explain that this is important for IGCSE English – both as a first and second language.) Correct spelling and grammar; identify where students have strayed from measured language. Students should be made aware of the importance of drafting, redrafting and proofreading for a task such as this.

Presenting a report to an audience

Read through the information on how to adjust a written report for oral delivery on page 43 of the Student Book and set the task. This is a good opportunity to practise public speaking skills, especially if you have a debating society or Model United Nations group in school. (You can find more about the Model UN on its official site (www.nmun.org) or by going to http://onlinemodelunitednations.org/middle-school-jro-mun.)

Pace, pitch and projection

Explain to students the meaning and significance of the following speaking skills:

Pitch – how low or high one speaks

Pace – how slow or fast one speaks

Projection – how loudly words are spoken (to make oneself heard across a large room); explain this does not mean shouting but projecting the voice

Clarity – how clearly people can hear what is said.

Arrange the class in small groups and ask them to find a short speech about the environment on the Internet or in a newspaper, or give them a copy of this speech about water in plastic bottles: 'H2O So You Know-Plastic Water Bottles: Bad For The Environment' from: http://www.kidzworld. com/article/17863-h2o-so-you-know-plastic-water-bottles-really-bad-for-the-environment.

Groups should find a space where they do not disturb others and take turns in reading their chosen speech aloud. Peers listen then give informative feedback on the speaker's pace, pitch, projection and clarity. Set a time limit and take feedback on troublesome or challenging areas such as projecting one's voice without shouting. (Girls with high voices should be advised to lower their tone for this.)

 ## Fitting sentences to purposes

The language practice task on page 22 of the Workbook is suitable for pair work. Introduce the topic by having fun with some overly formal expressions, such as 'Whilst engaged in the selection and cleansing of previously employed test-tubes, I turned to ascertain the nature of fumes spontaneously arising from a Bunsen burner, causing said test-tubes to . . .'

Note that some students will have greater difficulty with formal English than with informal English. If this is the case, record formal radio news reports or science programmes and give them listening practice with spot check questions to test comprehension.

Extension

Developing a formal vocabulary

How do we usually say the following words and phrases in a much less formal way?

(Example: ascertain = find out)

- Hitherto
- Notwithstanding
- Sporadic
- A resounding success
- A lamentable outcome

Students then choose three words and/or phrases and use them in sentences about the environment.

Public speaking

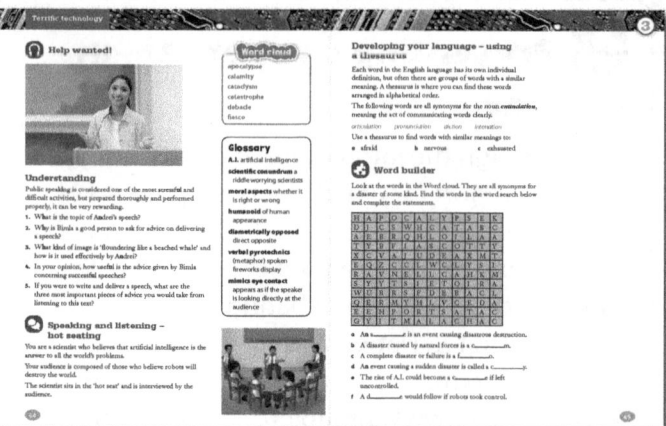

Student-book answers

🎧 Understanding

1. Technology/Do we really need A.I. or is it a catastrophe waiting to happen?

2. Bimla has experience of giving speeches.

3. A simile to show Andrei is 'out of his element', and struggling with the unknown.

4. Bimla's advice is very good, but accept any reasoned, justified answer.

5. Possible answers include: use cue cards; focus on the back wall; practise out loud; practise enunciation; make eye contact; mention negatives and discuss good points in detail.

Speaking and listening

💬 Hot seating

Students do this exercise as a whole-class activity. You may then develop it to give students more practice.

Organise the class into groups of five or six. Explain they will take turns being in the hot seat. You may need to establish a referee for each group, to ensure that students only use formal language. They must be polite at all times. Allow a few minutes for students to decide on their chosen topic. Put suggestions on the board, such as:

- Fossil fuels are a thing of the past, they pollute the air – their use should be prohibited.

- Plastics are not biodegradable – their use should be prohibited.

- Insecticides cause health problems and kill too many species.

Students may turn to the speech writing frame on page 47 of the Student Book to get ideas.

Using a thesaurus

a. Afraid: scared, terrified, petrified, alarmed, fearful, intimidated, cowardly.

b. Nervous: anxious, worried, apprehensive, concerned, uneasy, edgy, tense, overwrought, uptight.

c. Exhausted: tired, weary, worn out, fatigued, breathless, all in.

1. Motor car: automobile, horseless carriage, limousine, jalopy, saloon, hatchback, SUV, 4x4, etc.

   Building: apartment block, block of flats, mansion, cabin, bungalow, terrace, cottage, palace, etc.

2. The words that do not belong in the group are: submarine, aeroplane, ocean. The theme is space. Students may disagree on 'horoscope', but it is linked to star signs and the planets.

Word builder

Students find the words from the Word cloud in the word search and complete the statements.

H	A	P	O	C	A	L	Y	P	S	E	K
D	J	C	S	W	H	C	A	T	A	B	C
A	E	B	R	Q	H	L	O	I	L	A	A
T	Y	B	F	I	A	S	C	O	T	T	Y
X	C	V	A	J	U	D	E	A	X	M	T
E	Q	Z	C	C	L	W	C	L	Y	S	I
R	A	V	N	E	L	L	C	A	H	K	M
S	Y	Y	T	S	I	E	T	O	I	R	A
W	U	B	R	S	F	D	E	B	A	C	L
Q	E	R	M	Y	H	L	V	C	E	D	A
E	E	H	P	O	R	T	S	A	T	A	C
G	Y	I	T	M	A	L	A	C	H	A	C

a. An <u>apocalypse</u> is an event causing disastrous destruction.

b. A disaster caused by natural forces is a <u>cataclysm</u>.

c. A complete disaster or failure is a <u>fiasco</u>.

d. An event causing a sudden disaster is called a <u>calamity</u>.

e. The rise of A.I. could become a <u>catastrophe</u> if left uncontrolled.

f. A <u>debacle</u> would follow if robots took control of the world.

Workbook

🧩 **Words with similar meanings**

Students can do this activity for homework with the help of a thesaurus, or they can do it in pairs in class.

Extension

Word search

Provide students with printed 12 x 12 grids.

Ask them to choose either artificial intelligence and robotics or biology and the environment, and create a word soup with words in their chosen field.

Students then write out a set of clues under the grid, with one clue per word. (Example: A person who makes or works on robots = robotocist)

Students then swap papers and complete their partner's word search.

Finally, students check answers and discuss what made the task easy or difficult.

Vocabulary activity – Branches of science

Ask students to do an Internet search for different branches of science or use the *Oxford Thesaurus for Schools* inset on page 491 entitled 'Some branches of science'. Ask students to select five branches of science that they have not heard of before, or are unsure about, for example: *forensic science, mineralogy, oceanography, nanotechnology*. They should then investigate what scientists in these fields do, making notes. When they have finished, they share the names of these branches of science with a partner and ask them to guess what the scientists do.

Writing and performing a speech

Prior knowledge

Review prior work on tone and register in this unit. Remind the class of Andrei's concerns in the Listening task and Bimla's advice. Point out to students that they are now going to put this into practice.

Preparation

For maximum practice and engagement, do this as an individual task. Ask students to keyword the question: 'Is our increased use of artificial intelligence beneficial or dangerous?' Ensure everyone is familiar with the idea of 'beneficial'. Students then decide on: audience, purpose, length and scope.

Before asking them to begin, review the importance of the speech's structure; emphasise the need to create a sound argument leading to a convincing conclusion. A good way for students to learn about this is to underline topic sentences in their paragraphs after they have finished the first draft. Writing out these topic sentences should demonstrate their argument, and they can be used for cue cards.

Insist that students work on their own during the planning stage. They may use the ideas below and the writing frame on page 47 of the Student Book to help them. Later, students may work in pairs or small groups to practise their speeches.

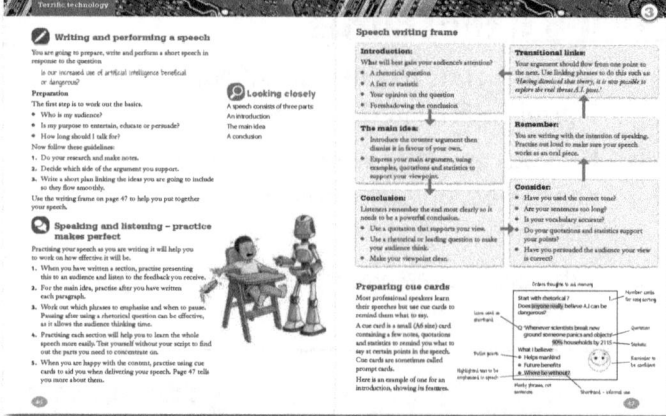

Speaking and listening

Practice makes perfect

While students are practising their speeches, single out the use of rhetorical language and ask them to use these questions with their peers, to test responses. Direct students to Workbook page 24 (see below); they should do this as homework while preparing their speeches. Remind them that the purpose of the opening is to be memorable and to sell; therefore it is not ideal for their formal discursive/argument speeches.

Provide blank cue cards or ask students to type up topic sentences in boxes on A4 then cut the page(s) into sections.

For A.I.

Helpful to humans

Does menial tasks

Does dangerous tasks

Does complicated tasks

Low maintenance

Cost effective

Reliable

Logical

Advanced technology

Against A.I.

Makes humans lazy

Takes humans' jobs

Will replace humans

Decisions based on logic not morals

Unfeeling and inhuman

Will become too intelligent so unpredictable

Too expensive to buy and maintain

Technology too advanced/complicated

Environmentally unfriendly

🧩 Writing a speech – the opening

Students should complete this activity individually.

1. Suggested answers:

   a. Weak and gives a negative impression. To be avoided.

   b. 'Unbelievable' and over-the-top. To be avoided.

   c. Memorable and suitable for the style of speech required. Effective.

2. This is a fun activity that allows students to play with language and its effect. If they have completed the PCM 'The Kitchen Robot' on the Teacher's Book CD, they can refer back to the seller's dialogue and use it as a model, if necessary.

Giving speeches

You could arrange for your class to present their speeches to the rest of the year group. Alternatively, you could arrange for an audience with colleagues in Science or IT.

Remind students of the importance speaking clearly and not rushing their words. After they have all finished, ask the class to give feedback on who spoke clearly, whose speech was particularly effective and make a few comments on the board about areas in which some or all of the class need to improve, for example, pausing for effect or to give listeners time to think, or projecting voices so they can be heard across a school hall or classroom.

An alternative or additional extension activity is to listen and compare different people giving speeches on a similar topic. Play the following two short speeches to the class (or select two by similarly disparate people in age and occupation). The first here is given by a Canadian schoolgirl, Severn Suzuki, speaking at the UN Earth Summit in 1992; the second is a short speech on the environment given by a professional actor, Leonardo DiCaprio. Ask students to make notes as they listen on pace, pitch and projection. Take feedback on how effectively they think each speaker conveys her/his message.

Known as 'the girl who silenced the world for six minutes', Severn Suzuki's speech is available on a number of YouTube sites: https://www.youtube.com/watch?v=IqrBzuOwGqQ

DiCaprio's speech can be found at: http://www.theguardian.com/environment/2014/sep/23/leonarodo-dicaprio-un-climate-change-speech-new-york

Progress check

Student Book progress checks are designed to help students revisit what they have learned in a unit in relatively informal manner. They should be completed in class if possible, and in silence, but it is not necessary to impose exam conditions. You may want to allow students to refer to both their Student Book and Workbook as required. When they have finished, read the answers aloud and let students mark their own or a partner's. Collect their answers later to see what progress students are making and what areas need repeating or practising.

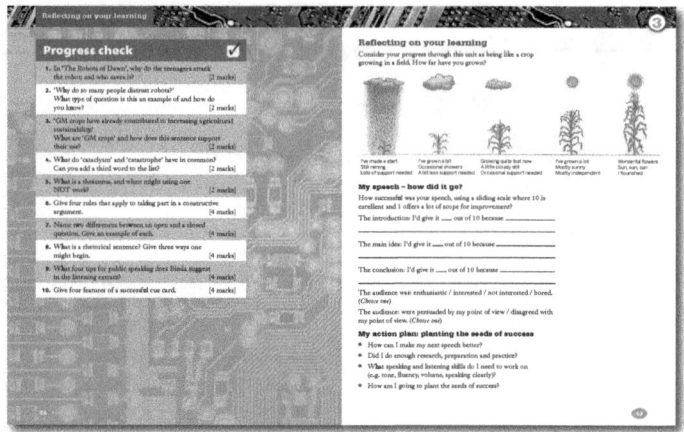

Student-book answers

1. A mean teenage prank; Baley saves the robot. [2]

2. Rhetorical, because there is no clear answer and no leading or loaded words. [2]

3. Genetically modified plants; sentence says they contribute to increased sustainability, so presents positive bias. [2]

4. Disasters; debacle, fiasco. [2]

5. Provides alternatives to a given word; context is important. [2]

6. Examine both sides of the argument; use formal, measured tone and language; no insults; no shouting; don't interrupt; listen. [4]

7. Open questions use: what, why, how; they cannot be answered with single words, they require thoughtful answers. Closed questions can use: do you, would you, can you, did you; they can be answered with yes/no or single-word response. Students give a suitable example of each. [4]

8. Used for dramatic effect and if in question form, does not require an answer; also used to draw attention to topic and/or speaker. Three examples required. [4]

9. Bimla's four tips could include: [4]
   - know your position on a subject (for or against) and start by presenting positive or negative arguments accordingly
   - begin with a rhetorical question
   - don't overwhelm the audience with your viewpoint

   - don't rush delivery
   - take care with body language
   - be informative and persuasive.

10. Features on cue card may include: bullet points to organise thoughts; statistics; quotations; personal shorthand; highlight point to be emphasised. [4]

Reflection

🧩 Reflecting on your learning

The reflection section in this unit uses growth as a metaphor for learning. Once students have completed their answers individually, take feedback. Spend a few minutes discussing with the class how they will use the different speaking and listening skills covered in this unit as they proceed through school and further education, then in their working life. Discuss why learning how to frame questions in different ways will be useful, and how, when we convey information, adjusting the tone of one's voice can be used for effect. Ask students if they are aware of doing this in real-life (not English classroom) situations. You can remind them that it is a strategy most children use instinctively when they want something or need to get out of trouble. Depending on your class, students may find discussing their 'plan of action' with a partner to be useful, but essentially this page is for personal reflection.

Students use the metaphor of growth to examine their personal progress.

Do a round-up of topics covered in this unit; discuss how these include skills of value across the curriculum that are applicable to further education and the world of work.

Once the class has completed the reflection section, round up the unit by going back to page 35 of the Student Book. Ask students how they now interpret the meaning of the quotation on knowing how to listen. Remind them that listening is a skill. At IGCSE, students need to be able to follow an argument and their contributions to discussions need to demonstrate they have listened *actively* and *attentively* to what has been said before. Take feedback on what students have enjoyed doing in the unit, such as the short plays, and make a list on the board of topics and language tasks they would like to revisit.

Science and technology unit quiz time

1. Rhetorical. No.
2. Any suitable definition.
3. **a.** Yes or no.
   b. Anything that guides the subject away from the question.
4. Tractor/harvester/insecticide/herbicide/fallow field/etc.
5. Sentence b), as it is more direct and immediate in a crisis.
6. Answers may vary slightly, but they are synonyms not connections.

   robot – android

   rocket – missile

   planet – world

   falling star – meteor

   moon – satellite
7. One sells robots; the other is a robot that sells.
8. Rhetorical question/shock tactic/engages on personal level/introduces opinion and topic/leading question.

A printable version of the full transcript for this unit is available on the CD.

End of unit listening activity

An interesting way to end this unit is to read Sylvia Plath's poem 'Mushrooms' to the class and encourage students to think about the silent power of the earth, and whether in the long run it might defeat both science and the way humans abuse it. The poem was first published in *The Colossus*, 1960. It can also be found on the Internet.

Mushrooms

Overnight, very
Whitely, discreetly,
Very quietly

Our toes, our noses
Take hold on the loam,
Acquire the air.

Nobody sees us,
Stops us, betrays us;
The small grains make room.

Soft fists insist on
Heaving the needles,
The leafy bedding,

Even the paving.
Our hammers, our rams,
Earless and eyeless,

Perfectly voiceless,
Widen the crannies,
Shoulder through holes. We

Diet on water,
On crumbs of shadow,
Bland-mannered, asking

Little or nothing.
So many of us!
So many of us!

We are shelves, we are
Tables, we are meek,
We are edible,

Nudgers and shovers
In spite of ourselves.
Our kind multiplies:

We shall by morning
Inherit the earth.
Our foot's in the door.

'Mushrooms' by Sylvia Plath

49

4 Unnatural nature

Setting the scene

Unnatural nature

Spend about 5–10 minutes drawing out students' ideas and prior experience in an informal way.

- Ask why people want to explore places that are thought of as hostile or extreme environments.

- Has anyone collaborated with a speaker or team in a debate?

- Ask if anyone has created a short summary out of a longer piece of writing.

- How do metaphors, similes, and personification help a reader to engage in what they are reading?

- When you watch a television documentary about dangerous animals or hostile places, do you ever stop to reflect on what the person filming or reporting is experiencing?

Reflection

Thinking time

You could start by asking whether students think they live in a hostile environment. Then take a moment to examine the words *hostile* and *extreme* in relation to places.

Throughout the discussion remind students to support their opinions with reasons (in preparation for the debate later). Ask if there is anywhere left in the world to explore.

Look at the quotations on page 50. 'Nature, red in tooth and claw' is a personification from 'In Memoriam' by Alfred, Lord Tennyson (1833). What does it suggest about Nature? Is Nature kind? Discuss places few people visit and why, such as the Arctic, deserts, jungles. If few people go there anyway, why should we 'Keep Out'? Do we know everything about Planet Earth? Should this century be about exploring the universe?

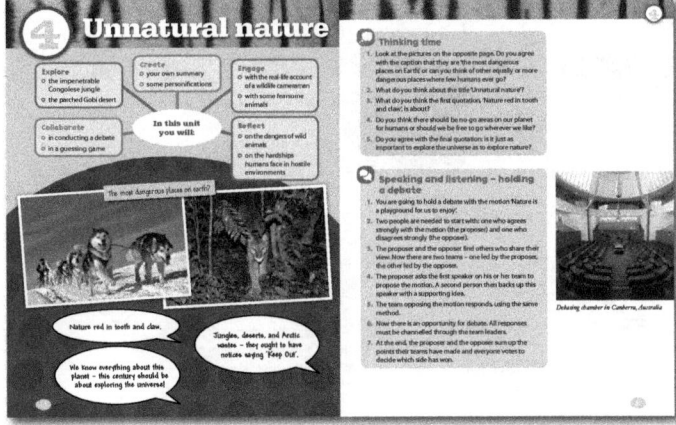

Holding a debate

Remind students how a debate is conducted: what a motion is, how it should be phrased, and the roles of proposer, opposer, and seconders. Discuss the implications of the motion 'Nature is a playground for us to enjoy'. You may need to spend a few minutes defining the concept of a 'playground' in this context. Clarify expressions such as 'at one with nature' and 'balance of nature', if required.

Organise two groups for the teams. Remind students that their opinions must be justified with sound reasoning. Make sure members of the audience understand how vital it is to listen and reflect on what they have heard, so they should make notes on what the speakers say before voting.

You could model examples of 'For' and 'Against' views, with supporting ideas and conclusions, to demonstrate how students' opinions must be justified by sound reasoning. For example:

View: It is wrong to think of nature as a playground.

Supporting idea: Examples of humans destroying wildlife could be given.

Conclusion: Wildlife declines and the balance of nature is changed.

Workbook

Debating

Page 26 of the Workbook gives students another opportunity to practise expressing personal views. They need to work in pairs, with students expressing opposing views, so this activity will work best in class.

Remind students that an argument has no value without a reasoned justification. Try to organise more vocal students in a team with students who

are less likely to express their opinions. Remind them that their contributions are of value, and that they should participate orally in the debate by asking questions if they are in the audience. Remind all students that active listening is also a necessary skill, which they can acquire with practice.

Remind the class that they should make notes, not write a full script. However, each of their arguments should be developed in some way to make it persuasive and valid.

Dictogloss

This is good listening practice that also helps students with summary skills. Choose a short informative text such as a news report or first-person account (see the sample 'Life at the North Pole' by Jan Gilling on the CD, or you could use the passage on page 29 of the Workbook). Ask students to listen as you read it aloud and to summarise the key points. Make copies for your class, but do not show them the text until after they have finished their summary of it from your dictation. Note that this is not a traditional dictation exercise, as students are expected to make only notes.

- Read the text to the class once in a normal speaking voice.

- Ask students to note down basic *wh-* points (who, what, where, when) from memory.

- Read the text again in a normal voice and ask students to note down numerical data (number of inhabitants, temperatures, etc). Then give them a few moments to expand their *wh-* notes.

- Read the text a final time and give students a few moments to complete their notes.

- Organise students into pairs or small groups then ask them to reconstruct the text from memory. Set a specific time limit that suits your class.

- When time is up, students exchange papers. While you read the text again, they tick the relevant points on their peer's reconstruction as they hear them.

- Read the passage one final time for peer marking, if necessary.

- Once you have finished the exercise, give students copies of the text and discuss what they found easy or difficult about the task.

A terrible place in the jungle

Prior knowledge

Mary Kingsley was born in England in 1862. She received no formal education and lived at home, caring for her invalid mother. Both her parents died in 1892. Kingsley then went to the Canary Islands and began her first West African trip in 1893, to complete studies begun by her father. A woman travelling alone was unheard of at this time. She sailed from Sierra Leone to Luanda then travelled inland from Guinea to what is now Nigeria. She collected scientific specimens, including insects and freshwater fish for the British Museum while she explored the lower Congo River. On her second trip, Kingsley travelled up the Ogowé (now the Ogooué) River by steamboat and canoe. She was the first European to visit remote parts of Gabon and the French Congo. Kingsley also climbed the south-east face of Mount Cameroon. Her controversial book *Travels in West Africa* (1897) shows her opposition to many European practices on the African continent. She returned to Africa in 1899 as a nurse and journalist, but contracted typhoid and died in 1900, aged 38.

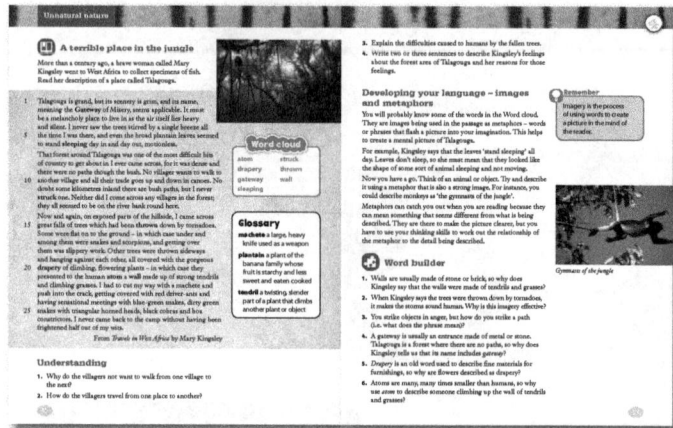

Vocabulary

A terrible place in the jungle

Remind students that Kingsley was writing in the 19th century. Ask how this affects how they should interpret words in the Word cloud, such as 'atoms' and 'drapery'. Also ask: How many different ways can we use the verb 'to strike'? How is it used in 'to strike a path'?

Draw attention to the fact that Kingsley is in a very remote, alien place, and how her impressions and feelings show in the expressions she uses. Also explore:

- the use of opposites in 'Talouga is grand, but its scenery is grim' and the description of the trees which harbour snakes and scorpions but are covered in 'gorgeous' flowering plants
- what 'sleeping day in day out' suggests
- how 'fall' is used in 'great falls of trees'
- a modern alternative for 'half out of my wits'.

Student-book answers

📖 Understanding

Give students time to read the text on their own, then read together as a class. Point out that the text was written in the 1890s, so some of the phrasing or words, such as 'drapery', may seem old-fashioned.

1. Kingsley says the forest around Talagouga 'was one of the most difficult bits of the country to get about in'. The forest is dense and there are no paths through the bush. Students may also infer that villagers may not want to travel on foot because it is a frightening place, as well as difficult to get through, due to the fallen trees full of scorpions, driver ants, and snakes.

2. They travel by canoe along the river.

3. It is difficult to get over the fallen trees and they hide ants, snakes, and scorpions. They create 'walls' of strong climbing plants that need to be cut down using machetes.

4. Kingsley finds the place grim, melancholy, and frightening, but with a certain beauty. She finds it one of most difficult places to get about in and she feels that the air is 'heavy and silent'. She is frightened of the snakes in the trees but she sees beauty in the flowers.

Images and metaphors

Discuss the imagery in 'the air itself lies heavy and silent' (line 3) and plantain leaves 'stand sleeping' (line 5). Discuss the language and imagery Kingsley uses.

You could also point out that we use nature and animal imagery all the time in everyday speech. Consider similes, for example: as busy as a bee, as brave as a lion, as quick as lightning. Point out that some cars are given the names of animals. What do the names 'Jaguar' and 'Cobra' suggest about the cars? Students could also think about the metaphors in the following phrases:

- she flew into a rage
- he wolfed down his food
- the singer croaked through the song
- a storm of protest.

Students then create their own imagery for their chosen creature.

 Word builder

The questions in this section consolidate language and reading skills, revisiting work covered orally, so you could ask students to work quietly on their own. They should write answers in full sentences, as good practice for later Checkpoint and IGCSE work.

1. Tree 'walls' are thick and can only be cut by a machete.

2. The imagery (personification) makes the tornadoes seem active, powerful, malevolent, violent.

3. This phrase means to find a path/to start to walk along a path.

4. Kingsley describes Talagouga as grim, silent, and melancholy, all words associated with misery. This is therefore a 'gateway' to a secret, hidden, sad place.

5. The flowers form a colourful pattern on the curtain of climbing plants over the fallen trees.

6. 'Atom' is used to give the sense that the humans are very small in contrast to the huge size of the trees.

Writing a letter

Page 27 of the Workbook asks students to write a letter for a specific audience – Mary Kingsley. Some students using English as an additional language may have difficulty identifying the difference between formal and informal registers, so remind the class how and why a letter such as this should be written in a formal to neutral register.

Give examples of formal/neutral/informal register before students start the task. Remind them to plan their three paragraphs so the letter has a clear structure and includes reasons based on what they have read in the Kingsley extracts. Point out that the convention for closing a formal letter to a named person is 'Yours sincerely'.

Writing a first-person account using figurative language

Now that students are familiar with how a first-person account can include more interesting and figurative language (imagery), ask them to write a short piece of travel writing or an extract from a journal about an interesting place. They should aim to use metaphors, similes, and personification in their writing. Remind them that their writing should express their feelings about the place they have visited, and it should also be entertaining.

This activity develops useful writing skills for IGCSE First Language English. It should be done individually. It could be set as a writing activity in class, with students working in silence but with the teacher helping as necessary, or you could set it as homework.

Students may find the following reminders useful:

- Start by setting the scene: who, where, when.
- Retell the events in chronological order – what happened, when.
- The final paragraph can link back to the opening lines.
- Use the past tense and the first person ('I').
- Use time connectives, e.g. meanwhile, much later, almost immediately, etc.
- Focus on one specific place, event, object, or person.

Verb tenses

Prior knowledge

Remind students of the difference between a phrasal verb and a one-word verb. Phrasal verbs generally contain a verb + adverb or a verb + preposition. Write a verb (e.g. *to break*) in the centre of the board and ask the class to suggest prepositions and adverbs to make it a phrasal verb (e.g. *break in* meaning to force entry for a robbery, or to *break up* a fight or *break up* at the end of term). You could then ask students to work together in pairs and jot down how many phrases they can think of with the verb *to make* (e.g. *make my way home, make my day, make up a story*).

In the first extract on page 54 of the Student Book there are: (to) *get up* and (to) *have*; in the second extract: (to) *carry out* (trade) and (to) *discover*.

Discuss how we use the simple present in habitual actions (e.g. I *go* to school every day). (You could also review the difference between *every day* and the adjective *everyday*, which is all one word.)

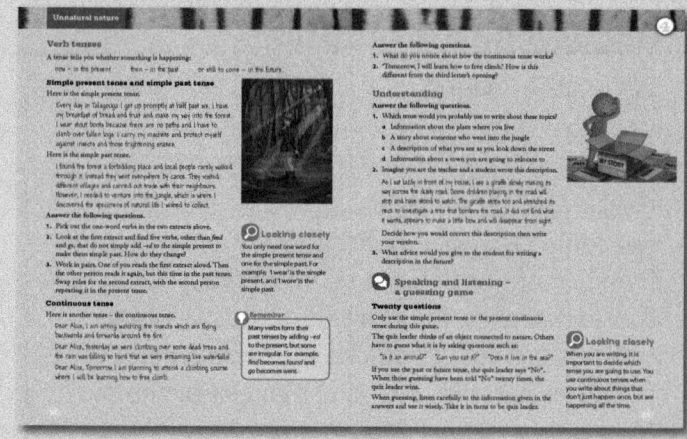

More able students who finish the activity faster than their peers can do another, similar activity employing alternative verbs in the relevant tense. This may include changing sentences slightly. For example, in extract 1, 'I get up' can be changed to 'I rise'. In extract 2, 'people rarely walked through it' could be changed to 'people rarely traversed' or 'made their way through it'.

Grammar

Simple present tense and simple past tense

In this section the focus is on one-word verbs.

1. The one-word verbs in the two extracts are: (extract 1) have, make, wear, carry, protect; (extract 2) found, walked, went, visited, discovered, wished. (Note both extracts also include modal verbs such as: I *have to* climb, I *needed to* venture.)

2. The irregular verbs (not made using *-ed*) are: (extract 1) get/got, have/had, make/made, wear/wore; (extract 2) find/found, go/went. Remind students of the spelling rule for verbs ending in a *-y* such as *carry/carried*.

3. This is a peer-correction exercise. For students who need more language support you may find it useful to ask each pair to make a list of the verbs in their (own) extract that should be changed before they listen to their partner do the oral activity.

Grammar

Continuous tense

1. Continuous tense verbs use *-ing* endings.

2. 'I am *planning to attend*' uses the present continuous to express the subject's intention to perform a future action. It suggests the subject is at the planning stage at this moment and something may prevent the action. 'Tomorrow I will learn how to free climb' expresses the subject's determination to learn to climb and expresses the intention that the subject will definitely do it.

Understanding

1. **a.** present
   b. simple past
   c. present continuous
   d. present continuous as a future form using *going to* and future tense with *will*.

2. Remind students that their choice of first verb should determine the rest of the paragraph: 'As I *sit* lazily…' or 'As I *sat* lazily…'.

3. Students should comment on how a writer's use of language contributes to the overall effect on the reader, using appropriate terminology to suggest the importance of the planning stage in any piece of writing. A quick *wh-* plan, for example, helps to prevent confusing tenses because it includes when the action takes place – past, present, or future. Proofreading and checking grammar before handing in work is another way to identify errors and eliminate confusing tenses.

A guessing game
Twenty questions

This is a variation on the Twenty questions game that starts, 'Animal, vegetable or mineral?' However, students need to be aware which tense they are using when they ask their questions. Review the present continuous tense and remind students how it differs from using the present simple tense for habitual actions, e.g. 'I get up every morning as soon as I hear the alarm' (present simple for habitual action); 'while I was getting up the alarm started ringing' (past continuous to show simultaneous actions).

Remind the class how important it is to listen to what each person is asking and to guess the answer correctly. Choose a student to keep the score, which should include the number of times the quiz leader says 'No'. The maximum number of questions is 20. Giving the scoring to a student will enable you to focus on how students formulate their questions and offer guidance, as well as decide what grammar areas need correction or improvement.

Know which tense to use!

Page 28 of the Workbook allows students to continue their work on tenses and consolidate their language awareness. In each case (teacher, observer, Claudia, Claudia's parent), students should write from a first-person perspective and in the tense requested. For students who need to work on their grammar skills, it would be better to do this activity individually, perhaps as homework. Students can then do the activity orally in class in groups of four, where each student takes a role and reads their sentence in character.

Speaking and listening – discussing big issues

Write the following issues on the board and add any other that relates to your area or country:

Building a dam

Producing genetically modified fruit without pips or stones (grapes/apples/apricots/peaches)

Arrange the class into groups of four or six and ask them to imagine they are in a social situation (not a formal debate) such as a family meal or with a group of friends. Name one student in each group as group leader. Ask groups to discuss one of the issues quietly and politely using the past and future tenses. They should include: how things used to be in the past; how the dam or new crops will make a difference in the future. The group leader should ensure conversation stays polite and reasonable, and make sure each person gets a chance to express his/her opinion. This is very good practice for future oral assessments and exams. Set a time limit and ask leaders to report back to the class on the following:

their group's topic of conversation

subjects they disagreed on

where they were in general agreement

if they had found any solutions to a problem.

If some of your class need more English language support write a few useful phrases on the board such as: *bearing in mind/you have to consider that/ yes, but don't forget/do you mean to say/look at it this way, if/that's one way of looking at it, but* etc.

Water! Water! Find me water!

Prior knowledge
The Gobi Desert

The Gobi Desert stretches across southern Mongolia and its border with China, and ranges from towering sand dunes to gentler terrain that is home to ibex, camel, and the rare Gobi bear. Beyond the mountains that lie inland from China's coastal plain, semi-arid steppe gives way to the Central Asian deserts, called gobis. The driest places support desert wildlife, but few people. The peripheral steppe regions are inhabited by herders, whose goats and horses feed on the region's meagre grass. To show students an aerial view of the Gobi you could use http://education.nationalgeographic.com/media/gobi-desert/. Another useful video of the Gobi, which shows the vast sand dunes in extremely cold weather conditions, is available at http://www.discovery.com/tv-shows/planet-earth/videos/camels-of-the-gobi-desert.

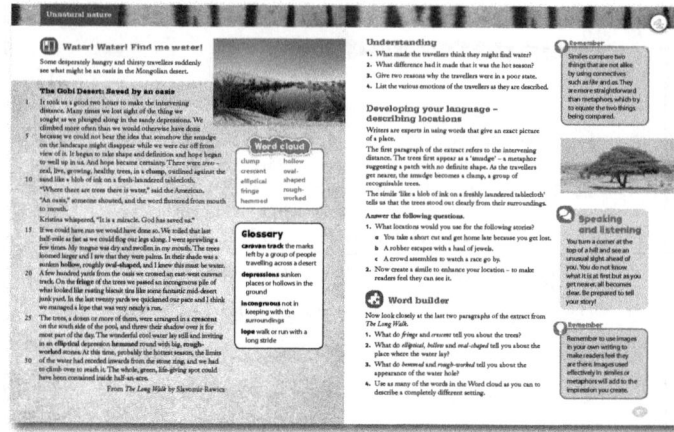

Vocabulary

 ## Understanding

The extract contains words with which some students may not be familiar. Read it with the class before starting on the Understanding section. Look at words such as: intervening, plunged, laundered, toiled (*to toil* as a verb), flog, loom, lope. Examine the phrase 'hope began to well up in us', as well as 'smudged on the landscape', 'freshly laundered', 'the intervening distance', and 'junk yard'.

The words in the Word cloud suggest shapes, patterns, and textures. You could invite students to divide the words into categories, then ask them to add some of their own, such as: bulge, square-shaped, frill, smooth.

Answers

1. The travellers see what they hope is a clump of trees, meaning an oasis.

2. Because it was the hot season the water level in the oasis had dropped, making it difficult to get to the water.

3. They had been walking in a desert with huge sand dunes and they had had no water to drink.

4. Exhaustion; happy that there might be water; afraid they are wrong (not an oasis); increasing hope (that it is); relief ("I knew this must be water"); surprise (they see rusty tins); delight/joy/happiness at getting to water.

Supporting students

To provide more help with unfamiliar words, you could extend the work on vocabulary to include work with a thesaurus, in which students find alternative words for: plunged, toiled, laundered, lope.

Developing your language

Describing locations

1. Suggested locations:
   a. Countryside or urban location.
   b. An urban location.
   c. A race can take place anywhere, including mountain bicycle races and the desert (Paris–Dakar), but here there is a crowd.

2. Students create their own similes to enhance their locations.

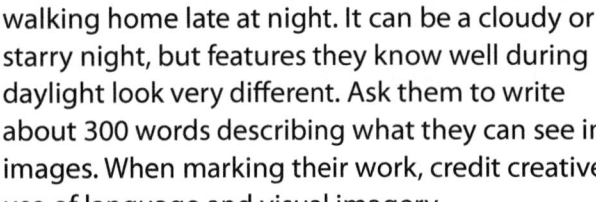

Speaking and listening

This activity can be done in pairs or small groups. Allow a few minutes for the class to prepare notes and create their imagery before starting the activity. Remind students to use descriptive language, including at least one simile, as they tell what they have seen.

If students require support in choosing a location, suggest that they are in a remote area and they see a railway line, then a railway station. A railway line *snakes* across the landscape or crosses the land *like a snake*.

Encourage peer sharing and some peer evaluation.

Word builder

1. The words describe the appearance (layout) of the trees. The palm tree leaves create a fringe on the edge of the clump, and there are trees set apart on the southern edge of the crescent-shaped patch around one side of the oasis.

2. The text describes how the oasis lies in an egg-shaped basin or depression.

3. These words describe how the oasis is surrounded or protected by roughly hewn stones (the work of man).

4. Make sure that students try to use all the words from the Word cloud to describe one setting, rather than using each word to describe different settings.

Extension

Writing – Creating visual images in words

Direct students' attention to the information in the 'Remember' box: 'Remember to use images in your own writing to make readers feel they are there. Images used effectively in similes or metaphors will add to the impression you create.'

Show students Van Gogh's painting 'Starry night', which can be found on http://www.vangoghgallery.com/painting/starry-night.html with detailed close-ups from http://twistedsifter.com/2013/07/detailed-close-ups-of-van-gogh-artworks. In pairs, students can discuss the shapes and colours and how they would convey these in writing. Then ask students to imagine they are

walking home late at night. It can be a cloudy or starry night, but features they know well during daylight look very different. Ask them to write about 300 words describing what they can see in images. When marking their work, credit creative use of language and visual imagery.

Workbook

Reading about settings

Page 29 of the Workbook gives students the opportunity to explore an extract about another extreme environment – the Arctic. This short extract is written in a very informal register.

Students can do this activity at home or in class individually, but you may find it useful to draw their attention first to some colloquial expressions such as 'Good luck!' and 'welcome to the tundra!' Discuss where and when exclamation marks have been used and why. Remind students not to use this style of writing in formal letters or school essays.

1. Whiteout, polar bears, mosquitoes.

2. A whiteout is a dense/heavy snowstorm covering/hiding everything, resulting in no or very poor visibility.

3. Plummets.

4. Disoriented.

5. Strong/effective insect-repellent is needed because of biting insects.

6. People walk in groups and carry rifles if there are polar bears near, and bear attacks are 'usually fatal'.

7. Students need to give a reasoned response justifying their views.

Extension

Identifying verbs and tenses

Ask students to colour in light blue all the verbs in the passage on the CD. (Do not let them use highlighters because this makes it very difficult to overlook mistakes.)

Once students have a good understanding of how the present tense is used in informative writing, ask them to divide the text into paragraphs.

Students can work in pairs for both tasks.

The conditional tense

Prior knowledge

Conditional sentences are generally formed using an *if* clause, but students may also be familiar with *provided* and/or *unless* in conditionals. The *if* clause can come before or after the main clause, as in 'If I can't come to your party, I'll call you,' or 'I'll call you if I can't come to your party.' We usually employ the present tense for the conditional ('If I can't come') and the future for the main clause ('I'll call you'). In question 1a, 'If we heat ice (present), it will melt' can be replaced with 'If we heat ice it melts.' In question 1b, 'If I stroke my cat too hard, it scratches me/will scratch me' is a type 1 conditional with a probable outcome. Students don't necessarily need to know that at this stage, but they do need to be aware of how tenses are being used in different clauses before they attempt questions 2 and 3.

Question 4 involves the type 2 conditional, when we do not expect the action in the *if* clause to take place or it is unlikely to happen (e.g. 'If I were to win the lottery, I'd go on a world cruise'.)

Review the first and second conditionals with the class and create some examples together before students complete this activity. They can work either individually or in pairs.

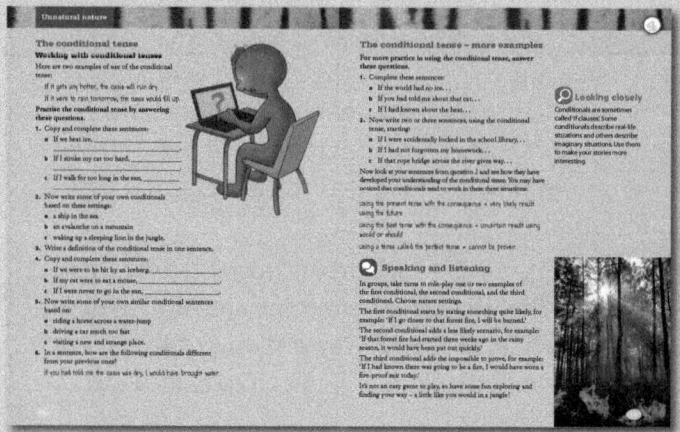

Grammar

Working with conditional tenses

Note that in the first example the verb 'gets' is in the present tense with future meaning, and the next verb 'will run dry' is in a future tense. The second example also expresses future meaning. In both cases the outcome depends on the preceding *if* clause.

Ask students to complete the answers to question 1 with present or future meanings. Suggested answers are:

1. **a.** If we heat ice, it melts/it will melt.

   b. If I stroke my cat too hard, it scratches me/ it will scratch me.

   c. If I walk for too long in the sunshine, I get very hot/I will get very hot.

2. Students create their own conditionals based on the settings in parts a–c.

3. Suggested answers could include: a conditional sentence shows what could happen if something else happens first; a conditional sentence is where what happens depends on the conditions in the first part of the sentence. A good answer would use phrases from your teaching session, such as: a conditional sentence is one in which the main clause depends on the *if* clause.

4. Students copy and complete sentences a–c by adding a main clause that depends on the given *if* clause.

5. Students' own answers based on the stated scenarios. Point out that a water-jump is a type of obstacle in horse show-jumping and cross-country competitions.

6. The third conditional is created when the verb in the *if* clause is in the past perfect (e.g. 'If I had known we were doing this, I would have brought my grammar book'.) The past perfect continuous can also be used (e.g. 'If I hadn't been wearing a seat belt, I would have been injured in the crash'.) In each case, the outcome depends on the *if* clause (e.g. 'If you had told me the oasis was dry, I would have brought water'.) (You didn't bring water because you didn't know the oasis was dry.)

   Technically, the verb in the *if* clause is in the past perfect conditional and the verb in the main clause is in the perfect conditional. The outcome could not or was not fulfilled because the action in the *if* clause did not occur.

The conditional tense – more examples

1. Suggested answers:
   a. If the world had no ice, we would always be hot/there would be no rivers.
   b. If you had told me about that cat, I wouldn't have touched it.
   c. If I had known about the heat, I would have worn a hat/brought plenty of water.

2. Give students an opportunity to have fun with the conditionals here. You could do it as pair work.

After working on the questions, ask students to read through their work on conditionals on their own and think about what they have found easy and/or difficult. Round up with a quick oral review. Ask students for an example for each of the three situations listed on page 59 of the Student Book. Finally, draw their attention to the Looking closely feature and check again to determine whether anyone is still having difficulties.

You can do this activity in groups. This activity may prompt some lively discussion, but keep students focused on the grammatical structures and remind them to refer to the situations listed in the Student Book to help them.

Using conditional sentences

Students can have fun completing this exercise, in which they practise writing conditional sentences with their own ideas. Be sure to check that their grammatical structures are correct.

Supporting students – Using conditional sentences

To give your students more practice in using conditional sentences, you could present them with an *if* clause and ask them to develop it into a paragraph, showing the possible outcome of the situation with a few more sentences. For example: 'If I were to be on a ship that sank in the Pacific Ocean, I would swim to a desert island. If there were trees, I would build a hut. If there were palm trees, I would use the branches to build the walls and use the leaves for the roof and floor.'

Stretching students – 'Escape'

Arrange students into small groups (maximum five). Tell them they have been on a school trip to a famous national monument such as the Tower of London, a palace or a museum. They have become separated from their group; it is now night time and the monument has been locked. They do not have mobile phones and have called for help but no-one has answered. They must decide how to get out of the building. Warn them that setting off a burglar alarm will result in arrest.

If possible, give groups an illustration or put an image on the board to help them visualise where they are. Do not assign group leader roles; leaders may emerge naturally from discussions. Each group must decide the following:

a. where they are locked in
b. what options there are to escape (through a window/fire escape)
c. what problems they may encounter.

Set a time limit and at the end take feedback. Allow each group a few minutes to explain what they did and why.'

Wild animals caught on camera

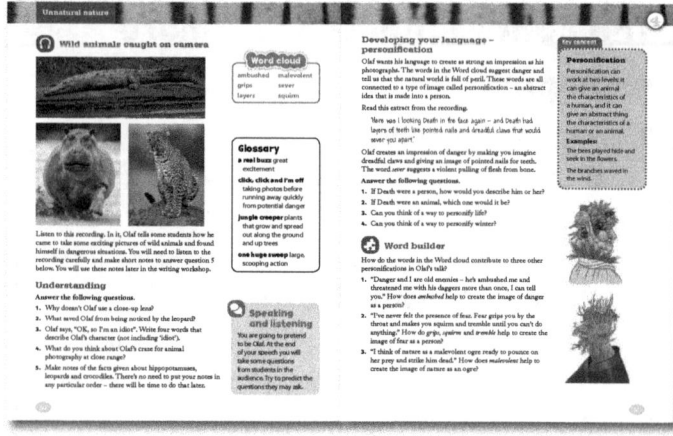

Listening

A wildlife photographer talks to a small group of students

Olaf: You want to see my wildlife photos? Right – here they are. I'll start with three of my favourites. By the way, I don't believe in close-up lenses. I'm the close-up – well, as near as I dare – click, click, and I'm off. Oh yes, Danger and I are old enemies – he's ambushed me and threatened me with his daggers more than once, I can tell you…

Student-book answers

🎧 Understanding

Allow students to listen to the recording before they take notes. You may need to play it twice more for them to complete their notes, but there will not be another opportunity, so make sure they pay attention. You could allow them to discuss what they have heard in pairs before moving on to the Understanding questions.

1. He does not like close-up lenses and gets as near as possible to his subjects.

2. Olaf was saved because the leopard couldn't smell him and the rain was so heavy he didn't hear him (a twig snapping or the camera clicking).

3. Suggested answers: adventurous, foolhardy, determined, brave, likes excitement.

4. Students' own answers. Make sure students justify their personal response.

5. Hippopotamuses: not cuddly; aggressive; huge (weight); good sense of smell; fast; ('like an army tank' is not a fact but a simile).

   Leopards: have patches of colour/spots on the body; one of the fastest animals; lash the tail and growl when angry.

   Crocodiles: eat everything, including stones; uses the tail to catch prey.

Speaking and listening

Students do the role-play activity in the Speaking and listening panel in groups. They take it in turns to be Olaf. Using their notes and what they remember from his talk, they respond to questions from their group in character.

Developing your language

Personification

Review personification and ask students if they can remember why Olaf said he was 'looking Death face to face'? Discuss the imagery in 'Death had layers of teeth like pointed nails and dreadful claws that would sever you apart.'

Draw students' attention to the Key concept feature on personification. Then allow them to formulate their ideas before answering questions 1–4. It would be better if they worked on their own for this activity and shared their ideas after writing down their answers.

Word builder

Students will have heard the words in the Word cloud in the context of Olaf's experiences. You could now ask them where and how they have heard the following in other contexts: ambushed (verb), grip (verb), layers (noun), malevolent (adjective), sever (verb).

Suggested answers:

1. Human beings ambush their enemies, and here danger is presented as a powerful enemy that is determined to get him one way or another.

2. The word *grips* suggests that fear is an enemy or opponent; 'squirm' and 'tremble' are bodily responses to fear.

3. 'Malevolent' alongside 'ogre', which is a typical monster in traditional northern-hemisphere folk tales, suggests the power and evil of nature.

You could also draw students' attention to the fact that Olaf's talk is informal and ask them to identify two informal phrases, such as 'Right – here they are'. Ask students if they remember anything else in the talk that sounded informal (e.g. 'How stupid was I?' or 'these close encounters give me a real buzz'). Then ask students how the phrase 'speaking of which' contrasts with how Olaf delivers his talk.

 Image explorer

Page 31 of the Workbook requires students to create word images of their own using given examples. Doing this task individually for homework will help students to take more responsibility for their own learning, but they need to know where they can find information if they have forgotten what a simile, a metaphor, or personification is. Suggest that they use the Internet or a dictionary to help them.

When the activity has been completed, students can share their ideas in class or with a partner. It would be useful if you also review what they have written, so you know where revision, support, or guidance is required.

Extension

Writing a travel guide entry

Ask students to write an entry for a travel guide called 'Get away from it all' about an inhospitable environment. The guide tells 'extreme tourists' what they will find in unusual locations and what they should pack in their luggage. Each entry should also include relevant illustrations, such as how to build an igloo or tree house and images of the scenery and wildlife.

Remind students of examples of inhospitable places in this unit, such as the dense jungle, Gobi Desert, or Arctic tundra. Also remind them that they must acknowledge the source of any material they use from the Internet or elsewhere. Students should complete this activity in pairs or small groups.

Extension

Vocabulary activity – Danger!

This task is suitable for students needing additional language support. Ask students to work in pairs. Provide each pair with a dictionary and a thesaurus. Tell them to find the words *danger* and *dangerous*. They should then make a list of different words for the noun and find its corresponding adjective. For example: hazard – hazardous; threat – threatening; peril – perilous

This language consolidation activity can be extended to give students practice in using vocabulary in context by asking individuals or pairs to choose three nouns and three different adjectives and use them in sentences. Individual students or pairs can then swap papers for peer-marking. Round up the activity by clarifying doubts and showing where some words for danger are not interchangeable, such as a harmful or deadly substance (poison) but not a harmful bend in the road.

Writing a summary

Prior knowledge

Being able to summarise in clear, concise language is a very useful skill for school work, for the workplace, and in the IGCSE First Language exam. Before students attempt their written summary, they should understand the purpose of summarising.

Write the following questions on the board, giving students a few minutes to discuss their answers in pairs or small groups before reporting back to the class.

- What do you think is meant by the term *summary*?

- Do you think writing a summary is a useful or important skill?

- In which other school subjects might you need to write a summary?

You could also give students this advice for summary writing practice:

- Avoid using highlighters, because once a word is marked it cannot be erased if you change your mind. Light-coloured pencils are better.

- Make notes on the text if you can, and use the margins for comments.

- Number the points in the text in the order you need them for your summary question. They don't always occur in that order in the text.

- If you have time, write out your main points in a list.

- Tick off the points you have included in your summary as you go along, to be sure you have included everything.

- Use short sentences and plain language.

- Never copy, quote, or 'lift' from the text – use your own words as far as possible.

- Count your words, and check your grammar and punctuation carefully.

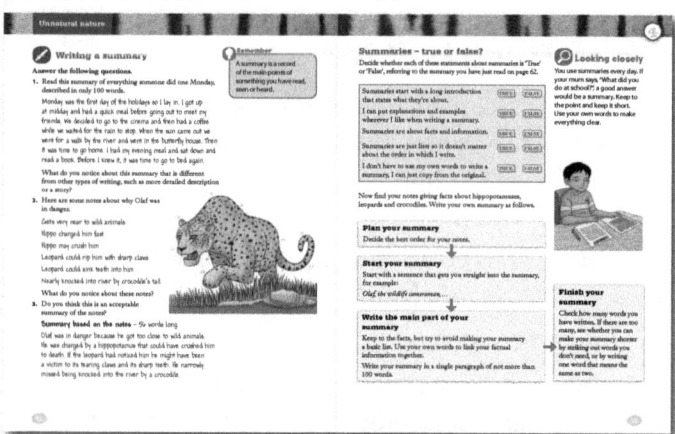

✏ Writing a summary

1. The summary is in chronological order. It is factual, concise, and contains no description or figurative language.

2. The notes contain what actually happened and what could have happened. They are not written in full sentences, typically omitting the definite article, punctuation, and descriptive detail.

3. Make sure students justify their point of view.

Writing

Summaries – true or false?

Only the third statement is true; the rest are false.

Students now write a summary of the notes they made on hippos, leopards and crocodiles in no more than 100 words. Remind them to keep checking they have followed the flowchart.

Writing a summary

Students should order their facts in a logical sequence such as:

1. Kangaroos live in Australia.
2. There are 34 million.
3. The name comes from 'big foot'.
4. They can leap at 20–25 km per hour.
5. They can swim.
6. They are nocturnal/come out at night.
7. They are shy.
8. Babies are called joeys.
9. The young live in a pouch on their mother's front.
10. They are edible.
11. Meat has little fat.

Students now write these facts in their own words, as far as possible in 60–65 words. Explain that if they do not reach 60 words it could be because they have left something out. They may need to write at least two rough drafts before handing in a clean, neat copy of their summary.

Extension

Supporting students – finding and writing facts

Direct students to an informative Internet site that gives factual details, for example, this site on the Galapagos Islands: http://whc.unesco.org/en/list/1. The text gives a lot of facts about the islands and includes interesting details, but it is written in what many students may find a challenging style, using a sophisticated vocabulary. Ask them to read the text but not to worry about the vocabulary they do not know; their task is to note down the facts. They should not include opinions or any extra details. For example: 'The Galapagos Islands are situated in the Pacific Ocean some 1,000 km from the Ecuadorian coast. This archipelago and its immense marine reserve is known as the unique "living museum and showcase of evolution" can be reduced to: *Galapagos Islands – in Pacific Ocean, 1,000 km from coast of Equador.*

When students have enough relevant facts, they should try to rewrite this information in their own words for a target audience such as a children's book or a school magazine for teenagers.

This activity gives students valuable practice in information retrieval. It also encourages them to try to understand new words in context and tackle more demanding texts. The writing task requires them to think about how we order and choose words to present information for target readers.

Extension

Writing to inform a specific audience

Ask students to write an entry called 'Do You Know?' on one of the following subjects for a children's encyclopaedia: container ships, ostriches, wild horses, electric guitars, the first steam engine, the Statue of Liberty. They may consult Internet sources and/or use the library, and they should write no more than 300 words.

Tell them to write their first version with a clear structure that has a beginning, a middle, and an end. They then write it out again but mixing up the sentences so there is no logical structure. They then give the jumbled version to a partner, who has to write it out again so it has a clear, logical structure. Students then compare the corrected versions against the originals.

This activity requires students to think about how they order information and involves writing clear and concise sentences for a specific audience. It is good practice for answering reading questions and writing summaries, articles, or first-person accounts.

Progress check

End-of-unit assessment

1. Animals are dangerous and Nature can also be cruel/dangerous. Accept ideas related to Nature as a predator. [2]

2. Talagouga was a 'grim' place, trapped in the jungle. [2]

3. There were no paths, large fallen trees, impenetrable undergrowth/creepers, snake-infested vegetation. Accept two reasons. [2]

4. Accept answers that show understanding of the imagery – an open space with a 'smudge' or 'blob' of colour seen from a distance. [2]

5. He says Mother Nature is not kind/a kind old lady but is more like a 'malevolent ogre'. [2]

6. Olaf was particularly fond of using personification. (He uses metaphors, simile and personification, but the personification is more memorable.) Examples include: danger as an enemy who threatens him with daggers; the hippo as 'a tonne and a half of amour-plating'; the leopard as Death with 'layers of teeth like pointed nails and dreadful claws that would sever you apart'; the crocodile as 'all teeth and a horrid grin'; Mother Nature as a 'malevolent ogre'. [4]

7. A motion is the topic/subject/idea being debated; a proposer presents the motion to the audience; an opposer argues against the proposer. People take turns to speak. Most debates have a chairperson to ensure they run smoothly. [4]

8. It was described as: a 'smudge on the landscape'; trees were in a clump 'like a blob of ink on a freshly laundered cloth'; there was a crescent of trees; the oasis is in an oval/elliptical hollow; it is 'hemmed round' with stones. [4]

9. Accept any first, second, or third conditional sentences if grammatically correct. [4]

10. This answer may include: do not copy from text; do not make a list; do not use flowery/descriptive language/keep to the word count; write in a clear, logical order; do not start with a long introduction or by setting the scene. [4]

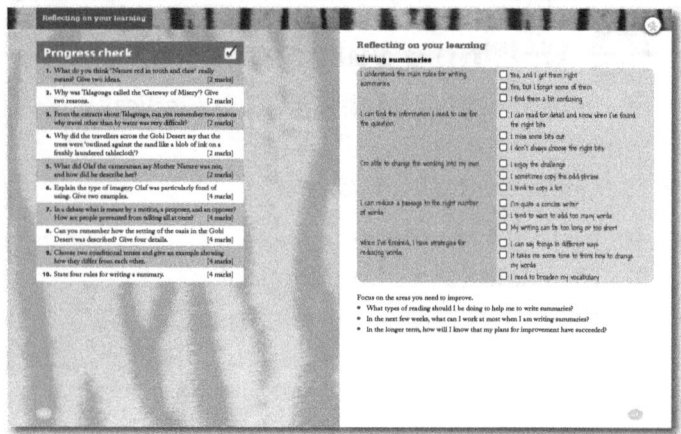

🧩 Unnatural nature quiz

Page 33 of the Workbook asks students to revisit topics, and review grammar and language learning they engaged with in the unit. Areas covered are:

- imagery in first-person accounts
- recognising and using metaphor, simile, and personification
- the effect of using powerful imagery on a reader or listener
- speaking in a debate
- justifying opinions
- reviewing verb tenses
- improving awareness of conditionals using *if* clauses
- recognising spoken informal language
- learning to write a summary and organising facts.

This activity should be used as an informal quiz and not summatively assessed. Feedback should, therefore, be formative and indicative of progress. You could assign this quiz as homework or do it as a classroom-based activity.

Reflecting on your learning

Discuss with the class how they will use the different writing skills covered in this unit as they proceed through the school writing essays and projects, and in exams. Go on to talk about how people in the workplace use writing skills in memos, reports, advertisements, emails, etc.

As a means of reviewing topics as well as the speaking and listening skills covered in the unit, ask the class to turn back to page 50 in the Student Book and look at the quotes again. Ask if, after what they have read, discussed and debated in the unit, they still believe 'Nature (is) red in tooth and claw'. Encourage students to give examples from the unit itself and provide examples from their own experience. Encourage students to separate and be aware of when they are using fact and opinion. Move on to consider the quotation about extreme environments such as Arctic wastes, jungles and deserts and if they still believe these places should be protected. If possible, call on views expressed earlier and re-examine original ideas in the light of material covered. You can use the third quotation about exploring space as a short final speaking and listening activity. This type of quotation is something students may choose to use for oral coursework or be presented with in assessments later in their school careers.

The reflection task is essentially an individual activity but you may find it useful to go back through the unit with your class and make a list on the board of all topics and activities they have enjoyed or would like to repeat, and those things they did not enjoy, but may need to do again. Briefly explore how our personalities influence what we read and do in everyday school life.

The Night World

Read this short description of the night world to the class once at a normal speaking pace. Then read it again more slowly and ask them to remember the names of all the creatures they hear. There are 17 if you count 'creepy-crawlies'. Students then make a list from memory, which they can compare with a partner. Do a final reading, asking students to tick off the animals on their lists.

The night-world, anywhere in the world, is very different from that of the day. Creatures that are blind or hide during daylight wake and go about their business the moment the sun goes down. **Spiders** take up position, ready to pounce on unsuspecting **beetles** and **cockroaches**, who in turn are tuning in their antennae for something tasty. **Centipedes**, **wood-lice** and all manner of **creepy-crawlies** edge out of cracks and crevices; even water that has barely survived the sun in warm puddles comes to life. **Owls** make eerie cries across a silent landscape, alerting **rabbits** and terrifying **mice**. Timid **deer** wander out of the safety of the trees to drink but there might be **foxes**, **jaguars**, **lions** or **leopards** slinking in the gloom. The **skunk** strolls alone, tail held high, warning none to come too close. **Bats** flitter hither and thither, and foolish **moths** seek any form of light to burn their wings and die in the instant. Night time is feeding time; it is when some creatures prey and others are preyed upon – and there's nobody there to witness the tragedy. Night time is another world wherever you are.

A printable version of the full transcript for this unit is available on the CD.

5 Fabulous hobbies

Super sports

Spend about 5–10 minutes with students, drawing out their views and prior experiences in an informal way. Ask them whether they have previously:

- explored how magazines are created for a target audience

- collaborated on planning or writing a real school magazine with a specific theme

- created material such as a review or report for a magazine

- engaged in playing lesser-known sports such as Ultimate Frisbee

- reflected on how they use different styles of formal and informal language.

Thinking time

The focus in this unit is reading magazines (which can be online). Draw out how and why students read magazines and what a school magazine can offer. If your school already has a magazine, discuss its form, content, and who reads it.

For question 2, define 'hobby' as a pastime and/or sport. For question 3, mention the phrase 'the mind's eye'. Questions 4 and 5 can be discussed in smaller groups, with a student from each group feeding back to class.

Explain that during this unit students are going to plan and write a school magazine with 'sports and hobbies' as its main theme. It can include a range of non-fiction texts, for example, articles, editorials, extracts from blogs, reports, and adverts.

Clarify what is meant by an editorial and the role of the editor. If you plan to develop this into a class activity with a complete magazine as its outcome, ask students to think about what areas they might like to focus on in their writing.

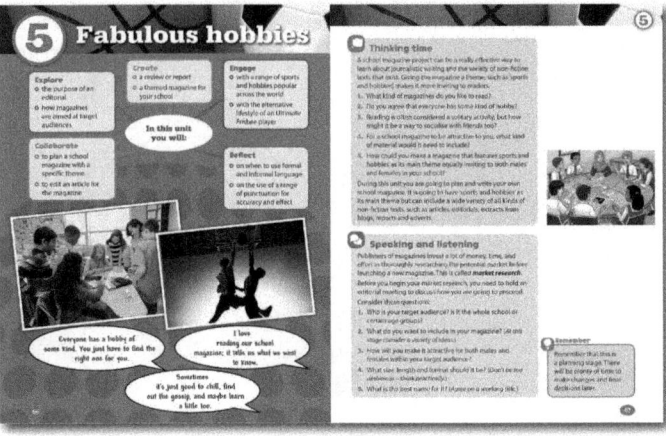

this may be the first time they have been in the library to read a magazine or seen different types of magazines and academic journals. It is an excellent way to encourage reluctant readers to engage with material they may otherwise not encounter.

Market research

This activity is designed to raise awareness of target audiences. Set it as homework, so that students think about the nature of magazines individually. If students do not buy magazines, suggest they go online, search for 'teenage magazines' and select two. Be advised: these will be mostly American, and *Cosmopolitan* is considered teenage material. Alternatively, choose two magazines for students to work from on their own. They may use sports or hobby magazines, such as those on football or horse-riding.

Review students' completed work and/or allow students to compare findings in pairs. They should consider their findings in relation to their planned 'sports and hobbies' magazine.

Speaking and listening

Launching a new magazine

Discuss question 1 as a class. Then arrange the students in groups, each with a designated spokesperson. Round up after a given time, putting decisions on the board. Students should copy these down if the class will go on to create a real magazine.

Extension

Introducing house style

A good way to introduce the style of magazine writing and the concept of house style is to allow students to leaf through and compare popular magazines and journals. If possible, take your class to the school library and give them a wide selection to browse through such as *National Geographic*, *New Scientist* and less academic magazines. You can also ask students to bring in newspaper weekend supplements. Using contrasting publications such as *National Geographic*, a literary or arts journal and a popular high-street magazine such as *Hello*, ask the class to identify the different ways text and images are laid out. Show them where the proportion of images is greater than the related texts and ask why editors have made this decision. Students should also be able to comment on fonts, headings and subheadings, bylines and the nature of photography (colour, paparazzi distance shots etc). Ask why it is important for a magazine to have a particular 'look'.

Leave students to continue reading through magazines for the rest of the lesson as they choose; this will help when they come to prepare their own material later in the unit. For some,

Editorials

Prior knowledge

Elicit how students have written magazine-style material in English before. Ask if they are aware of the role of a magazine editor. Explain that a features editor is responsible for the content and quality of the publication, and must ensure that stories are engaging, informative, and apt for the target audience. Editors set the tone of each issue and write 'editorials' that include their opinions.

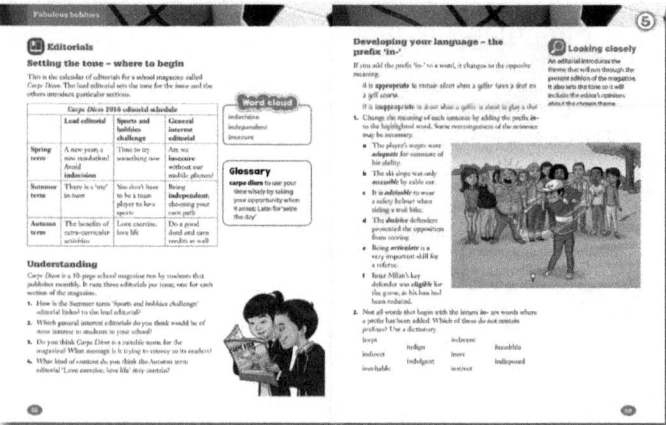

Student-book answers

📖 Understanding

1. You don't have to be a team player to enjoy sport/not only team sports.

2. Accept any well-reasoned answer.

3. *Carpe Diem* = Latin for 'seize the day'. Message is: live life to the full/don't waste your time. Accept any well-reasoned response.

4. Accept any answer along the lines of: healthy mind and body/fit for anything new/healthy and fit for sports and activities.

Extension

Comparing editorials and articles

If your class have access to computers in lessons ask them to do a search for online magazines on a specific sport or hobby such as ice dancing, horse-riding or stamp collecting. The objective is to find two or three issues that cover the same topic and compare the ways different magazines present similar material (proportion of image to text, point of view etc.). Students do not need to write anything, but they should read the texts thoroughly to become more aware of how online media presents a point of view, and how online editors also have to make decisions about text and format. This is also a good introduction to formal and informal registers for page 70 of the Student Book.

If necessary, model how to search for and select magazines. You may need to keep a careful watch on what your class is accessing for

suitability. If this is a concern, do this activity yourself beforehand and specify exactly which magazines your class should look at. If there has been a recent international sports event in your country or area you could ask students to look at magazines from different countries to see how they cover the same event in different ways.

Set a time limit, call a halt and take feedback orally.

Workbook

🧩 Editorials

1. Any three facts from: the Premier League is commonly known as EPL; it is watched in over 200 countries; it has a potential audience of over 4 billion; its domestic television deal is worth £1 billion.

2. EPL has become too big. The main problem she refers to is its size: 'thousands of devotees', 'juggernaut of such size and scope', 'the bigger problem'.

3. Negative comments, such as 'predictable conclusion', 'what have we learnt? Very little', suggest the author does not approve of the EPL.

4. Students should mimic the semi-formal writing style and include reasoned opinion(s).

The prefix '*in-*'

1. a. The player's wages were <u>in</u>adequate for someone of his ability.

    b. The ski slope was <u>in</u>accessible <u>except</u> by cable car.

    c. It is <u>in</u>advisable to <u>not</u> wear a safety helmet when riding a trail bike.

    d. The <u>in</u>decisive defenders <u>could/did not prevent</u> the opposition from scoring.

    e. Being <u>in</u>articulate is a <u>disadvantage/ problem</u> for a referee.

    f. Inter Milan's key defender was <u>in</u>eligible for the game as his ban <u>was still in force</u>.

2. inept; indigo; inert; indulgent; instinct

Supporting students – Practising prefixes

Give students a 12 by 12 empty grid and ask them to write in the words 'impossible' and 'possible', 'independent' and 'dependent'. They may then complete their grids putting in words with their opposite, choosing words whose opposites require the *in-* or *im-* prefixes (indecision, indefinite, immoral etc.). Allow students to use dictionaries. Remind them to keep a list of all the words they have used. When they have finished their word search, they pass it to a partner to complete and mark it against their list.

This activity can be extended or repeated in different ways to practise opposites with *ir-* and *il-* prefixes as well.

Looking at a writer's point of view

Provide the class with a variety of daily newspapers and/or magazines with sports columns, or ask them to open an online magazine. Students find a short article about a sport of their choice and decide on the writer's point of view. They then copy down opinion words and phrases to support their ideas. Students can do this in pairs, but they must both write down their findings, which they should keep for use later in the unit.

Using the prefix '*in-*'

1. The team lost because of too much <u>indecision</u>.

2. A round the world yachtsman needs to be <u>independent</u>.

3. <u>Inactivity</u> is a state of doing nothing that leads to a lack of fitness.

4. No one believed the tennis star as he was being <u>insincere</u>.

5. The defence conceded five goals because it was <u>insecure</u>.

6. The club could not pay the players' wages because there were <u>insufficient</u> funds.

Formal and informal register

Prior knowledge

As some students may not be familiar with English language magazines, use a popular monthly magazine to demonstrate use of semi-formal register for a more personal tone. Review the rule 'the more serious a piece of writing, the more formal the tone', using an academic journal as an example.

As a warm-up activity, arrange a sequence of very short role-plays in pairs or groups, where students are speaking to:

1. a judge/referee
2. the head of a school
3. a sibling with whom they never agree
4. a friend.

The subject matter under discussion is a student who has been disqualified from a competition – wrongly, in the student's opinion.

Set a two-minute time limit for each role-play. Draw attention to how we automatically moderate speech according to who is listening. Students will now take this a step further in their writing.

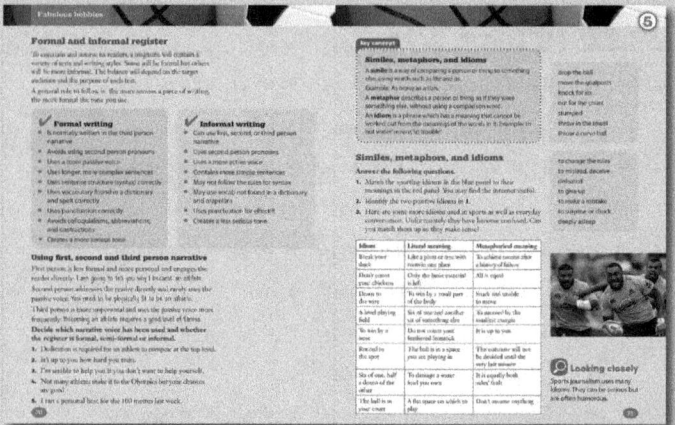

Grammar

Using first, second and third person narrative

Review the following and model on the board, as necessary:

- first, second, third person narrative
- passive/active voice
- the effect of simple sentences to grab attention.

	Narrative voice	Register
Dedication is required for an athlete to compete at the top level.	3rd	Formal
It's up to you how hard you train.	2nd	Informal
I'm unable to help you if you don't want to help yourself.	1st	Semi-informal
Not many athletes make it to the Olympics but your chances are good.	2nd	Semi-formal
I ran a personal best for the 100 metres last week.	1st	Semi-formal

Similes, metaphors, and idioms

1. Answers:

move the goalposts = to change the rules

throw a curve ball = to surprise with the unexpected

knocked for six = to surprise or shock with upsetting news

out for the count = deeply asleep

stumped = confused, unsure how to proceed

throw in the towel = to give up

drop the ball = to make a mistake

2. 'Move the goalposts' and 'out for the count' are the only two that are NOT negative idioms.

3. Answers:

Idiom	Literal meaning	Metaphorical meaning
Break your duck	To damage a water fowl you own	To achieve success after a history of failure
Don't count your chickens	Do not count your feathered livestock	Don't assume anything
Down to the wire	Only the basic material is left	The outcome will not be decided until the very last minute
A level playing field	A flat space on which to play	All is equal
To win by a nose	To win by a small part of the body	To succeed by the smallest margin
Rooted to the spot	Like a plant or tree with roots in one place	Stuck and unable to move
Six of one, half a dozen of the other	Six of one and another six of something else	It is equally both sides' fault
The ball is in your court	The ball is in a space you are playing in	What is done next is up to you now

 Using the prefix *in–*

1. indecision
2. independent
3. inactivity
4. insincere
5. inadequate
6. insufficient

Consolidating language awareness – Tone and register poster

Choose two very different types of recent or on-going individual and team sports/hobby events, such as a chess championship and the Dakar Rally, or

⬅ gymnastics and a football cup. Ask students to find examples of how these have been reported. They should copy and paste online material that includes:

● the name of the source
● the byline or name of the reporter for each sport
● examples of language used to report the two events that we rarely use in everyday speech
● a brief comparison of the language used (semi-formal, very informal, very descriptive, etc.).

Alternatively, ask students to bring articles into class.

Arrange groups and ask each group to paste their examples onto a poster. They should then label the different types of language, highlighting the use of formal, semi-formal, and informal register.

Students then write a paragraph or two on how different sports organisations and/or media groups vary the way in which they report events, to best suit their target audience.

Prior knowledge – A host of hobbies!

Return to the discussion on hobbies or sports that students enjoy and identify two students who like and hate the same activity. Ask them to share their point of view with the class, explaining why they hold their opinions. Then ask the class to make a brief list of the least rewarding pastimes they can think of. As they feed back to the class, write on the board the adjectives they are using. These may fall into two lists, positive and negative. Return to this when students have finished the Speaking and listening activity on page 73 of the Student Book.

When students have finished reading 'A host of hobbies!', ask if this has modified their opinions and discuss how an individual's imagination and creativity operate when choosing a hobby.

Watch the clip from *Billy Elliot*, which shows when Billy, who is at the gym for boxing lessons, first encounters ballet. Follow this up with a scene at the end of the film, where Billy is an accomplished ballet dancer. To learn more about the Billy Elliot, the boy who gives up boxing and becomes a professional ballet dancer, go to: https://www.workingtitlefilms.com/films/view/film/6/billy-elliot

The beginning of the movie, when Billy first discovers ballet is in the clip: https://www.youtube.com/watch?v=i0p2X2rQ6Ag

The final scene, which should not be missed, can be found at: https://www.youtube.com/watch?v=TSTw8wOlBGY

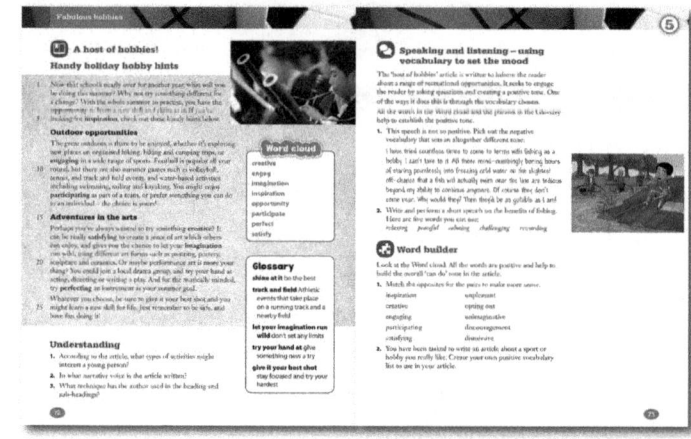

Speaking and listening

Using vocabulary to set the mood

The activities can be done in pairs.

1. Negative vocabulary: I have tried countless times; can't take to it; mind-numbingly boring; pointlessly; on the slightest off-chance; tedious.

2. Students write and perform a short speech on the benefits of fishing to each other.

Student-book answers

📖 Understanding

1. Anything – music, sports, arts.
2. Second.
3. Alliteration.

Vocabulary

Word builder

1. inspiration – discouragement
   creative – unimaginative
   engaging – dismissive
   participating – opting out
   satisfying – unpleasant

2. Students may use a thesaurus, working in pairs. To get them started, direct them to the following words: beneficial, satisfaction, enjoyable.

Workbook

Using vocabulary for effect

1. Answers:
   - Positive: intriguing, rewarding, unique, captivating, informative, entertaining, fascinating, countless appealing tales to tell.
   - Negative: pointless, mind-numbing, tatty (pieces of second-hand paper), futility, anti-social, uninteresting.

2. Students write a descriptive paragraph about a sport or hobby they either like or dislike. They need to write from their own biased perspective.

Extension

Writing an editorial

Give students the PCM with the article on skateboarding from a school magazine (found on the Teacher's Book CD). Ask them to read the article and then to write their own article in a semi-formal to formal, balanced style. When marking, credit insight, the way the topic has been examined and the article structured, and the student's writing style, including technical accuracy.

Extension

A fun way to explore just how many different sports and hobbies there are is to play the game Categories. Ask students to write the letters of the alphabet down the side of a blank page and across the top write the words 'individual', 'pairs', 'team'. They then write in as many sports and hobbies as they can think of in these categories. Set a time limit. The winner is the person with the most sports and hobbies. This game can also be played in pairs or small groups, but you will need to set a time limit.

Write out the format on the board and explain they must name a sport or hobby for each letter of the alphabet in each category if possible. Give a few random examples to get students started such as:

	Individual	Pair	Team
B		bobsleigh	
C	crotchet		cricket
D	diving		
K	knitting		
X	xylophone		
Y			yachting

Using punctuation accurately

Prior knowledge

Before students begin this part of the unit, do a quick review of the names of punctuation marks. Ask which they find most confusing and why. Check that they know the difference between a dash and a hyphen, and why we often use dashes in informal writing.

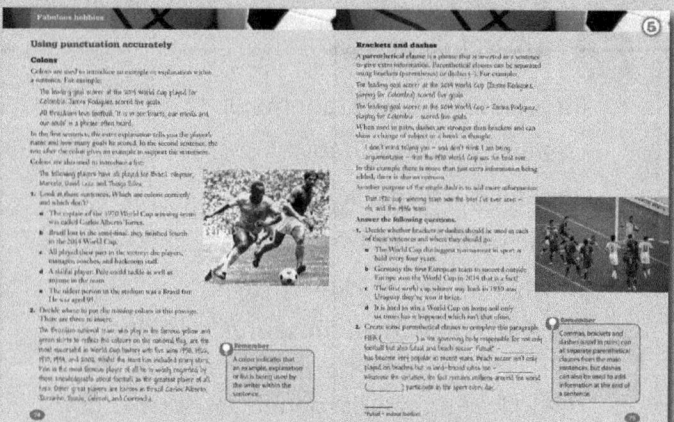

Student-book answers

Colons

1. a. incorrect
    b. correct
    c. correct
    d. incorrect
    e. correct

2. Three colons inserted, as shown below.

    The Brazilian national team, who play in the famous yellow and green shirts to reflect the colours on the national flag, are the most successful in World Cup history with five wins: 1958, 1962, 1970, 1994, and 2002. Whilst the team has included many stars, Pele is the most famous player of all: he is widely regarded by those knowledgeable about football as the greatest player of all time. Other great players are heroes in Brazil: Carlos Alberto, Jairzinho, Tostão, Gérson, and Garrincha.

Student-book answers

Brackets and dashes

1. a. The World Cup (the biggest tournament in sport) is held every four years.
    b. Germany (the first European team to succeed outside Europe) won the World Cup in 2014 – that is a fact!
    c. The first World Cup winner way back in 1930 was Uruguay (they've won it twice).
    d. It is hard to win a World Cup on home soil (only six times has it happened – which isn't that often).

2. Suggested answers are given below. Also accept alternatives that fit with grammatical construction.

    FIFA (<u>football's governing body</u>) is the governing body responsible for not only football but also futsal and beach soccer. Futsal – <u>indoor football</u> – has become very popular in recent years. Beach soccer isn't only played on beaches but in land-bound cities too – <u>wherever there's a sandy pitch</u>. Whatever the variation, the fact remains millions around the world (<u>amateur and professional, young, and not so young</u>) participate in the sport every day.

Using punctuation accurately

1.
   a. 'Ever since I was a child I have listened to all kinds of music: slow, fast, modern, and old-style.'

   b. 'It would be wonderful if I could meet my favourite rock star: I would be overawed.'

   c. To start a band you need: guitars, keyboards, drums, and a singer.

   d. 'I love the sound of a steel guitar: it is so relaxing.'

   e. 'I've played live concerts in all the world's major cities: London, Cairo, New York, Mumbai, Moscow.'

2. Students write out the sentences again, adding brackets or dashes.

   a. Beyonce was born in Houston, Texas, but has moved to Los Angeles, California – having once lived in New York.

   b. She is a now a solo artist – having made her name in the group Destiny's Child – and has sold over 75 million records worldwide.

   c. Beyonce has won many music awards and is a leading figure in the music industry. She is also a successful businesswoman.

Extension

Practising correct punctuation

Ask students to copy a paragraph from a novel they are reading or an article in a magazine, but without any punctuation, capital letters, or full stops.

Then arrange the class in pairs and ask students to swap papers. Each student inserts the punctuation they think is appropriate.

Students then compare their corrected paragraph with their partner's chosen text.

Finally, students write another short paragraph in the same style on the same topic. This can be peer marked or you can collect in the work of each pair and check their progress.

Extension

Playing with punctuation

There are dozens of interactive punctuation games available on the Internet. Ask your students to find a game for a punctuation mark of their choice such as a hyphen or colon and play the game. If you have time available students could try several games.

The class should then split into groups and discuss what game they tried, how effective it was in consolidating what they already knew and/or how good it was at explaining what they found confusing. Ask students to compare the difference between practising punctuation in class and on a screen. They could then be encouraged to devise their own grammar/punctuation games, either to be done in class with pen and paper or on a computer.

It's the ULTIMATE thrill!

Prior knowledge

Before you play the audio recording, review the vocabulary in the Word cloud and ask students to supply more formal alternatives. Ask the class how their informal language differs from their parents' colloquial expressions, because idioms and expressions change with each generation. Ask whether they know these words: fab (used by the Beatles in their first film) for fabulous; wicked; brilliant; tickety-boo; top-notch.

Before starting the Student Book and Workbook activities, spend a few moments discussing the difference between colloquial expressions and poor grammar. Are students aware of the difference? Can they tell whether someone 'speaks badly' out of choice, or because they do not know they are making mistakes (for example, 'me books')? Does this matter?

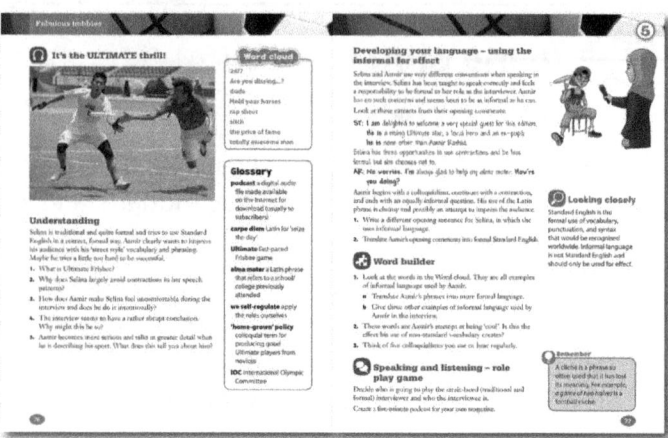

Student-book answers

📖 Understanding

1. Ultimate Frisbee is a self-regulated sport.

2. Selina is conducting a formal interview and is more conservative by nature.

3. Aamir makes it sound as if he disapproves. Accept reasoned answers as to whether this is intentional.

4. Selina does not want to play/be with Aamir.

5. Aamir becomes more serious because he's discussing something he is knowledgeable and passionate about. It suggests the cool image is a pose, or that he has a serious side to his nature as well. Accept any well-reasoned alternatives.

Student-book answers

Using the informal for effect

1. 'Hi, and welcome to our cool school podcast . . .', or similar.

2. 'No need to apologise. It is a pleasure to assist my old school. How are you?', or similar.

Vocabulary

🧩 Word builder

1. **a.** Answers are as shown in the table below.

Informal phrase	Formal meaning
24/7	seven days a week
Are you dissing?	putting down/ criticising
dude	man/boy
hold your horses	wait a moment
rap sheet	report/school file
sitch	situation
the price of fame	the result of being well-known
totally awesome	impressive
man	an empty phrase – accept reasonable translations such as 'you know'

b. The other examples of informal language used by Aamir are: yeah; it kicks traditional sport; real quick.

2. Accept reasoned responses depending on opinions about use of non-standard vocabulary.

3. Students supply five colloquialisms they hear regularly (recall from pre-teaching session).

When to write informally

1. Students match the type to the purpose and decide on formal, informal or both. Answers are as shown below.

Feature	Purpose	Formal or informal?
Editorial	Offers opinion on topic	Formal
Index of features	Factual list	Formal
Review	Writer's opinion	Formal/semi-formal
Letters page	Personal opinions	Depending on writer/informal
Advertisements	Depending on target audience	Semi-formal/informal
Reports	Describing events/eyewitness descriptions	Formal/semi-formal
Interviews	Depending on target audience	Semi-formal
Articles	Informative accounts that may include opinions	Formal

2. Incorrect use of grammar ('me' for 'my') and colloquialisms ('cool', 'no way'); also, very personal ('Please, please help me!!!').

3. Students reply to the letter in a similar informal register. When they have finished, ask them to identify which is informal language and which is bad grammar.

Role-play game

Arrange the class in pairs. Students now create a five-minute podcast for their own magazine, which they can record.

Recording real interviews

Arrange students in groups and ask them to watch a few minutes of interviews with sports personalities (you can use online videos, such as those available on YouTube). Ask the following questions:

- Do the speakers (interviewer and interviewee) express themselves well?

- Could someone who is not keen on the sport follow the discussion?

Writing a report

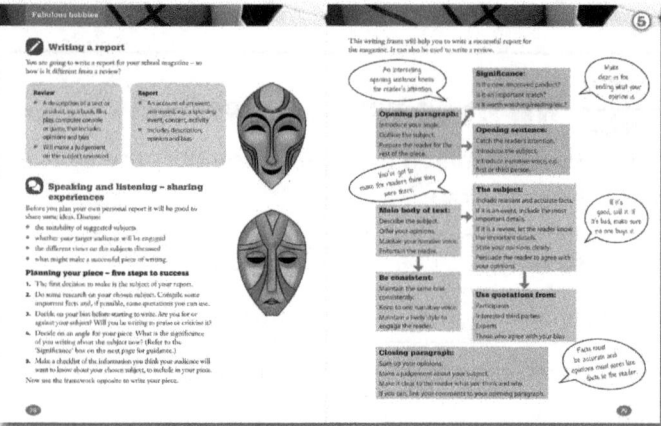

Writing

✏ Writing a report

While students may share ideas in the Listening and speaking (planning) activity, the writing task is best carried out individually, because students are learning and practising useful writing skills for their future Checkpoint and IGCSE assessments.

When marking students' reports, credit content and use of language. The report should be a clear account of the event witnessed and include interesting description as well as comments that reflect the writer's opinion and/or bias. Students have been working on more advanced punctuation in this unit so credit correct use of punctuation and more ambitious sentence grammar. Your feedback on essays should include this where relevant.

This activity can be developed for the class magazine and you can ask students to find appropriate images or photographs to go with their reports. However, if they are using photographs from the Internet they must be aware of the rules for using intellectual property and credit photographers.

Speaking and listening

💬 Sharing experiences

Students share ideas in small groups or in pairs. Encourage them to make notes individually during their discussions.

- If students struggle to select an idea, suggest 'Ultimate Frisbee' or a less well-known sport. Give them time to find the necessary information. Alternatively, ask the class to attend a school sports competition and plan a report on that as a real event.

- Students should then research their chosen subject, compiling facts, relevant data/history and, where relevant, including quotations.

- Review point of view and bias; let them decide whether they are writing to praise or to criticise.

- Review what is meant by 'angle'.

- Finish by directing the class to the writing frame on page 79 of the Student Book.

More able students will now benefit from working on their own, coming to you for guidance only. Less confident students may need to go through the writing frame with you before starting their reports.

Insist students proofread carefully and redraft as necessary for effective use of English. They may use a thesaurus and/or dictionary.

Marking criteria: mark each report for form and content, giving ample feedback. Language should be in an appropriate register for the target audience. Reward the use of more sophisticated punctuation covered in this and previous units. Spelling should be correct.

Writing a review

1. Over-priced and under-powered.
2. Came second/inferior.
3. More powerful/less expensive.
4. Objective.

Marking reviews: students should write their reviews in a similar formal register and be objective. Language should be precise and concise.

Class magazine project

Having nearly completed this unit, students are now well equipped to write and produce a class or year-group magazine. Ask them to search online for information regarding who works on a magazine. Useful details can also be found at: http://work.chron.com/types-jobs-magazine-publishing-9486.html.

Take feedback and make a list on the board of all the posts that need to be covered, from content writers in different field (arts/entertainment/sports) to the vital editorial team, who will put the material together and proofread articles. Having established who is needed, students may volunteer to take on roles or you can arrange groups to take care of different aspects such as content writing, editing, illustration and photography.

Alternatively, ask students to arrange themselves into an editorial team, with features editors such as team sports editor, athletics editor, hobbies and pastimes editor, etc. Each editor needs at least one writer who will help create material. They also need proofreaders and photographers and/or illustrators.

Set a deadline and specify how many pages the magazine should contain. Provide paper as required. You could set aside a school week to produce final drafts and create the hard copy. This activity enables students to practise a wide range of valuable skills. It is also excellent preparation for producing coursework folders and working in teams later in their school careers.

If you do not have sufficient time to complete a full magazine, ask students to form pairs and deconstruct an existing magazine. They should bring in a magazine, read the contents page and match each topic heading to the relevant editor or writer. They may then physically take the magazine apart to show who was responsible for what. For example, they could take all the cookery pages out, staple them together and write the cookery editor's name and the photographer's name on them. This helps to show just how much work goes into creating a monthly magazine.

Progress check

Ask students to do this short test in silence on their own.

Unit test mark scheme

1. Purpose: to introduce the monthly theme/set the tone; written by: editor. [2]

2. Latin; 'seize the day'. [2]

3. Award 1 mark for explaining the difference in meaning (one positive, the other negative), and 1 mark for explaining that the prefix inverts/changes the meaning. [2]

4. Colloquialisms. Award 1 further mark for a suitable example. [2]

5. Idioms. Award 1 further mark for a suitable example. [2]

6. Award 1 mark each for any four appropriate qualities, e.g. engages target audience/ topical articles/relevant to students/ interesting to read/accurate facts/ maintains theme. [4]

7. Accept any two features of formal writing and any two features of informal writing from the list that appears on page 70 of the Student Book. Award 1 mark per feature. [4]

8. Accept any four relevant details found in the text 'It's the ULTIMATE thrill'. Award 1 mark per detail. [4]

9. Award 1 mark each for any two relevant differences. Award 1 mark each for any two examples that exemplify these differences, e.g. a book review as opposed to a sporting event. [4]

10. Award 1 mark each for any four steps to successfully writing a report from the five featured on page 78 of the Student Book. [4]

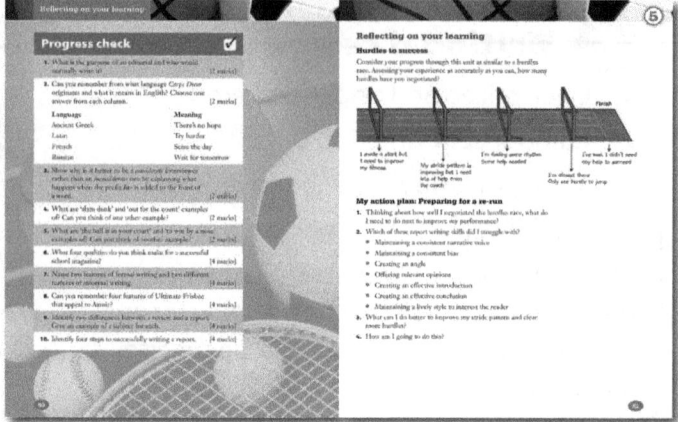

🧩 Reflecting on your learning – Hurdles to success

Take a few minutes to reflect on the content of this unit (see questions on page 80 of the Student Book for a quick reminder). Elicit whether students are familiar with the metaphor of 'hurdles' and ask if they found any along the way; if so, what were they, and to what extent do they feel they have successfully jumped or overcome them? Students should make a note of areas where they still have doubts and prepare an 'action plan'. By now, students should be more aware of the need to take more responsibility for their own learning. Encourage the students to do this reflective assessment in silence and independently.

Culture unit quiz time

1. Answers are as shown in the table ('F' stands for formal and 'I' for informal).

Editorials	F
Reviews	F
Reports	F
Interviews	I
Human interest articles	F
Topical articles	F
Advertisements	I
Letters page	I
Games page	I

2. **c.** It introduces a theme and offers an opinion that sets the tone.

3. Any reasonable explanation that explains the idiom, i.e. that circumstances changed considerably between the beginning and the end.

4. Students underline: delights, loves, freely, magnificent, blessed, marvellous.

5. Students rewrite the sentence as follows: These four clubs were founding members of the Premier League: Liverpool, Manchester United, Arsenal, and Chelsea.

6. **c.** A question and answer section.

7. Any two reasons from: a change of subject/a break in thought/to separate parenthetical clauses/extra information being added to the end of a sentence/an opinion being given.

A printable version of the full transcript for this unit is available on the CD.

Reflecting on your learning

If necessary, explain the metaphor for learning in this unit as the hurdles race. Students can do this activity in pairs, but ideally they are monitoring their own progress so they should be given time to think about it and answer the questions on their own. Spend a few minutes discussing with the class how they may use the different writing skills covered in this unit as they proceed up the school and in their working life. Review how the media use an 'angle' and the other bullet points.

As a means of reviewing topics and speaking and listening skills covered in the unit, ask the class to turn back to page 66 in the Student Book and look at the quotations again. Ask if, after what they have read and heard in the unit, they now think there are hobbies or pastimes they might enjoy that they had never considered before. Move on to consider the quotations about reading a school magazine and ask if they now have a better understanding of what creating a magazine actually involves. If possible, call on views expressed earlier and re-examine original ideas in the light of material covered.

Round up the discussion by asking who in the class would like to be a professional sports player, athlete, or who might like to develop a hobby they enjoy outside school into a career. Would anyone now consider working in the print media? While students are speaking, encourage them to substantiate their views, ideas and opinions. This is very good practice for oral assessments in IGCSE English.

6 Alarming journeys

Learning objectives

In this unit, students will:

- Conduct a discussion, drawing together ideas and promoting effective sharing of ideas. **Pages 82–83** *8SL6*

- Explain how specific choices and combinations of form, layout and presentation create particular effects **Pages 84–85** *8Rv5*

- Extend vocabulary by noting down powerful words in books read. **Pages 84–85 and 90–91** *8W02*

- Confidently use a range of sentence features to clarify or emphasise meaning, e.g. compound nouns or prepositional phrases. **Pages 86–87** *8Wp3*

- Trace the development of a writer's or a poet's ideas, viewpoint and themes through a text and relate these to other texts read. **Pages 88–89** *8Rv1*

- Explain, using accurate terminology, how language is used to create effect, e.g. personification, figurative language, imagery, patterns and structure in the use of language, use of dialect or informal language. **Pages 88–89** *8Rw4*

- Spell most words correctly, including some complex polysyllabic words and unfamiliar words. **Pages 90–91** *8Ws1*

- Learn the spelling of difficult and commonly misspelled words and develop strategies for correcting spelling. **Pages 90–91** *8Ws2*

- Apply editing and proofreading skills to a range of different texts and contexts. **Pages 90–91** *8W01*

- Create and control effects by drawing independently on range and variety of their own vocabulary. **Pages 92–93** *8Wa6*

- Identify the most appropriate approach to planning their writing in order to explore, connect and shape ideas. **Pages 94–95** *8Wa1*

- Compare poems from different cultures and times, commenting on poets' use of language and imagery to develop similar themes and elicit responses from the reader. **Pages 94–95** *8Rw3*

Setting the scene

Spend about 5–10 minutes with students, drawing out their views and prior experiences in an informal way. Ask them whether they have previously:

- thought about exploring Mount Everest
- collaborated in a word-association game
- created stories to tell aloud
- engaged with how a mountaineer might feel about his or her climb
- reflected on what makes a journey special or unusual.

Reflection

 Thinking time

Look at the quotations on page 82 of the Student Book and discuss with the class what the heading 'The way not taken' may mean. It relates to a famous poem by Robert Frost about wondering what might have happened on the 'road not taken'.

Discuss different forms of travel for the first quotation then let students think about a journey as a metaphor: 'our journey through life'. Introduce the idea that how we respond to these quotations might say a lot about how we think. Explore different approaches and attitudes to journeys and ask students to consider the quotation about the best bit of a journey being coming home. Take into account that some

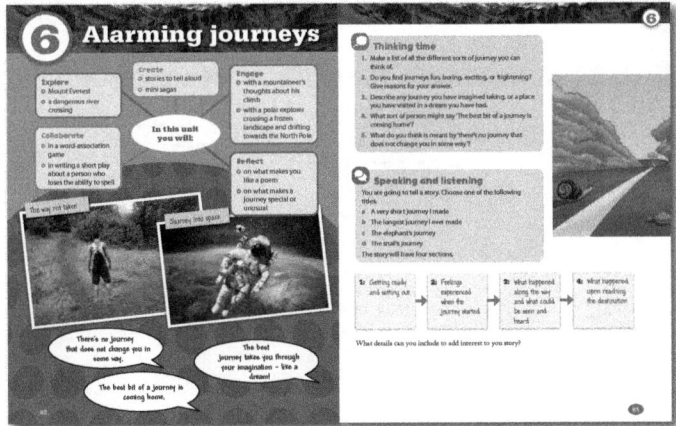

students may have different concepts of 'home': a country, city, a house, and/or a family. Students may be more comfortable discussing questions 4, 5, and 6 (on page 83) in groups of their own choice. Ask them to organise themselves into small groups, but appoint a spokesperson in each group to feedback to the class.

Speaking and listening

Allow students to choose their own groups of four. They each select one of the story titles and arrange their ideas into four sections. They should be encouraged to speak without much planning, largely making it up as they go along. This is a formative fun activity, but set a time limit to help provide focus.

Workbook

 Discussing journeys

This small group activity can be arranged after you do the class discussions on journeys or the Speaking and listening task. Ensure students are aware that these journeys have a 'scary' element. Encourage them to make notes; they should keep them for work on mini sagas later in the unit.

Extension

Direct students' attention to the photograph and quotation 'The way not taken'. Show how 'two roads diverged'. Read Frost's 'The Road Not Taken' to the class and ask them if it is about a journey, or a journey not taken. It is available at: http://www.poetryfoundation.org/poem/173536 and various other Internet sites, some with evocative images.

The poet says he took the 'the (path) less traveled by / And that has made all the difference'. Frost may be suggesting that he chose the path in life to be a poet, and that made his life what it is, but still he wonders what might have happened had he chosen the other route. As a listening exercise, ask the following questions when you have finished the second reading.

- At what time of year did the poet see the paths? (Autumn)
- What reasons does he give for choosing the path 'less traveled'?
- What do you think the poet means by: 'Yet knowing how way leads on to way, / I doubted if I should come back'.
- What atmosphere or tone do the words create?
- If the tone of this poem is calm, or melancholy, why might standing at a crossroads or where one path splits into two make one anxious?

The Road Not Taken

Robert Frost (1874–1963). Mountain Interval. 1920

Two roads diverged in a yellow wood,
And sorry I could not travel both
And be one traveler, long I stood
And looked down one as far as I could
To where it bent in the undergrowth;   5

Then took the other, as just as fair,
And having perhaps the better claim,
Because it was grassy and wanted wear;
Though as for that the passing there
Had worn them really about the same,   10

And both that morning equally lay
In leaves no step had trodden black.
Oh, I kept the first for another day!
Yet knowing how way leads on to way,
I doubted if I should ever come back.   15

I shall be telling this with a sigh
Somewhere ages and ages hence:
Two roads diverged in a wood, and I—
I took the one less traveled by,
And that has made all the difference.   20

Conquering Mount Everest

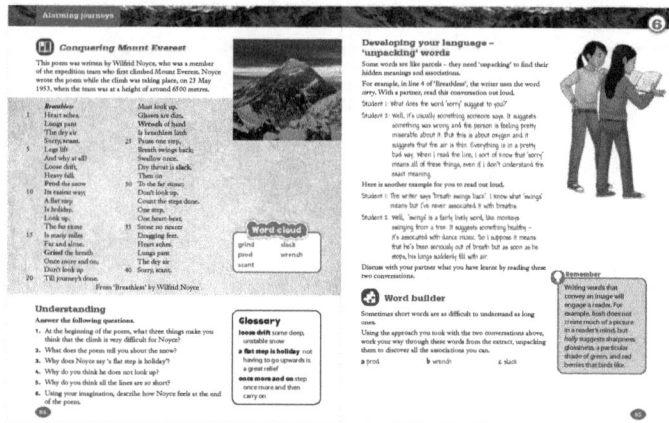

to them. They may use their notes and Noyce's poem to help them. Set a maximum of 200 words. Ask them to use their five senses as they describe their (imagined) experience, but they should not tell a story. When they have finished, students may read their journal entries together, and compare and contrast their different points of view or emphasis.

Extension

Writing a journal entry – Climbing Mount Everest

There are a number of videos available on the Internet that give a sense of the sheer distance involved in reaching the summit of Everest, and the appalling dangers climbers face. These two are taken from climbers' helmets and are available on You Tube: https://www.youtube.com/watch?v=moBJMGNSql4 and https://www.youtube.com/watch?v=pKq-3H04SkQ.

Ask students to watch, then individually make notes on their first impressions about the location and dangers, and the physical difficulties climbers experience. They should then form small groups and discuss their ideas together. Name group leaders, set a time limit and take feedback. Now return to Noyce's poem and give students a few minutes to compare their notes and what they have discussed with what Noyce sees and feels. When they have finished, tell students to imagine they are part of a team climbing Mount Everest. Ask them to write an entry in their journal describing their location and what is happening

📖 Understanding

1. 'Heart aches, / Lungs pant'; 'Loose drift, / heavy fall' (of snow); 'scant' air.

2. It is loose, heavy, and deep.

3. Because 'a flat step' requires much less effort to climb.

4. Repetition of 'far' suggests huge distance to summit. The poet is discouraged by the distance and the height, and is thinking of giving up on his quest to get to 'The far stone'.

5. Form represents steep incline.

6. As the poem comes to a close, Noyce is 'no nearer' and 'dragging feet'; his heart still 'aches' and the dry air is thinner. Allow students to express their own ideas, using quotations to support their views.

'Unpacking' words

Start by asking students to complete this section on their own, so they can formulate their own ideas and questions, before opening it up for class discussion. Spend time looking at words that 'move', such as 'wrench' and 'prod' (also in the Word cloud). Allow students a few minutes to work in pairs to discuss the conversations and ideas of layered meaning and unpacking words. They should be making notes as they do each of these activities, which they will use later. Students should then work individually to unpack:

a. prod (as a verb)

b. wrench (as a verb)

c. slack (as an adjective).

Discourage students from using a dictionary but help them with how words (verb/noun/adjective) are used in the poem.

Words that suggest images can then be developed. For more examples, suggest these ideas:

- a river as a torrent, brook, stream, meandering
- rain as drizzle, cloud-burst, downpour, shower.

Ask what these descriptive forms of rain and rivers suggest through the words we use.

Investigating dangerous climbs

Ask students to find out about mountain climbing in other countries, for example, Mont Blanc in the French Alps, Mount Whitney in the USA, or Aconcagua in Argentina. They should read articles about the location and if possible find a first-person account of the experience of climbing their chosen peak. Then each student takes the role of a returning climber and in pairs students take turns to interview each other.

Unpacking words

Students can suggest a wide range of possibilities to describe what they imagine. Share their ideas in a short whole-class feedback session or ask them to review their work in pairs.

Extension

A personal poetry anthology

Students create their own poetry anthologies by copying out short poems they enjoy, or stanzas from longer poems. These poems can be illustrated and kept in a folder. You can set aside one lesson a month or focus on this activity during specific periods (for example, the end of term). You will need to provide paper, blank and lined, and a wide range of poetry books for students to choose from. Discourage any use of the Internet. The activity here is to copy exactly what a poet has written by hand. This helps students to appreciate a poet's diction, how and why poets have constructed stanzas, and how poems are punctuated. The act of copying by hand will seem old-fashioned, but it is a valuable exercise. Students may include poems from lessons. At the end of the year they can take their folders into the next year group. By IGCSE level, each student should have an interesting selection of poetry and a much better appreciation of the use of language for specific effects.

Prepositional phrases

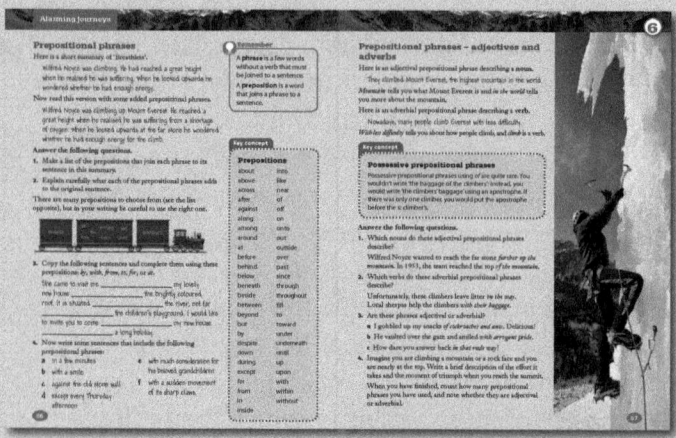

Student-book answers

Prepositional phrases

The following activities can be peer marked.

1. up/from/of/at/for

2. Students should demonstrate awareness of how a noun or pronoun relates to the sentence: the position or direction of a person or thing (up/down/along); when something happens (after/before); a connection (with/like).

3. She came to visit me *at* my lovely new house *with* the brightly coloured roof. It is situated *by* the river, not far *from* the children's playground. I would like to invite you to *come* to my new house *for* a long holiday.

4. Students make sentences that include prepositional phrases. These can be peer marked.

Prepositional phrases – adjectives and adverbs

If you are in a largely bilingual classroom, spend a few minutes looking at possessive prepositional phrases in translation and how direct translation can sound awkward. For example, 'the baggage of the climbers' is a correct construction in some languages, but in English we generally use the Saxon genitive ('the climbers' baggage'). This can be confusing for some Latin language speakers in particular (and result in an apostrophe being employed with plurals as well).

Answers

1. stone; the top

2. leave; help

3. a. adjectival; b. adverbial; c. adverbial

4. Descriptions should include the effort it takes and the moment of triumph. Students then count prepositional phrases they have used, and note whether they are adjectival or adverbial.

Workbook

 A prepositional verse

This page of the Workbook should be attempted individually, to enable students to consolidate work done in class, and then shared in small groups or pairs for peer marking.

A prepositional verse:

> I met a creature
>
> *at/on* the top step
>
> *of* the staircase
>
> *on* the carpet
>
> *with* six creepy-crawly legs
>
> *at/of* five centimetres long
>
> I took it
>
> *from* its hiding place
>
> *in/on/into* my shaking hand
>
> *at* greatest peril
>
> *to* my fragile sanity
>
> I couldn't bear to kill it so it went
>
> *into* a pretty little box
>
> *on* the windowsill
>
> *under/beside/by* the floral curtains
>
> *until/till* some later time.

My annoying little sister happened to find the box and, being inquisitive, had to discover what was in it.

Extension

Prepositions in song lyrics

If students are still struggling with prepositions, use the lyrics of a song to help them see how these little words provide more information in a sentence. An easy example is the old song 'A Windmill in Old Amsterdam' by Ronnie Hilton. There are various sites on the Internet with the lyrics, some of which can be screened on a smart board, so students can identify the prepositions during the song itself.

Grammar

Practising prepositions

To give students a better idea about how we use prepositional phrases, ask them to try writing a paragraph using as few as possible. Ask them to write down three things they do each school morning in the present tense, using only a subject/verb/object sentence order as far as possible. If they use a preposition they should underline it. For example: *I wake up* (verb + preposition). *I catch the bus. I come to school.* They should now expand on each of these sentences to give the reader more information. *I wake up when the alarm goes off at seven o'clock. I catch the bus at the end of my street.*

Working in pairs, and using the rules for 'Prepositional phrases – adjectives and adverbs' on page 87 of the Student Book, students now colour in their prepositional phrases using yellow for adjectival phrases and green for adverbial phrases. They then take turns to explain how their prepositional phrases give information.

As extra practice for students needing more language support, ask them to write out as many prepositions as they can think of (or use the list on page 86 of the Student Book) on pieces of card and cut them out. Students form pairs and tell each other what they have been doing during the course of the day, or what they have done in the past hour. Each time one of them uses a preposition, the other has to give him/her the appropriate word from their cards. For example, if Student A says '*I woke up*', Student B hands over the *up* card. '*I put my bag under my chair*' = *under* card.

Drifting

Prior knowledge

Fridtkof Nansen (1861–1930) was a Norwegian scientist and explorer, most famous for his North Pole expedition of 1893-96. His boat, the *Fram*, was designed to be carried along in the drifting ice without being crushed by it.

Before reading the poem, establish what they think the Arctic might look, feel and sound like, and how an explorer in the nineteenth century might have felt about going there for the first time.

Read the poem aloud to the class and ask what they think it is about. Then allow them to read it for themselves, review the words in the Word cloud and take feedback. Go through the words in the Glossary box and read the poem aloud to the class again, before students complete the Understanding section on their own.

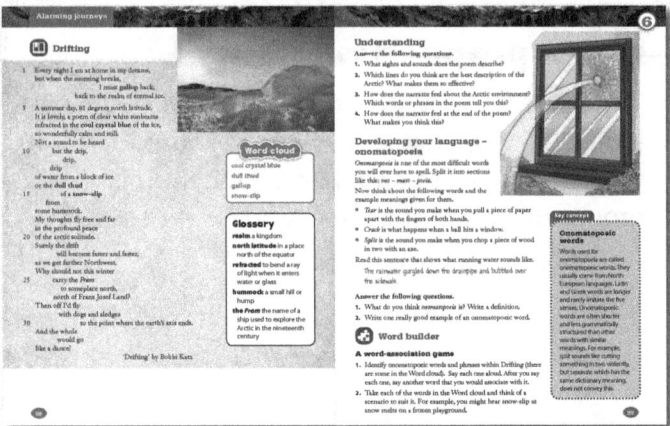

Student-book answers

Understanding

1. Sights include the 'the realm of eternal ice' and 'cool crystal blue of the ice'. Sounds include the 'drip, drip, drip of water' and the 'dull thud of a snow-slip'.

2. Students' personal responses should be supported by quotations from the text.

3. The narrator seems to feel very peaceful and thoughtful. Towards the end of the poem he is excited. Accept responses backed up with quotations from the text.

4. He seems to feel excited about reaching the North Pole. Justification from the poem could include 'faster and faster', 'off I'd fly' and 'like a dance!'

Vocabulary

Onomatopoeia

Students should work through this section individually before feeding back to the class. Enjoy the different sound words they suggest.

1. Sound words.

2. Accept: buzz, zoom, splat, etc. Also accept invented words often used in comics, such as: ka-boom!

Extension

Cartoon onomatopoeias

A fun way to practise using onomatopoeias is to ask students to create cartoon strips. Give them a choice of situations such as at a car or motorbike race, at the fair or in a city street, then ask them to create a character in a dangerous situation. They should draw a comic strip describing what happens to him or her.

Tell them to include as many sound effects as possible. When they have finished, arrange small groups and ask students to take turns 'talking through' their comic strips with the relevant onomatopoeias. Be warned, this can get noisy.

Vocabulary

Word builder – A word-association game

For question 1, arrange the class in pairs; students take turns with word associations.

For question 2, they may work together to think of a scenario.

Making a big splash!

Students should do the first activity on their own, to determine how their mouth forms the words 'push' and 'pull'. After finishing the poem they can discuss their answers as a class.

For the second activity on the poem 'Jazz Fantasia', accept words that are not strictly onomatopoeic but that suggest a sound, such as 'sob' and 'drum'.

Answers: drum, batter, sob, ooze, husha-husha-hush. Students should be able to explain that these words describe the sounds the jazz band is making.

Extension

Class activity: rhythm in poetry

'Drifting' is a very effective poem, but has a fairly loose rhythm. As an extension activity, you could move on to look at a poem with a very strong rhythm. *The Night Mail* is a documentary film made in 1935 about the mail train from London to Glasgow. Part 3 includes the famous poem by W. H. Auden, written for the film. There are various clips on YouTube and other sites on the Internet.

This footage gives students a good idea about steam trains and shows how a poet can create rhythm through words. It will be necessary to explain some diction, such as 'postal orders'.

To consolidate work on rhythm, you could listen to this extract from a recent electronic music version of 'Night Mail' using Auden's words, found at https://soundcloud.com/psbhq/night-mail-radio-edit.

If you are not able to show *The Night Mail* documentary film clip, read this extract from the poem to the class and ask them to listen for the rhythm. Explain that 'crossing the Border' refers to the train crossing into Scotland. Note that this published text differs slightly from the earlier version used in the film clip.

Night Mail

I

This is the Night Mail crossing the Border,
Bringing the cheque and the postal order,

Letters for the rich, letters for the poor,
The shop at the corner, the girl next door.

Pulling up Beattock, a steady climb:
The gradient's against her, but she's on time.

Past cotton-grass and moorland boulder,
Shovelling white steam over her shoulder,

Snorting noisily, she passes
Silent miles of wind-bent grasses.

Birds turn their heads as she approaches,
Stare from bushes at her blank-faced coaches.

Sheep-dogs cannot turn her course;
They slumber on with paws across.

In the farm she passes no one wakes,
But a jug in a bedroom gently shakes.

II

Dawn freshens. Her climb is done.
Down towards Glasgow she descends,
Towards the steam tugs yelping down a glade of cranes,

Towards the fields of apparatus, the furnaces
Set on the dark plain like gigantic chessmen.
All Scotland waits for her:
In dark glens, beside pale-green lochs,
Men long for news.

III

Letters of thanks, letters from banks,
Letters of joy from girl and boy,
Receipted bills and invitations
To inspect new stock or to visit relations,
And applications for situations,
And timid lovers' declarations,
And gossip, gossip from all the nations,
News circumstantial, news financial,
Letters with holiday snaps to enlarge in,
Letters with faces scrawled on the margin,
Letters from uncles, cousins and aunts,
Letters to Scotland from the South of France,
Letters of condolence to Highlands and Lowlands,
Written on paper of every hue,
The pink, the violet, the white and the blue,
The chatty, the catty, the boring, the adoring,
The cold and official and the heart's outpouring,
Clever, stupid, short and long,
The typed and the printed and the spelt all wrong. (...)

From 'Night Mail' by W. H. Auden

Spelling round-up

Prior knowledge

Start with a spot-check spelling test with the whole class before students open their Student Books. Select ten frequently misspelled words, do the test then put the answers on the board. Students swap papers and peer mark. Ask if they have any tricks for remembering spellings such as:

- necessary (one c, two s)
- professional (one f, two s).

Show students the 50 words and ask what they think is the best way to learn them and why spelling matters. Remind them that computer grammar and spell checkers aren't always reliable.

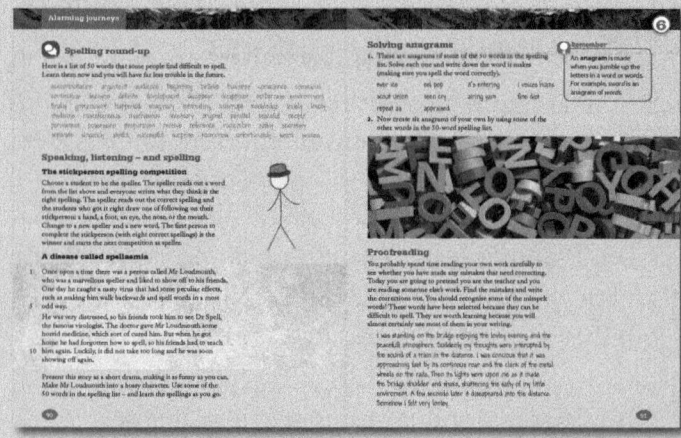

Speaking and listening

💬 Speaking, listening – and spelling

The stickperson spelling competition

This is a group activity. Each student needs paper on which they draw a copy of the incomplete stickperson.

Choose one student to be the speller; he or she reads out a word from the list. The class write what they think is the correct spelling. The speller then reads out the correct spelling and the students who got it right draw one of the following on their stickperson: one hand, one foot, one eye, the nose, or the mouth. Change to a new speller and a new word. The first person to complete the stickperson (eight correct spellings) is the winner and starts the next round as speller.

A disease called spellaemia

Organise students into groups for this role-play game. They should present this story as a short drama, making it funny and Mr Loudmouth bossy. They should use some words in the spelling list, and learn the spellings as they go.

Vocabulary

Solving anagrams

1. Explain how to do an anagram; for example, 'sword' is an anagram of 'words'. Then students can do the practice in pairs.

   Answers to anagrams:

   - ever ice = receive
   - eel pop = people
   - it's entering = interesting
   - I voices hums = mischievous
   - scout union = continuous
   - seen cry = scenery
   - airing yam = imaginary
   - fine diet = definite
   - repeat as = separate
   - appraised = disappear

2. Students create six anagrams of their own using other words in the 50-word spelling list. Some students may find this quite challenging, so they could work together or do it as homework, without time pressure.

Proofreading

Corrected spelling mistakes are shown below underlined.

> I was standing on the bridge enjoying the <u>lovely</u> evening and the <u>peaceful</u> atmosphere. Suddenly my thoughts were <u>interrupted</u> by the sound of a train in the distance. I was <u>conscious</u> that it was approaching fast by its <u>continuous</u> roar and the clank of the metal wheels on the rails. Then its lights were upon me as it made the bridge shudder and shake, shattering the <u>safety</u> of my little <u>environment</u>. A few seconds later, it <u>disappeared</u> into the distance. Somehow I felt very <u>lonely</u>.

Extension

Travel vocabulary

Ask students to turn back to the first page of this unit and look at the two images of a man looking at two paths and an astronaut in space. Write on the board *a journey* and ask students to suggest alternative nouns (stroll, voyage, trip, expedition, etc.). Give students a thesaurus and ask them to find five more words for different kinds of journey. They should make a list then use each of their words in sentences to demonstrate meanings. For example, *expedition: The scientists went on an expedition to Alaska.*

When they have finished, students compare their words with a partner and decide who has got the most unusual word and who has got the most original or entertaining sentence. Set a time limit and take feedback. Write students' words on the board and ask for definitions. The class should add any new words to their lists.

This activity can be developed by asking students to write a short first-person account of a real or imaginary journey, using the past tense.

🧩 Spelling word search

Students should find 10 words in this word search from the poem 'Drifting' then write out the correct answers under the grid. The words are:

- sledges
- latitude
- eternal
- thoughts
- surely
- drift
- axis
- profound
- crystal
- solitude

W	J	P	Y	W	K	X	D	E	Z	Q	Q
S	C	R	Y	S	T	A	L	E	P	O	Z
T	H	O	U	G	H	T	S	L	M	L	L
E	T	F	X	T	C	O	C	X	A	Z	A
H	F	O	Q	D	S	A	K	J	T	J	T
Z	N	U	U	F	F	A	Z	O	J	B	I
Q	B	N	Q	E	T	E	R	N	A	L	T
H	A	D	Q	S	L	E	D	G	E	S	U
C	X	A	W	N	U	D	R	I	F	T	D
W	I	R	X	S	U	R	E	L	Y	S	E
E	S	W	Q	G	N	H	R	L	V	D	D
Z	Z	S	O	L	I	T	U	D	E	C	Q

1. Example = eternal
2. Drift.
3. Surely.
4. Sledges.
5. Axis. The Earth/the world.

   Students will need to refer back to the end of the poem to answer the second part of the question.

Content and language in poetry

Prior knowledge

Briefly review why a poet may want to write a poem. Return to 'Breathless' and 'Drifting' and ask what experiences led poets to write these poems. Discuss how emotions play a part in creativity then ask how a group could create a poem. Remind students what a haiku is and ask if they have read any or created their own haikus before.

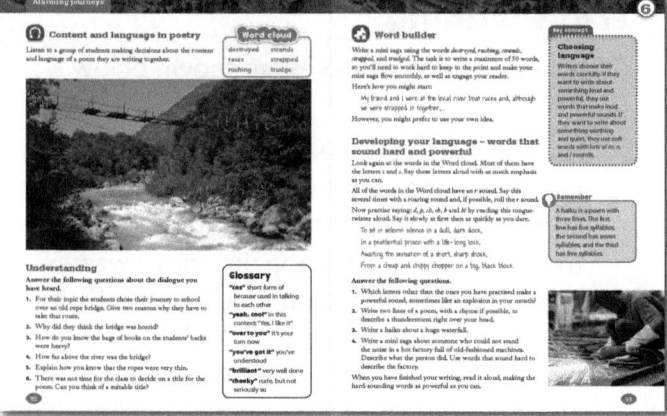

💬 Speaking and listening

Tell the students they will now hear a class writing a poem together. Play the recording and review the words in the Word cloud. Point out how the dialogue in the Glossary box is colloquial and hasn't been used in the class poem.

Student-book answers

🎧 Understanding

1. Their road is closed because of a landslide; there is rushing water.
2. The bridge is made of thin rope and high above the river; it looks and feels dangerous.
3. 'load'
4. 'high'
5. The ropes are described as 'lines' and 'strands' and 'a spider's web'.
6. Title could be 'Rope Bridge' or any suitable alternative.

Vocabulary

Word builder

Explain that a mini saga can be as few as 50 words, and it often has a twist at the end. Students should use: *destroyed, rushing, strands, strapped,* and *trudged.* They can also use their notes from the beginning of this unit, when they were creating stories to tell aloud. Ask students to work on their own, allowing them sufficient time to make a rough draft, redraft, and proofread. Look out for creative storylines and technical accuracy (stress the importance of proofreading).

Extension

Class poem activity

If you would like to do a class poetry writing activity similar to the one on the recording, suggest specific situations and or times of the year to help students choose a topic. The recording takes advantage of a recent weather event that affected the students' daily lives, but if such a dramatic experience is not available to you in your area, specify a time or place.

Students can then start work in groups, choosing the form and content for their poem, deciding whether they want free verse, rhyming couplets, or quatrains, etc. Name one student in each group as leader: their role is to adjudicate when there is any dispute, ensure each person is involved, and report on their group's ideas during feedback. Set a time limit and bring the class together.

If you have a large class, students can continue the writing process in their groups, or you can all work together. If working in groups, set a time limit and collect in completed verses or poems. These can then be merged together to create a longer poem if suitable.

Words that sound hard and powerful

Direct students back to the Word cloud and ask them to read the words aloud, emphasising the harsh consonants. They can practise saying *d*, *p*, *sh*, *ch*, *b*, and *bl,* and reading the tongue twisters aloud. Depending on the nature of your class, you can start to introduce consonance and review alliteration here. Explain that this is not only used in poetry: prose writers use the sound of words for effect as well. (This point is useful for question 4 on mini sagas.)

Ask students for other tongue twisters, and identify those that use harsh and soft consonants apart from the usual alliteration.

Questions 1 and 2 can be done in pairs.

For question 3, students should start by making a word list for a waterfall. This can be done with the class or in groups or pairs, but the final haiku should be written individually. Remind students how to create a haiku in three lines: five syllables; seven syllables; five syllables. Direct the class to the Key points before they begin.

As questions 3 and 4 are demanding, offer students the choice of one or the other, or set one as homework. Questions 3 and 4 are best done individually for maximum consolidation.

Answers

1. p, b, k, t
2. Students' own answers.
3. Students write a haiku; they should use the form five syllables, seven syllables, five syllables.
4. Students write their own mini saga. Ensure they use words that sound hard to describe the factory. When they have finished, students read their work aloud, emphasising the hard-sounding words.

🧩 Creative writing

Look out for vivid description and personal response, especially where students attempt to use unusual adjectives and sound words. As there is no opportunity in the Workbook to redraft, students should proofread their work in class, correcting any spelling mistakes themselves, before handing it in. They can then read their descriptions aloud.

This writing exercise is very good practice for writing at IGCSE. A descriptive writing task does not need to have a beginning, middle, and end. The object is to focus on powerful language using the five senses as far as possible. Aural imagery is an important aspect of descriptive writing (see Extension activity below).

Aural imagery

This extension task gives students a chance to develop skills with aural imagery introduced in this unit. Remind them that alliteration is restricted to the beginning of words then introduce the following terms:

- Assonance: the repetition of similar vowel sounds, as in the tongue twister 'Moses supposes his toeses are roses'.
- Consonance: the repetition of similar consonant sounds, especially at the ends of words, e.g. 'dark dock' and 'black block'. Consonance can occur anywhere in the word – beginning, middle, or end.

'Thistles' by Ted Hughes (available as a PCM on the CD) is a good way to practise 'listening' to aural imagery. The diction reproduces the harsh, dry sound of spiky thistles and the much softer, more vulnerable sound of 'hoeing hands'.

Writing about a poem you like

Prior knowledge

Ask students what needs to be included when writing about a poem and write their replies on the board. Review strategies students may know and check whether these are still appropriate now they are developing better language awareness and can name more literary features. Tell students that in this part of the unit they will be consolidating language skills learned earlier and applying editing skills. Leave comments on the board for students to use later in the lesson.

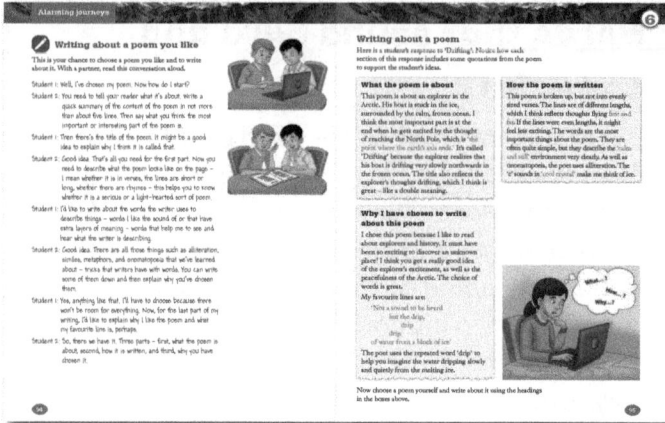

Writing

 Writing about a poem you like

Working with a partner, students should read the conversation on page 94 of the Student Book aloud.

The key elements in the conversation to be included when writing about a poem are:

- what it's about – summary
- title
- structure in verses
- tone, i.e. serious or 'light-hearted'
- layers of meaning in words and phrases
- style – literary devices such as alliteration, imagery, onomatopoeia
- personal response – why the student likes the poem.

Once students have read the conversation, identify these points and go back to what you already have on the board. Tick off what is there already and add new points. The next objective is to decide on a suitable order for the points. Student 2 says, 'Three parts – first, what the poem is about, second, how it is written, and third, why you have chosen it.'

Writing

Writing about a poem

Direct students to the response to 'Drifting'; ask them to read silently before discussing the content. Depending on your class, you may want to draw attention to the over-colloquial use of 'great' in the response and ask what words would sound better.

Give students a selection of poetry books or photocopies of poems with aural imagery and powerful words for them to choose from. The writing activity should be done individually. When marking responses, look out for the structure of essays and how students have incorporated what has been covered in this unit.

Workbook

Responding to a poem

This activity on Chatterjee's 'Hungry Ghost' can be done in class or set as homework. If done in class, you may wish to draw out the descriptive language used by the poet (e.g., floating) and how she journeys through time, back to when she was a child. Students can then examine situations where they may also feel like a hungry ghost, and write a short poem about it.

1. Exciting atmosphere, full of 'spicy scents', amazing 'sights' and noisy with 'shouts'.

2. The world is like a busy market place; busy people trading commodities; a reflection of how the world has become obsessed with material goods. Accept relevant suggestions.

3. The poet wishes to be a child again, when she was carefree, and had the freedom to 'float' amongst the stalls.

◀

Extension

Comparing poems from different epochs – The sounds of winter

This activity can be done as homework/ independent research after students have worked through the extension on layers of meaning in poetry.

Ask students to research Part 1 of 'The Rime of the Ancient Mariner' by Samuel Taylor Coleridge and 'The Snow Man' by Wallace Stevens. These poems are also available on the CD. Ask them to make notes on how each poet presents ice and snow. The first was written by an English poet in 1834 while the second was published a hundred years later by an American. Ask students to read the two poems and make notes on how they are similar and different. Focus on how each poet conjures sound or uses its absence, and on the different presentations of ice and snow.

Extension

Layers of meaning in poetry

A useful way to introduce students to 'layers of meaning' in poetry is to demonstrate how a haiku contains images and thoughts in very few words, then move on to a short poem that also presents images and thoughts. More than any other type of poem, Japanese haiku are a way of seeing the physical world and our existence within it. You can find some very good examples at http:// examples.yourdictionary.com/examples-of-haiku-poems.html#iHpmomClGPQgB38L.99

Ask students to create a haiku or a very short poem of their own about the where they are at this moment. For example:

Scratched desk and scratched board,

I listen and I wonder,

Will this ever end?

Now move on to examine a short lyric poem where a poet expresses his/her thoughts on a topic you have recently covered. If possible choose a poem your students are unlikely to have seen before. Below is a poem for this unit on journeys by Rabindranath Tagore, a Bengali poet, philosopher, artist, playwright, composer, and novelist from India, who won the Nobel Prize in Literature. Ask students to read the poem

➡

themselves. Tell them to speak the words silently in their heads, or they can say the words out loud if you have a big enough room for them to speak without disturbing each other. Tell students that poetry is written to be spoken – that way you can hear the sound of the words and their rhythm.

Take feedback on first impressions and make notes on the board. Now read the poem to the students and clarify any vocabulary problems such as 'futile' and 'clamorous'. Ask for new thoughts on the following:

- Where is the speaker?
- What time of year is it?
- Why does the speaker feel restless?

Remind students to find words to support their ideas.

The Boat

I must launch out my boat.
The languid hours pass by on the
shore – Alas for me!

The spring has done its flowering and taken
   leave.
And now with the burden of faded futile flowers
   I wait and linger.

The waves have become clamorous, and upon
   the bank in the shady lane
the yellow leaves flutter and fall.

What emptiness do you gaze upon!
Do you not feel a thrill passing through the air
with the notes of the far-away song
floating from the other shore?

Now ask students to re-read 'The Road Not Taken' by the American poet Robert Frost and compare and contrast it with Tagore's 'The Boat'. Aspects students might want to compare and contrast are: time of year; age of the speaker (persona); form of travel; nature of the journeys; their personal thoughts and feelings. Students can do this activity in pairs or small groups. Take feedback and ask how the poets are using the natural world (a forest and a river or lake) to talk about human emotions.

Progress check

Ask students to complete this test in silence on their own.

Unit test mark scheme

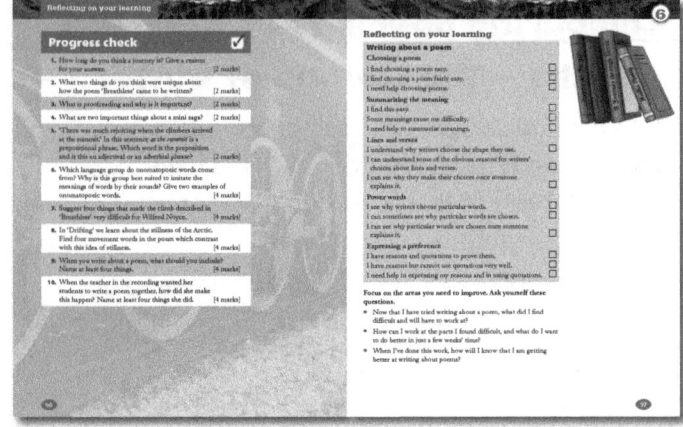

1. There is no specific answer, but award 1 mark for references to length, time, and/or purpose. Any reasonable answer for the second mark, but length may be related to the person or creature making the journey and the reason for it. The second part of the answer should develop and explain the first. [2]

2. It relates to the first successful climbing of Everest (1 mark). It was written during the actual climb/at a unique location and height (1 mark). [2]

3. Proofreading is when you re-read the whole of what you have written for errors and changes (1 mark). It is important because it saves you from making mistakes and it gives you the chance to improve your expression and the content of your work. (1 mark) [2]

4. A mini saga is short – in this example, 50 words in length (1 mark) – and there is a twist at the end (1 mark). [2]

5. 'At' is the preposition (1 mark) and the phrase is an adverb because it tells you where they arrived (1 mark). [2]

6. North European (1 mark), and the words tend to be shorter and less grammatically structured than other words with similar meanings (1 mark). Award 1 mark each for any two appropriate examples of onomatopoeic words (2 marks). [4]

7. Award 1 mark for *any four* of the following (encourage students to give more than four answers):
   - He couldn't breathe.
   - Every step upwards was very difficult.
   - There was a heavy fall of snow.
   - The stone seemed miles away/didn't seem to get closer.
   - His heart and his limbs ached.
   - He couldn't bear to look up. [4]

8. Award 1 mark for any of the following:
   - gallop
   - fly (line 18)
   - faster and faster
   - fly (line 28)
   - dance [4]

9. Award 1 mark for *any four* of the following (encourage students to give more than four answers):
   - a summary of the content
   - the most important part of the poem
   - the reason for the title
   - the shape
   - the language
   - favourite lines
   - a reason for choosing the poem
   - quotations. [4]

10. Award 1 mark for *any four* of the following (encourage students to give more than four answers):
    - She got the students to decide on a topic.
    - She asked them for a first line.
    - She asked them to suggest adjectives for nouns.
    - She chose the best ideas.
    - She asked them to find the best words.
    - She helped them decide what came next.
    - She made them read parts out often.
    - She encouraged them to use devices such as rhyme and alliteration.
    - She stopped them from writing too much.
    - She sent them away to think of a title for the next day. [4]

| tour | Visiting different places or sites in a country, city, or building | Not a single journey to one destination |

2. Link the words to their definitions.

preposition	=	Used with a noun or pronoun to show how things are related, e.g. place, position, or time
phrase	=	A group of words that form a unit within a sentence, often without a verb
prepositional phrase	=	A phrase with a preposition and its object

3. In the first instance, 'fly' refers to the narrator's thoughts (students might also point out the alliteration). In the second instance, the narrator imagines travelling to the north.

4. a. Moveless fish/silver reeds in a silver stream.

   b. Students explain their answers; they should demonstrate awareness of syllable and softness of sounds (assonance/sibilance, if taught).

Listening

A printable version of the full transcript for this unit is available on the CD.

Reflection

 ## Reflecting on your learning

Writing about a poem

The reflective exercise on page 97 of the Student Book is designed to help students focus on their strengths and weaknesses, and also what they enjoy doing in English lessons. Reviewing students' responses will help you to prepare more work on poetry skills, whether to develop students' strengths or help them overcome weaknesses. The work covered on poetry here is an important aspect of preparing for both IGCSE English as a First Language and IGCSE English as a Second Language, because it enhances language awareness. Writing about poems and being able to discuss form and content is also a vital skill for IGCSE Literature and later. At this stage, what students are doing will help them greatly with their reading and writing skills for Checkpoint.

Workbook

Journeys unit quiz

1. Answers are given in the table below.

	Definition	Different from *journey* because…
journey	Travelling from one place to another	
trip	Short visit to a particular place	Trip suggests you return home soon. On a journey you are going somewhere. Examples: a business trip, a school trip
expedition	Travelling with a group of people, perhaps somewhere remote	Going somewhere unknown but planning return/ adventure/ discovery

 **Heroic history**

Learning objectives

In this unit, students will:

- Explore why certain texts are important within a culture and show awareness that the context in which a text is written and read affects its meaning. **Pages 98–99 and 100–101** *8Rv3*

- Comment on implied meaning, e.g. writer's viewpoint, relationships between characters. **Pages 100–101** *8Ri1*

- Experiment with different ways of structuring and presenting texts, appropriate for different audiences and purposes. **Pages 102–103** *8Wt1*

- Confidently use a range of sentence features to clarify or emphasise meaning. **Pages 102–107** *8Wp3*

- Identify relevant points, synthesising and summarising ideas from different parts of a text. **Pages 104–105** *8Rx1*

- Use a range of cohesive devices with audience and purpose in mind. **Pages 104–105** *8Wt2*

- Develop ideas to suit a specific audience, purpose, and task. **Pages 106–107 and 110–111** *8Wa2*

- Write in a range of forms for a variety of purposes. **Pages 106–107 and 110–111** *8Wa4*

- Create and control effects by drawing independently on the range and variety of their own vocabulary. **Pages 108–109** *8Wa6*

- Identify the most appropriate approach to planning their writing in order to explore, connect and shape ideas. **Pages 110–111** *8Wa1*

Setting the scene

Heroic history

Taking about 5–10 minutes, draw out students' ideas and prior experience in an informal way.

- Discuss myths and legends that students may know or have studied at school.

- Develop this to ask about popular folk heroes in their culture, and how and why heroes still feature prominently on television and in movies.

- Try to bring in the difference between a fictitious superhero such as Superman or Batman and a classical hero they may have studied, such as Hercules or Theseus.

- Ask if anyone has explored folk tales and myths in other lessons. If so, when and why?

- Has anyone collaborated in a real interview?

- Ask students if they think it is possible to work together to improve their grammar, for example, in planning paragraphs or understanding how to write sentences.

- Ask if anyone has created their own myth or legend with a typical legendary hero.

- Before closing, direct students' attention to the quotes on page 98 and ask: How many students think history is only facts? Do we need to study myths and legends as history?

Speaking and listening

21st Century Hall of Fame Tribunal

This activity can be carried out as homework, as preparation for the Speaking and listening activity on page 99 of the Student Book.

Explain that a tribunal is a committee appointed to hear evidence and give judgements in a dispute. Ask students to choose two real people who deserve to be remembered as heroes of the 21st century. Students should research their lives and construct an argument for why they should be remembered. Students present their nominees to a group who act as a tribunal. Set a time limit for the tribunal, which can be carried out as a whole-class activity or in groups of 6–8. The material students gather for this tribunal activity can be used again for the balloon debate at the end of the unit.

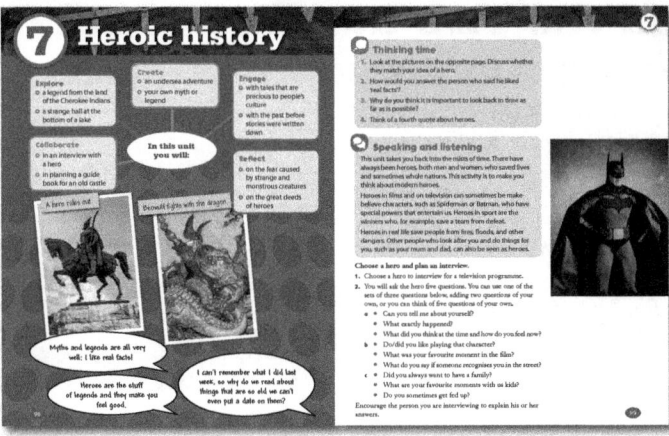

Speaking and listening – interviewing people

On page 50 of the Workbook students are asked to plan who they want to interview and the questions they will ask. You may want students to do this activity before asking them to work on the interviews suggested in the Student Book. You could ask students to perform the interviews in pairs, then the class could comment on how well the questions encouraged the interviewee to talk about him/herself.

Reflection

 Thinking time

You could start by asking students whether young people nowadays need to bother about folk culture and stories that have come to us from what we call 'the oral tradition'? If so, why?

Ask students to work in pairs or small groups, with a note-taker, to discuss the pictures and the questions on page 99. Set a time limit and round up by asking for feedback from each spokesperson. Students should be aware they are discussing ideas and opinions, so they need to justify what they say with reasoned arguments.

Speaking and listening

Extension

Young Theseus – a hero in the making

Tell students the story of Theseus from Greek mythology: a legendary king of Athens who as a young man killed the terrible Minotaur in the labyrinth under the palace of King Minos of Crete. Use the extract about the early life of Theseus from the CD either as a class or independently. Ask the class to make notes on the character, personality, or qualities of Theseus when he was young, which they may use later.

Point out that, although the extract ends with Theseus meeting problems in Athens, he evidently overcame them because he went on to fight the Minotaur and become King of Athens after his father died. Ask students to speculate on how Theseus demonstrated he was the king's son and not a rival for the throne.

Answers to the question should include details such as: Theseus shows he is a determined young man because he perseveres with the huge rock and takes on a challenge in walking overland to Athens. He shows he is brave in walking across the country, knowing the dangers that exist. He shows he is strong because he eventually moves the boulder and defeats the club-wielding robber. Answers to question 3 should draw on Theseus's personality and details from the beginning of the story. Look for evidence of creative thinking that includes something of the boy's ingenuity and/or determination not to be outdone.

Planning an interview with a modern hero

Students will develop their ideas on folk and classical heroes, and think about modern heroes. Briefly discuss films with make-believe characters such as Spiderman or Batman, where the hero has special powers. Talk about how sports heroes are generally the winners. Then go on to talk about how heroes in real life can be 'ordinary' people, such as mountain rescuers, lifeboat crew, firefighters, and ambulance crew. Also ask if people in caring roles, such as parents, could be considered 'unsung heroes'.

Students will conduct an interview for a television programme, asking the interviewee a total of five questions. Support them as they choose a set of given questions and add two more or create their own questions. Once students have made a start, ask them to pause and reflect on how the questions draw out the interviewee's answers so the audience learn more about them. Discuss how questions need to be phrased to avoid a 'yes/no' response.

'The Legend of Catahecassa and the Two-horned Snake'

Prior knowledge

The Cherokee were the original residents of the south-east region of the USA, including Georgia, South Carolina, Virginia, and Tennessee. They were spoken of as 'people who live in caves', so they would have been very familiar with the snakes native to their region. The original Shawnee homeland was what is now Ohio, Kentucky, and Indiana, but the Shawnee travelled as far north as New York and as far south as Georgia. It is likely that the young Shawnee in the legend was 'trespassing' on Cherokee territory when he was captured.

Also draw out students' ideas on the difference between a myth and a legend. One possible interpretation is that myths are a way of explaining what were once considered to be inexplicable natural events, such as earthquakes, volcanoes, and fire; legends contain an element of truth that has been exaggerated in the retelling, such as in the story of Robin Hood.

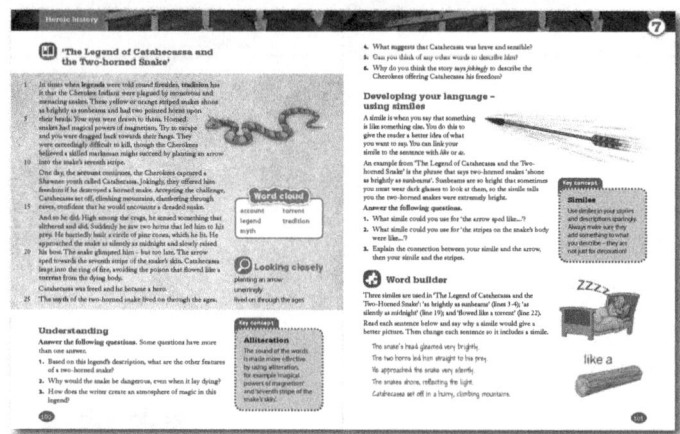

Vocabulary

'The Legend of Catahecassa and the Two-horned Snake'

After students have read the passage, remind them of the previous discussion. Look at the sentence 'The myth of the two-horned snake lived on through the ages' (line 25) and ask if students would categorise the story as a legend (as in the title) or as a myth, and why.

Consider the phrases 'planting an arrow' and 'lived on through the ages', asking students to find another way to say them in the context of the reading. The first could be replaced with 'placing an arrow' (in the target/snake/seventh stripe); the second (the story) 'was told through history/ever after'.

Go over the examples of alliteration from the passage (lines 6 and 10) in the Key points box. Ask how this alliteration affects the way students read the story. Talk about creating powerful description, what it adds to written fiction, and to the way we hear myths and legends when stories are told aloud. Also review how alliteration is used in poetry, if you have already covered this.

Student-book answers

📖 Understanding

1. The snake has two horns, yellow and/or orange stripes, and is very bright.

2. The snake would be dangerous even when dying because the body emits poison.

3. The writer creates an atmosphere of magic through simile and alliteration, and powerful, memorable description (e.g. 'as silently as midnight').

4. Catahecassa was brave and sensible because he took on the challenge and planned what to do.

5. Other words to describe him: courageous, determined, careful, a good shot.

6. 'Jokingly' is used because the Cherokees didn't believe it could be done.

Vocabulary

Using similes

Remind students of the work they did on figurative language in Unit 4, then ask them to look at the examples of similes from the Cherokee/Shawnee legend. Remind them that this story comes from a long time before electricity, so there were no neon colours or headlights!

Suggested answers:

1. Like lightning.

2. As bright as a fresh orange .

3. Students explain their choice of words.

Word builder

Give students a few minutes to work on their own then take feedback about how the sentences could be improved to make them more visual and exciting. Ask the class for suggestions for appropriate similes and go through each sentence orally. Alternatively, ask students to work in pairs to create effective imagery, then take feedback.

Suggestions:

The snake's head gleamed *like a bright burning flame.*

The two horns led him to his prey *as if he were trapped in a magic spell.*

He approached the snake *as silently as moonlight shines at night.*

The snakes shone *like an evil glow worm,* reflecting the light.

Catahecassa set off in a hurry, climbing mountains *as fast as the wind.*

Your opinion

Page 51 of the Workbook asks students to compare two short stories and explain their preferences. You will need to hand out the short extract on the CD, which is from the prose version of the Beowulf story. Students read this and compare it with the legend of Catahecassa. If they cannot decide which is the better of the two, they must also explain why that is. The bullet points will give some support so they can do this writing exercise individually. When marking, take into account how students have structured their writing, bearing in mind the work they have done earlier on organising sentences in a paragraph. Also take into account how they have justified opinions, and used discourse markers and connectives to lead to a conclusion.

Oral presentation – Mythical creatures and beasts

Ask students to find out information about mythical creatures or beasts that occur in traditional cultural tales, or from stories that they know. They should choose one and write about the following:

its origin – where and when it first appears in folk tales or myths

what it is like

why people feared it

whether we ever see or hear about it nowadays

if they think the creature really existed, and if so what it might have been.

If you would like to prepare some visual aids for this writing task go to: http://www.mythical-creatures-and-beasts.com/mythical-creatures.html which has many images of very different creatures. Ask students to start by making notes for homework. They should then write up their notes in class for a short presentation using images from the Internet. You can extend this activity by asking them to write up their material in an essay. Mark for the following criteria: evidence of research and critical thinking; originality in choice of subject and plausible interpretations; appropriate use of English and technical accuracy. This writing task can also be developed as a whole-class project on mythical creatures.

At some point during the activity, ask students to think about how modern television and films use ancient mythological creatures. The dragon Smaug in *The Hobbit*, was adapted by Tolkien from the dragon that sleeps on treasure at the end of the Beowulf saga (see page 104 of the Student Book). The same dragon/treasure motif appears in other Norse legends such as that of Sigurd or Siegfreid.

Paragraph building

Prior knowledge

Start by asking students if they can remember when they first began to use paragraphs, then ask them to write down two reasons why they are useful. Take feedback and ask the class to expand on the following ideas: Paragraphs are a way to organise ideas; they make writing easier to read; they make a piece of writing more visually pleasing. Now ask students to explain what a 'topic sentence' is and how it works in a paragraph.

If possible, show the class: a page from an academic journal or an old-fashioned textbook where the paragraphs are very long; a page from a novel they are reading; a page from a newspaper (where paragraphs are at sentence or even clause length). Ask them to compare and contrast the different formats and suggest why the writers have used paragraphs in different ways.

You can now give them two extracts without paragraphs – one should be fiction, the other non-fiction. Ask them to work in pairs and mark where paragraphs should go, using the // symbol. Then ask students to identify and underline topic sentences in the non-fiction. Take feedback, encouraging students to explain their decisions and reasoning.

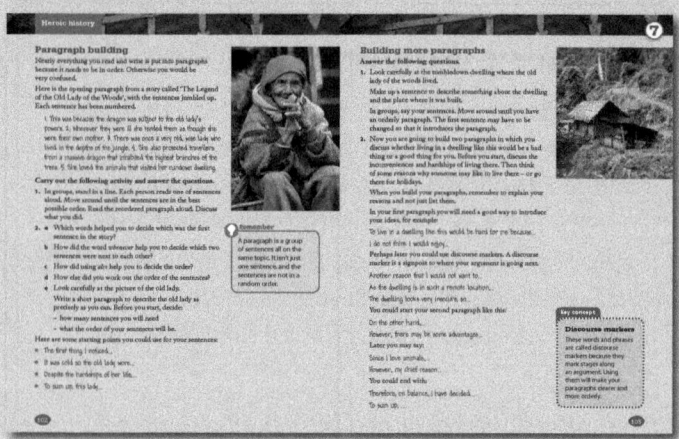

Grammar

Paragraph building

The exercise on the opening paragraph of 'The Legend of the Old Lady of the Woods' is a group activity. Arrange the class into groups of five and give each student in each group a number from 1 to 5. Set a clear time limit for students to rearrange the sentences, and themselves, as described in the activity. Groups then read their sentences aloud in the new order and discuss any discrepancies. Point out that students will need to make notes to answer question 2e.

Answers:

1. The order should be: 3, 5, 2, 4, 1.

2. **a.** 'There was once…'

   b. The word *whenever* needs a subject (the animals), provided in the previous sentence.

c. *Also* is used to link one thing (the travellers) with something similar (the animals) in the previous sentence.

d. Answers could range around the logic of what is happening or the sequence of events.

e. Students could describe her first, before settling on the running order of the sentences.

Supporting students of all abilities

Before students write their paragraphs, you could have a round of class story-telling. Ask the whole class to stand in a circle or against the walls if you have limited space. Explain they are going to tell a story, but they may only supply one sentence each. Start with a well-known tale such as 'Little Red Riding Hood' and provide the opening sentence, 'Once upon a time there was …'

You can develop this form of story-telling so that each student provides only a phrase or clause that ends with a conjunction or connective, such as *then* or *unfortunately*. In each case, give students the opening sentence.

Monitor the progress of the stories, so students stay in the same tense. Put the plot back on track when it gets too convoluted or fantastical.

Building more paragraphs

1. This question is another 'active grammar' activity, but this time students choose what to say and the order in which to say it. Arrange students into groups of five and ask them to look at the picture on page 103 of the Student Book.

2. Before students write their paragraphs, get them to discuss the inconveniences and hardships as a class or in pairs/groups. Encourage them to make notes.

You could also recap on discourse markers, including the examples given. Make sure students understand how to use them and how important they are in signposting the direction of an argument, making paragraphs more orderly, and meaning clearer. The first sentence for paragraph 1 has been modelled to help students begin one way or another, and there are suggestions for the last sentence. Keep reminding them to explain their reasons and not simply list them.

Crazy paragraphs

On page 52 of the Workbook students reorganise sentences to make a paragraph. The correct order is:

Yesterday I woke up from a long sleep and looked at my watch. It was eight o'clock! With a sinking feeling, I realised I'd be late for work. I had overslept so there was absolutely no time for my daily shower. I threw on my clothes and rushed downstairs. Grabbing a piece of bread, I rushed to my car. Of course it wouldn't start and therefore I'd have to catch a bus. It was already 8.40 a.m.

Supporting students – Creating paragraphs

To provide more practice in using paragraphs and discourse markers ask students to write out a well-known story, such as Little Red Riding Hood, as fully as possible without any paragraphs. Students should write as much as they can, adding details to the story as they go along. When they have finished, they swap papers with a partner and proofread each other's writing. Proofreaders should put in the // mark where they think new paragraphs should start. Partners can then discuss whether discourse markers helped them to decide on paragraph breaks, and how the different stages of the known story required new paragraphs.

Take this a step further by asking students to write an original story for homework. Provide the subject and location if your students struggle with creative writing, and if necessary specify a minimum of 150 words. Repeat the partner proofreading exercise in class and take feedback. Ask if it was more difficult to decide where paragraph breaks should go because they did not already know the story.

To consolidate this exercise, students may then cut up their stories at paragraph breaks to form jigsaw readings. They now exchange their cut-up stories with another person (not previous partner), who has to reassemble the story.

'Beowulf, the Mighty Hero'

Prior knowledge

'Beowulf' is a heroic tale told in verse in a tenth-century manuscript but dating back as early as the sixth century. Written in Old English, it tells of the legendary hero Beowulf, who saves Danish King Hrothgar's court from a terrible marsh-dwelling monster called Grendel. He then kills the monster's mother and, much later in life, engages in mortal combat with a dragon. The prose passage in the Student Book is taken from after the fatal maiming of Grendel, when the monster's mother seeks her revenge.

The poem tells us that Grendel cannot bear the sound of merry-making or music, and at night goes on murdering rampages in King Hrothgar's great feasting hall called Hearot, taking men as they sleep. For 12 years, there is no feasting or joy because everyone is so afraid. Beowulf comes to Heorot, saying he will save them from the monster. Once more there is the sound of joy in the feasting hall. Beowulf pretends to be asleep and manages to overcome Grendel when he arrives. Grendel limps away to die in his marshy home. Unfortunately, Grendel's mother, who lives beneath a lake, seeks revenge. Beowulf follows her to her lair and only manages to overcome her after a tremendous fight.

There are many versions of this story, including Seamus Heaney's wonderful verse translation, which is a great source if you are doing kenning with your class.

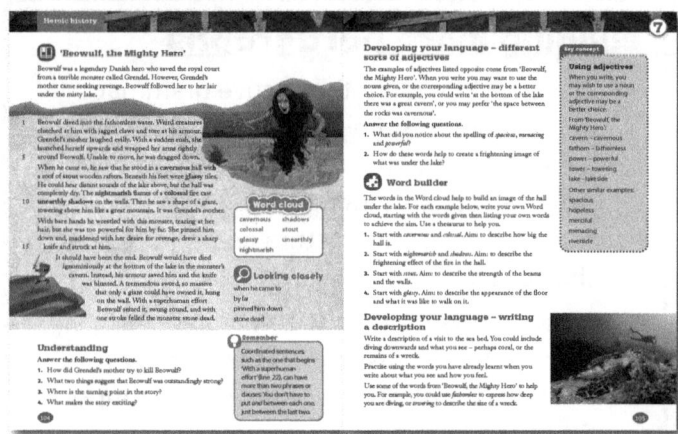

Vocabulary

In this passage, Beowulf goes to Grendel's mother's lake. You might like to go through the words in the Word cloud before students start reading. Ask them what impressions words such as *cavernous, colossal, nightmarish, unearthly* have on them, and what they might expect in the reading. Ask them to find the meaning of *fathomless* and what it suggests about a lake. Also look briefly at the phrases in the Looking closely feature, asking students how we use them and to suggest alternatives.

Student-book answers

📖 Understanding

1. Grendel's mother tries to kill Beowulf by dragging him down to her lair, pinning him down, and stabbing him.

2. Accept any two from the following suggestions: Beowulf must be outstandingly strong because Grendel's mother is described as being 'colossal', or like a giant, but he still tries to wrestle her; when he fails to defeat her with his 'bare hands' he uses a tremendous sword; he is also described as having 'superhuman' strength because he fells her with one blow.

3. The turning point is 'It should have been the end' on line 16.

4. The story is exciting because it combines dramatic action/adventure with well-chosen description. It seems impossible that the hero will survive, so there is an element of surprise and satisfaction.

Different sorts of adjectives

Briefly show how adjectives can be made out of nouns by adding a suffix such as: *-ous, -less, -ful, -ing*. Study the examples given. Note how spellings vary with *-ous* endings: cavern<u>ou</u>s, courage<u>ous</u>, spac<u>ious</u>. Then look at fathom<u>less</u>, merci<u>ful</u>, power<u>ful</u>, tower<u>ing</u>, etc.

Answers

1. Make sure students understand that *-ful* is added without altering the noun form *power*. However, in *spacious* the 'e' is replaced by 'i' and the suffix *-ous*; in *menacing* the 'e' is simply replaced by the suffix *-ing*.

2. The words *spacious*, *menacing*, and *powerful* give a frightening image of what was under the lake because they suggest a vast open space full of menace and the she-monster's power.

Word builder

Students need a thesaurus for this activity. Establish that the words in the Word cloud help to build an image of the hall under the lake as a huge place full of menace. Encourage students to keep the same mood/atmosphere in their own word clouds. Accept any words that convey the aims given.

Writing a description

Start by asking if any students have been diving. Discuss how our senses are affected by being underwater. Remind students that when they write a description they need to use their five senses, although in this case smell, taste, and hearing may not be very relevant. If no one in the class can describe the sensations from experience, ask students to imagine what it must be like to dive down and find things like coral or a wreck on the sea bed. Remind them to use as wide a vocabulary as possible and, if they use a thesaurus, to be careful of context. Words from the Beowulf extract are acceptable if used in an appropriate way.

When marking, take into account how students have created a sense of place and used descriptive words and phrases. Paragraphs should be in a meaningful order.

Dragonland

On page 53 of the Workbook, students identify typical visual characteristics of dragons, then write a paragraph about them. Suggested visual characteristics are: long tail; tail with sharp spikes; wide 'flappy' wings; hard skin like armour; forked tongue; pointed teeth; breathing fire; ridge of sharp spikes on the back and neck.

Remind students to use their own words as far as possible when writing their paragraphs. When marking, tick off each item and award marks for correct use of English and grammatical accuracy.

This activity is best done in class.

Improving your writing

Revisit the short extract on the CD, which is from the prose version of the Beowulf story. Students will have looked at it for the Workbook activity 'Your opinion'. Hand out copies to those who no longer have them. You could use it as a short text to discuss alliteration. Discuss the way alliteration (e.g. 'shape slid', 'huge and hairy', 'slightly stooping') has been used to create Grendel as a menacing monster.

Alternatively, you could use the extract for a writing exercise in which students say what happens next. They could finish the scene so that it includes Beowulf's fight with Grendel, to show how Grendel runs back to his marshy lair mortally injured. Make sure they focus on description, using alliteration and similes.

Building stories and information texts

Prior knowledge

If possible, start this part of the unit by looking at copies of brochures or pamphlets for tourist attractions or museums. Ask students to comment on layout and direct attention to how readers use this material. Direct their attention to topic sentences. Ask students how and why they used paragraphs in their stories earlier in the unit, and if they can apply similar rules to writing non-fiction and information texts. Review and recycle how we use discourse markers and connectives, which students may know as 'linking words' or 'linking phrases', and ask students to supply useful phrases. Write their examples on the board and add others, such as: *consequently, as a result of this, in order to, nevertheless, therefore,* etc. The 'Writer's Toolkit' on page 661 of the *Oxford English Thesaurus for Schools* has a useful section on working with paragraphs and using linking words.

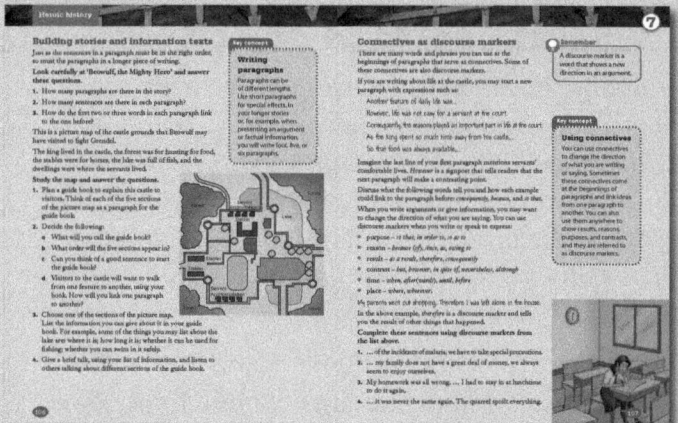

Grammar

Building stories and information texts

Ask students to turn back to 'Beowulf, the Mighty Hero' on page 104 of the Student Book and answer the questions.

Answers

1. There are four paragraphs.

2. Number of sentences: five in paragraph 1; six in 2; two in 3; five in 4.

3. The links work in the following ways: 'When he came to…' (paragraph 2) refers to the fact that Grendel's mother has dragged him to the bottom of her lake; 'With bare hands…' (paragraph 3) shows Beowulf has no weapon; 'It should have been the end…' (paragraph 4) shows Beowulf has almost no chance of survival against a huge monster wielding a sharp knife.

Discuss how paragraphs can be of different lengths. Point out that short paragraphs can be very effective in fiction, but that longer paragraphs are usually needed for presenting an argument or factual information.

After students have studied the map of the castle grounds on page 106 the Student Book, discuss the components and talk about what life in the castle may have been like. Then briefly review how non-fiction texts differ from fiction.

1. Explain that students are going to plan a guide book to explain this castle to visitors. They will write five paragraphs, each one focused on one of the five sections: castle, forest, stables, lake, dwellings.

2. Point out that they need to decide the order of their paragraphs, bearing in mind that visitors to the castle will use it as a guide as they move from one area to another. Remind them to use connectives and discourse markers to link the paragraphs.

3. Students who need more support could use the bullet list to write about the lake. Others could use it as guidance for their list on a section other than the lake.

4. Depending on the size of your class, you could do this task as a whole-class activity or in groups. Each student should give a brief improvised talk using their list, then listen to others talking about different sections of the guide book. Asking students to speak to the group using only their notes is very good practice for speaking assessments in the IGCSE English exams. The content of this unit (on discourse markers and connectives) should also help them become more aware of how they need to deliver information in an ordered sequence.

Connectives as discourse markers

Look at the suggested discourse markers and discuss how a new paragraph might be started with: *Another feature of; However; Consequently; As the; So that*. If necessary, model ideas on the board.

Review how a discourse marker indicates a new direction in a piece of writing, and talk about how the words should link to the previous paragraph. Go over the use of *consequently, because, so that*. Point out that we also use these words when we are speaking. In casual conversation we may use less formal expressions such as 'Ah, but…' or 'Hang on a minute, you said…', but the purpose is the same.

Before students start to complete sentences 1–4, discuss how the first word after the gap may limit their choice. For example, the words in sentence 1 start with *of*, so they can't use *Owing to*. You may want to explain why 'Due to' is a better alternative to 'Because of' when starting a sentence.

Answers

1. Because of (reason)
2. Although (contrast)
3. As a result/consequently (result)
4. Afterwards (time)

Don't argue with me!

Page 54 of the Workbook gives more practice in using discourse markers in conversation. When marking, make sure students continue in the same tense as the modelled sentences and pay attention to grammatical accuracy.

Discourse marker posters and wall charts

Arrange your class in pairs or groups of three. Provide them with eight sheets of coloured card or coloured paper, or one large sheet of card which they should divide into eight sections. Tell them they are going to make discourse marker posters or a wall chart. Write these eight headings on the board: *Adding; Sequencing; Illustrating; Qualifying; Comparing; Contrasting; Cause and effect; Emphasising*. Then give two examples for each heading (mix in less familiar words such as *whereas* with those students will all recognise):

Adding – *and, furthermore*

Sequencing – *meanwhile, secondly*

Illustrating – *such as, for instance*

Qualifying – *but, that is to say*

Comparing – *in the same way, likewise*

Contrasting – *whereas, on the other hand*

Cause and effect – *so, hence*

Emphasising – *above all, especially*

Hand out dictionaries and ask students to find the word *whereas*. Ask for alternative ways to say it (*but, in contrast to*, etc). Explain they can use their dictionaries to find more words for their posters in this way. Alternatively, allow them to use the Internet. There are many sites offering grammar support, but try to prevent them simply copying without understanding the vocabulary.

If you have a class with stronger students, you can develop this activity into a map-making exercise. Students reproduce a map of the London Underground, for example, or a local area, using the eight headings as routes from a central point: words and phrases for those headings become the names of stations or places on the way to the eight destinations.

Should myths and legends be in History or English lessons?

Prior knowledge

This part of the unit looks at the differences between what we categorise as history and what is myth or legend. You could start by asking students to think about their school subjects and make a Venn diagram showing how they overlap. Science, for example, includes Maths and English; History includes Geography and English. Once they have begun to appreciate how subjects overlap, focus on History and ask them to define it. If/when students suggest it is a record of 'real events', ask them to expand on what they mean by 'real' and how we can know. This should lead them to discussing documents or recorded events in writing. After this, remind them that the story of Beowulf was written down, but it tells of events that were part of the oral tradition many centuries before. Try to get students to think about how and why people told stories in the distant past and lead on to whether myths and legends might be based on real events. Ask what they think 'folk memory' means and ask for examples. Later, students will be looking at how we use different words to describe something that is old: while they are talking, try to get them to qualify what they are saying about the past, using terms such as classical, ancient or primitive civilisations. Depending on time, you could ask why we study ancient civilisations in school, and whether this belongs in History or should go in Art, Science or Geography.

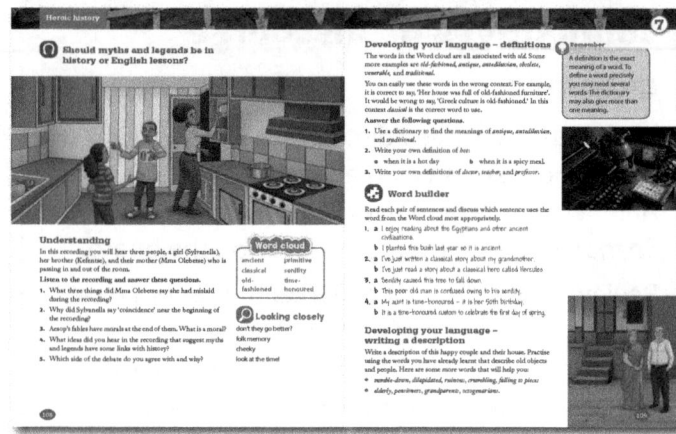

2. Sylvanella says 'coincidence' because they have been doing the same topic in different lessons.

3. A moral is a piece of good advice about life.

4. Ideas that link myths and legends with history are: oral tradition; folk memory; stories about people; stories about life before writing or printing started.

5. Kefentse says 'History is facts' and myths belong in English lessons. Sylvanella is not so sure and says stories of heroes are a way of conveying ideas of leadership. Students must justify their views.

Extension

Supporting students

Before moving on to the next section, which looks at the words in the Word cloud, some students may benefit from work on choosing appropriate words for the context. Ask students to make a quick list, without using a dictionary, of words and phrases meaning *new* or *young*. Ask them how these words are used in different contexts. For example, a baby can be new (or *young*) but not modern; we can watch an old movie but not a young movie.

Student-book answers

Understanding

After the first listening, draw students' attention to the register. Ask if this is a formal or informal conversation. Students should quote examples to support their answers. For example, it's informal because Sylvanella says, 'We got taught about a guy called Aesop'.

You could also discuss the words and phrases: 'don't they go better', 'folk memory', 'cheeky' and 'look at the time'. Which is the odd one out? (The odd one out is 'folk memory' because the others are colloquial expressions.)

1. Mma Olebetse mislaid a saucepan, her cellphone, and car keys.

Vocabulary

Word builder

Answers

1. a is correct. Civilisations can be ancient; one-year-old bushes are not.

2. b is correct. Stories about heroes of the ancient world are classical; grandmothers are not that old.

3. b is correct. Human beings can grow senile; trees cannot.

4. b is correct. Customs can be time-honoured because they are repeated time and again, but people cannot.

Definitions

Discuss the words in the Word cloud and the other examples given. Make sure students understand that some words can be used only in very specific contexts and definitely not in others. Ask them to suggest other examples where that is the case. Draw out that they need to pay attention to context clues to find the most appropriate word.

You could do a short activity on how we use words for *old* in different contexts by displaying a palace and/or ancient ruins, an elderly grandmother, a prehistoric cave-dweller, a typewriter, a traditional dance, a man or woman in fashionable 1960s clothes, etc. Ask students which of the following words apply to each image and why: ancient, classical, old-fashioned, primitive, senility, time-honoured. They may suggest alternatives or use their thesaurus to find more words.

Students' answers to the activities will vary. The terms in question 3 have slightly different connotations in some countries, so ask students to do this for English-speaking countries only, and only if English is their first language.

Writing a description

Students should study the picture on page 109 of the Student Book then write a description of the couple and their house, to practise using words that describe old places and elderly people.

Sample vocabulary is provided to describe the old house: *tumble-down, dilapidated, ruined, ruinous, crumbling, falling to pieces;* and to describe the people: *elderly, pensioners, grandparents, octogenarians*.

Pin down the meaning!

The activities on page 55 of the Workbook should be done in class, as the first two require students to work in pairs. In activity 1, one student can read all the definitions provided or students can take turns. You will need to organise activity 2 so that one student in each pair cannot see the words to be acted out.

Answers

1. **a.** maggot; **b.** lava; **c.** dormant; **d.** sleeper; **e.** boxcar; **f.** carton.

2. Students could prompt each other by saying which words are nouns and which are verbs.

3. Students work individually to invent definitions for the words without reference to a dictionary.

4. Students pair up again to compare and assess their work on activity 3.

Stretching students – The oral tradition

Ask students to think about something that has happened in the recent past, a very exciting event and/or something that involves a very courageous or outstanding person. Accept a wide range of people from famous sports heroes to world leaders. Tell students to make a few notes, briefly describing the following: location, event, people involved. Once the note-taking has finished, arrange the class in groups of four or five. Ask them to sit in a circle and imagine they are living ten centuries in the future. In turn, they tell of their legendary event, describing their hero in language that will leave their listeners in awe. Remind them this must be entirely oral; they may not read from their notes. If necessary, they can invent new parts to their story, embellish on facts, and generally make it up as they go along. Students then choose the best from their group and come together as a class to retell their tales. Round up the activity by showing the parallel between what they have been doing and how history was conveyed before humans had pens and paper.

My superhero legend

Prior knowledge

Ask students to talk about the following statement in pairs: 'The greater the monster, the greater the hero'. Take feedback from the class and revisit material covered in this unit about dangerous beasts and mythical monsters. Now ask them to think of the monsters as metaphors. The 'monster' could be a threat to people's security or aliens from outer space (as in Star Trek movies), or a secret organisation (as in James Bond movies). Draw out ideas about how superheroes act and what they achieve (restoration of order and peace for their community). Ask for examples from popular fiction and comic strips (Superman, Batman, Spiderman, etc.). Get students to talk about the dangers, threats and menaces these famous superheroes overcome. Then ask for the typical qualities of superheroes: how many of them have magical powers and/or superhuman strength? Remind students of the reading about Theseus, a hero in the making, before starting the writing task 'My superhero legend'.

Extension

Describing people – personal qualities

Ask students to work in pairs and make a list of words and phrases to describe personality traits or character. Give the examples of *brave, courageous, persistent* and any other words students have been using in this unit. The *Oxford School Thesaurus* has a comprehensive list on page 412 but encourage your students to work on their own before referring to a thesaurus. They should then separate their words into positive and negative traits. When they have done this, ask them to create a Venn diagram with three circles: one for positive qualities, one for negative qualities, and one where the qualities overlap, such as being persistent, ambitious, or easy-going, which can all be both positive and negative according to the situation.

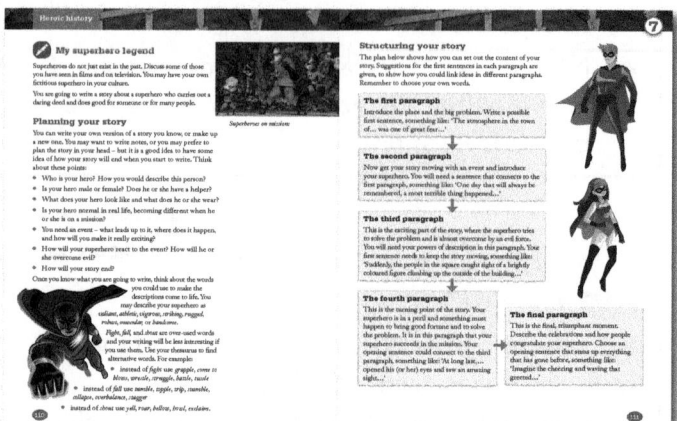

Planning your story

Discuss the qualities that popular superheroes are supposed to possess, then move on to talk about imaginary superheroes in films and television, such as Batman, Superman, and Superwoman. Students can then talk about traditional heroes in their own cultures.

Explain that students are going to write a story about a superhero. They can adapt a well-known tale and tell their own version or invent a completely new hero/heroine using the bullet points on page 110 of the Student Book.

Any form of planning on the board, such as a mindmap or a *wh-* plan, will help students plan the elements of their story. Remind them that it is very important that they know how their story is going to end before they start, even if they do not want to write down their plans. Remind them also that, once they have decided who and what to write about, they should think about the sort of vocabulary they need to use to create atmosphere and make descriptions come to life. Warn against using clichés and over-used adverbs such as *suddenly*. Read through the vocabulary on page 110 and clarify any doubts.

Structuring your story

Encourage students to use the paragraph planner on page 111 of the Student Book. You could use the Freytag pyramid (available online) to extend and support stronger students as they structure their stories. Help all students to become more aware of how a storyline and action progresses through scenes in paragraphs. You could explain how each paragraph in a short story has one key piece of information, event, or scene.

Award marks for: originality or how students adapt a well-known tale; how the story is structured and paragraphing; interesting use of vocabulary; grammatical accuracy.

Workbook

Writing an alternative ending

Page 56 of the Workbook asks students to imagine a new version of paragraphs 4 and 5 in their superhero stories. Remind them to change the atmosphere in the final paragraphs by choosing descriptive words and phrases carefully. In preparation, you could ask students to offer atmospheric words and phrases from their writing in order for the class to make suggestions for creating the opposite atmosphere. Students should carry out this activity independently.

Listening

ALBION: Islands of Giants

Read the following story to the class then ask what this version of various old folk tales explains. (The text is an amalgam of various myths and folk tales that serve to explain the geography of the British Isles.)

ALBION: Islands of Giants

In the beginning, it is said, there were Giants. These Giants strode out of Africa across the Middle Sea. They crossed Europe scattering stones this way and that across rich and fertile lands. They picked up vast boulders and chucked them down again just for fun, and because they could. Sometimes they lifted rocks from mountainsides and hurled them at each other. Giants were always argumentative. But sometimes, in quiet places, where the land was flat and green, they stopped, and arranged specially chosen stones to suit their fancy, leaving lines which started with the rising of the sun and closed with the dying of the moon. Sometimes they arranged circles inside circles. No one knows why.

Well, as it is told, the Giants crossed Europe from south to north and when they came to a narrow strip of water they crossed it in one stride then

stopped. They had reached a group of irregular shaped islands. As far as they could see – through the mist and fog – there were very few humans around. None of the Giants knew who owned the islands, so the leader of the Giants said he would have them, and he gave the biggest island the name Albion. Some say this was because it was white round the edges and *alba* means white. Some say he named it after himself.

Why these Giants began their journey from the continent of Africa, which was big enough for them, then stopped when they got to the small islands of what we call Britain nobody knows...

Whatever their reasons for coming, they settled in Britain for 600 years. But their race was doomed. There were far too many male Giants, and as everyone knows, when too many males get together someone always starts a fight. These Giants were forever squabbling and scrapping over bits of land and any other excuse that came into their fat heads. They got more bad-tempered with each passing year, until they were so disagreeable they couldn't stand the sight of each other. Eventually their numbers declined so drastically that there were just a few living in the south and west. Knowing their days were numbered, and being of a nasty disposition, they did as much damage to the landscape as they could. They shifted whole chunks of land, pushing granite into sheer cliffs where cliffs weren't necessary; they upturned huge boulders and left boggy swamps to trap ponies at night; they dropped large rocks around the coastline so fishermen would have trouble getting back to their families. There seemed no end to their geographical mischief. Then they started to terrorise natives, for they had realised, too late of course (Giants were never very bright), that there were not going to be any more 'Rock Movers' on Albion unless they found human wives.

But then, to their horror and shame, the last three remaining Giants noticed mortals were moving boulders and worse, finding ways round obstacles. Their fury was colossal. Giant Cormoran in Cornwall, Big Bolster in the Midlands and Tom Hickthrift in Norfolk, the last of their race, did their best to frighten little humans to death, but it was all too late and eventually the three disappeared altogether. Nobody was sorry to see them go.

Progress check

Progress check

Progress checks are designed to help students revisit what they have learned in a relatively informal manner. They should be completed in class if possible, and in silence, but it is not necessary to impose exam conditions. You may want to allow students to refer to both their Student Book and Workbook necessary. When they have finished, read the answers aloud and let students mark their own or a partner's. Collect their answers to see what progress students are making and what areas need repeating or practising.

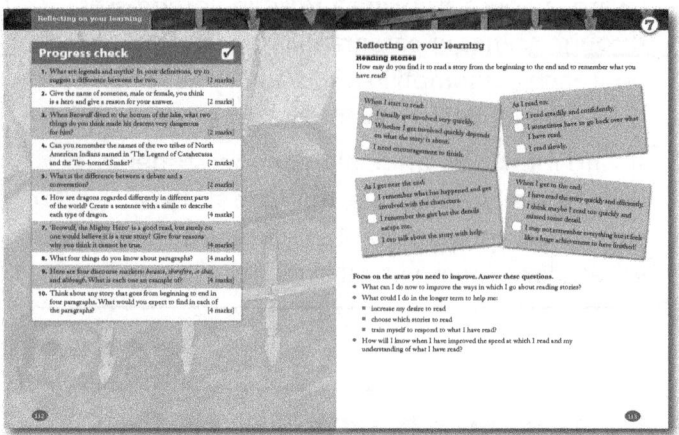

Student-book answers

End-of-unit assessment

1. Legends tell tales about classical heroes, while myths can include fantastical creatures. [2]

2. Students must supply reasons for a complete answer. [2]

3. Creatures clutched at him and he was trapped in Grendel's mother's arms. [2]

4. The two tribes of North American Indians are Cherokee and Shawnee. [2]

5. A debate follows a formal structure; a conversation is informal. [2]

6. Dragons are dangerous in northern Europe but seen as kind/benevolent in Asia. Students create two similes, one to describe each type of dragon; award 1 mark for each appropriate simile. [4]

7. Students answers will vary, but they must give four reasons. [4]

8. Accept details such as: story order; discourse markers; new topic; connectives; sentences in order; showing scenes in a story; giving information in non-fiction. [4]

9. These discourse markers have the following purposes: *because* (reason), *therefore* (result), *so that* (purpose), *although* (contrast). [4]

10. Students outline the structure of a story in four paragraphs: introductions, exciting details, turning point, triumph. [4]

Extension

Heroic storytelling

Remind students of the storytelling they did in class earlier in the unit, where each person had to supply a sentence or a phrase. Arrange two or three big groups, or keep the class together, and ask them to make a big circle. This time they are going to tell a heroic tale combining as many heroes, monsters and situations from the unit as they can. Tell them they should each supply a full sentence, and as far as possible keep the story logical. Start by giving one of these sentences as the opening line: *Long, long ago there lived a terrible fire-breathing dragon in a mountain.* Or, *long, long ago there lived an evil, man-like beast in a swamp, his name was Grendel.*

Reflection

Reflecting on your learning

Students should think about the way in which they read stories and answer the questions individually. Discourage conversation to avoid peer influence when answering.

Ask students to makes notes on areas in which they need to improve, so they can revisit them later in the term to check whether they are making progress.

Workbook

Heroic history quiz

The quiz on page 57 of the Workbook is designed for students to see what they have learnt and revisit some of the topics.

Areas covered in the unit are:

- reading myths and legends from different cultures
- interviewing a real or fictitious hero to understanding the qualities that make a hero
- imagery in myth and legend narratives
- alliteration and similes
- ordering sentences and structuring paragraphs in fiction and non-fiction
- combining paragraphs with connectives and discourse markers
- using a thesaurus to increase vocabulary
- using vocabulary in context
- structuring a story using turning points.

Answers

1. The two-horned snake had magical powers of magnetism because people's eyes were drawn to it.

2. Students sentence will vary.

3. 'Like a wounded animal' is a simile that shows the girl howls as if in pain.

4. Discourse markers are words and phrases that show the direction of an argument.

5. A turning point in a story is when the narrative takes a new direction for good or ill.

6. Aunt Germ = argument; Overcoats Inn = conversation; Eat bed = debate.

7. False; an octogenarian is in his/her eighties.

8. Students' personal choices.

Reflection

💬 Reflecting on your learning

Spend a few minutes discussing with the class what and how they read, then let them fill in the answers to 'Reading stories' on their own. Depending on your class, you may want to develop these answers into a class discussion or arrange discussion in groups. You could form three groups: those who read a great deal for pleasure; those who read only when they have to; and those who admit to never finishing anything they start unless it's in class. Appoint group leaders; their role is to control discussion, take notes and feed back to the class. Give each group the following three questions:

1. Why do we read?

2. What do we read for pleasure or out of choice?

3. How does reading help us in our daily lives?

Spend a little time discussing alternative activities to reading for pleasure, and whether these also 'help us in our daily lives'. You could at this point explain how seeing life through another person's eyes helps us to understand human relationships better.

Once the class has completed the reflection section, return to the quotations in the Student Book. Ask students if they now see the statement that, 'Heroes are the stuff of legends and they make you feel good' in another light. Draw out whether heroes do make us feel better. Take feedback on what students have enjoyed doing in the unit, and make a list on the board of topics and language tasks they would like to revisit.

Listening

A balloon debate

Five famous heroes are in a in a hot air balloon. They may be real people from history or figures from folk tales, myths and legends. The balloon is losing height rapidly and will soon crash because it is too heavy. It is decided that only the bravest and best person should remain in the balloon to live on in folk memory. Each person in the balloon is given up to three minutes to tell the audience why they should live on in legend. The audience must listen to what all five say and interrogate them as to their real worth. The audience then votes on who should jump out and who should remain in the balloon. Each hero continues to plead for and justify his or her life until only one remains to land in safety.

Suggest a list of real people and folk heroes, and ask students to suggest more. Then choose the first five students for the balloon journey and ask them to select their personas. You may want to give them a few moments to prepare notes. The audience can also do on the spot research to prepare their questions. Alternatively, ask the crew of the balloon to speak off the cuff and start the activity immediately.

Listening

A printable version of the full transcript for this unit is available on the CD.

Learning objectives

In this unit students will:

- Give short presentations and answer questions, maintaining effective organisation of talk. **Pages 114–115** *8SL1*

- Comment on how a writer's use of language contributes to the overall effect on the reader, using appropriate terminology. **Pages 116–117** *8Rw1*

- Explain, using accurate terminology, how language is used to create effect. **Pages 118–121** *8Rw4*

- Explore the range, variety and overall effect of literary, rhetorical and grammatical features used by poets and writers of literary and non-literary texts, considering informal or formal style as well as the choice of words to create character. **Pages 120–121** *8Rw2*

- Make relevant notes when researching different sources, comparing and contrasting information. **Pages 122–123** *8RO3*

- Draw on their knowledge of a variety of sentence lengths and a wide variety of sentence structures, including complex sentences, and apply it to their own writing to make their ideas and intentions clear and create a range of effects. **Pages 122–123** *8Wp1*

- Comment on implied meaning, for example, writer's viewpoint, relationships between characters, ironic effect. **Pages 124–125** *8Ri1*

- Experiment with different ways of structuring and presenting texts, appropriate for different audiences and purposes. **Pages 126–127** *8Wt1*

- Work in groups to formulate ideas and plans of action. **Pages 126–127** *8SL7*

- Develop skills in solo, paired and group assignments, including role-play and drama. **Pages 126–127** *8SL8*

Setting the scene

Exciting escapades

Begin this unit by asking students to think about the texts they read in the course of a normal day (at home, in transit, at school). What would it be like if we couldn't read any of these? Direct attention to the title of the unit and clarify meaning of 'escapade' (a reckless adventure). Ask how this title might relate to reading or writing. Bring the discussion round to how children's books traditionally included exciting adventures without parents, for example, *Treasure Island* by Robert Louis Stevenson.

Be aware that some students may not have access to books in English at home, so during the course of this unit arrange with your school librarian to do lessons in the library if need be.

Spend about 5–10 minutes with students, drawing out some of their prior experience in an informal way. Ask them whether they have previously:

- explored how writers 'hook' readers with their story openings

- collaborated in structuring stories

- created a presentation about books and reading

- engaged with an extract from a novel by Khaled Hosseini

- reflected on which books and authors they most enjoy reading and why.

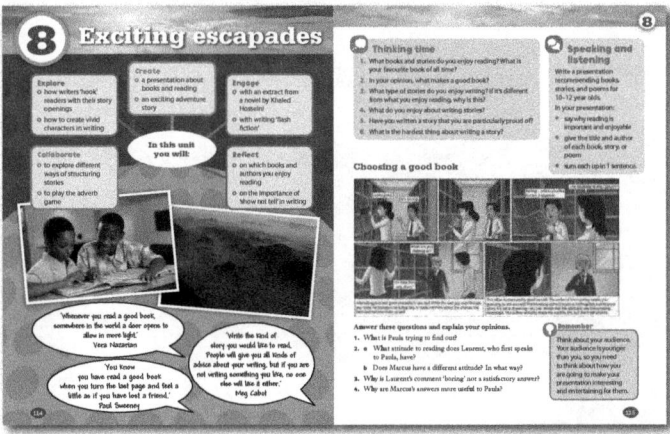

Ask students to read the cartoon on page 115 of the Student Book on their own. Then review the questions with the class, discussing different responses. Alternatively, ask students to write their answers in full sentences and explain their reasoning. Some suggested responses are given below, but accept valid alternatives.

1. Paula is trying to decide which book to choose, and asking for an opinion.

2. **a.** Laurent does not enjoy reading and/or finds it difficult to finish a book.

   b. Marcus reads widely and thinks about what he's reading.

3. 'Boring' gives no reason or criteria – it is a personal response that tells you more about the speaker than the book.

4. Marcus's answers are more useful because they mention character, plot and setting, plus the author's aims or technique.

Reflection

 # Thinking time

Take a few minutes to read through the quotations on page 114 with the class. Allow them to work out the metaphor of a door opening 'to let in more light' on their own, and take feedback before examining the next two quotations.

If you have a fairly large class, arrange students into groups to discuss the 'Thinking time' questions. Assign group leaders and set a time limit. Take feedback from leaders and identify popular genres and titles. Briefly review what makes these books successful. Make notes on the board for question 6 and draw out students' attitudes to writing stories. If possible, leave titles of popular novels on the board for later in this unit.

Workbook

 # My favourite book

If possible, set students the task on page 58 of the Workbook before they complete their Speaking and listening presentations for younger readers, as described on this page. Remind them that a summary is not the blurb on the back of a book. Students may peer mark, but if you are doing this activity early in the academic year, collect in books to see what your class has been reading.

Extension

Speaking and listening

 # Presentation – Books, stories, and poems for children aged 10–12 years

To help groups focus on the age group and type of material for this task, suggest they think about a particular class they were in themselves, or name a class in your school and if possible arrange to make presentations there. Assign group leaders and ensure that all students are actively involved, not just one or two doing the writing. Set a time limit, possibly the end of the next lesson.

 # Making a book trailer

Ask students to work with a partner or small group to create a video for a book trailer. It may include a short reading or a selection of key moments from the opening or early part of the story for a target age group, similar to a film trailer. Students may use sound effects, music, visual aids, or puppets to bring stories to life.

Set aside a lesson for students to show their trailers to the class. If making a video is not possible, ask students to perform it as a television trailer.

For an example of an excellent trailer, search for 'The Golden Compass trailer' on YouTube (the film version of *The Golden Compass* by Philip Pullman).

Tribes

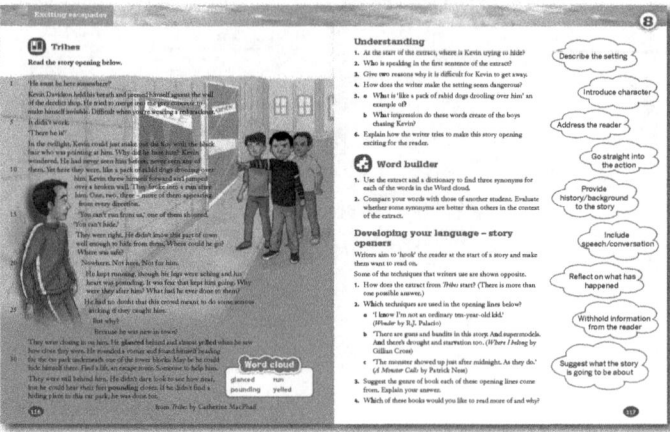

Vocabulary

 Tribes

Ask students to read the text on page 116 of the Student Book on their own. Suggest they refer to dictionaries if necessary for words such as 'derelict', 'merge', and 'drooling'. Students should answer the questions in full sentences and explain their reasoning. Mark their work and give feedback on their comprehension techniques (quoting, reported speech, and so on).

This activity provides good practice for Checkpoint and IGCSE exams later.

Student-book answers

 Understanding

1. Kevin is trying to hide against a derelict shop wall.

2. A boy with black hair (who is pointing at him).

3. Accept two reasons from: he doesn't know the area; they appear from many directions; there are a lot of them; he is running out of breath/getting tired.

4. The setting seems dangerous because of a sense of abandonment: 'derelict', 'broken'. There is a sense that the concrete tower blocks loom and the car park is an open (dangerous) location.

5. **a.** A simile.

   b. Dangerous/aggressive/mad (rabid) dogs; word 'pack' suggests hunting dogs or wolves.

6. Students should give reasons for their opinions and show understanding of Kevin's

situation. The final sentence should make them want to read on to see whether he is captured or escapes, and what the 'pack' wants.

Vocabulary

 Word builder

Ask students to do this task individually or in pairs. They may peer mark, but check they understand 'run' is being used as a noun.

1. Glanced: looked, peeked, peeped, glimpsed.

   Pounding: stomping, thudding, clumping, clomping (accept noise of running words).

   Run (accept nouns for 'broke into a **run**'): trot, jog, sprint, dash, race.

   Yelled: shouted, called out, bellowed, roared, howled, screamed.

   Accept any other suitable alternatives.

2. Ask students to find the best substitute for words in the Word cloud and to compare their choices with a partner.

Story openers

This task should be carried out individually. Students may share their thoughts and ideas afterwards.

1. The author goes directly into action with a boy trying to hide. Accept valid alternatives; there is more than one possible answer.

2. a. Introducing the character

   b. Suggesting what the story is about.

   c. Going straight into the action.

3. Students should explain their answers, but generally the opening lines suggest:

   a. Sci-fi ('not ordinary') or first-person life story, possibly a school story.

   b. Adventure.

   c. Sci-fi or fantasy.

4. Students give their personal responses to the question.

Telling

Read the famous opening page of *The Hobbit* by J. R. R. Tolkien, available on the CD. Ask students what this page contains that has made millions of people of all ages want to read on for the past 80 years. Then ask them to form small groups and *from memory* answer the following question: What is it about the setting and **character** of Bilbo Baggins that make readers want to read on?

Remember

The exercise on page 59 is a useful homework activity, but if you think students may not have books in English at home, encourage them to do the task in the school library. If students struggle to express themselves in English or have only been in your school for a short time, you could do this task *with* your students in the library.

For question 1, students are tasked to find three good opening sentences, copy them out, and explain the authors' techniques. They should explain their opinions. For question 2, they write an opening sentence with a convincing 'hook' for three different stories, hinting at the genre.

Extension

Library activities

The Workbook task above can be developed in different ways for students who have less English than their peers, or for high-flyers. The former can work together to select texts and openings, and make a list for the librarian of books to suggest to students in their situation. Alternatively, high-flyers and avid readers can make a display for the library, showing good openings and suggesting titles for their age group.

Adverbs and adverbials

Prior knowledge

Spend 5–10 minutes drawing out students' knowledge of parts of speech. Ask them what they remember about adverbs and adverbials from the preceding year or work already covered in this book.

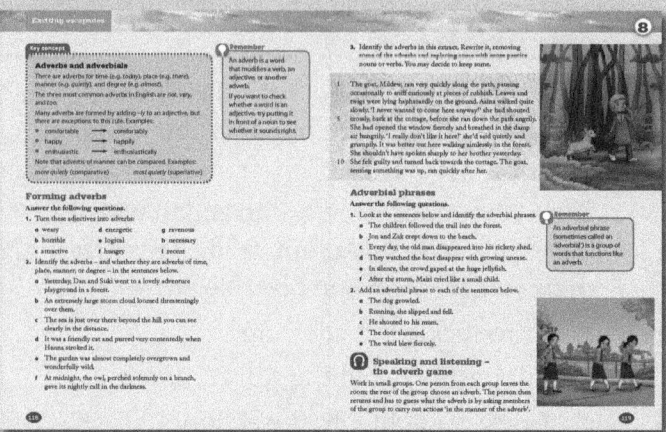

Grammar

Adverbs and adverbials

Start by modelling adverbs of time, place, manner, and degree on the board.

Explain that many adverbs are formed by adding –*ly* to an adjective, but there are exceptions to this rule and different spellings, for example: *sadly, comfortably, happily, enthusiastically*. Remind students of the comparison rule similar to polysyllabic adjectives: *more* and *most*.

Grammar

Forming adverbs

1. **a.** wearily
   b. horribly
   c. attractively
   d. energetically
   e. logically
   f. hungrily
   g. ravenously
   h. necessarily
   i. recently

2. **a.** *Yesterday* = time (Note: *lovely* is an adjective)
   b. *extremely* = degree; *threateningly* = manner
   c. *there* = place (*beyond* can be an adverb or preposition); *clearly* = manner
   d. *contentedly* = manner (Note: *friendly* is an adjective)
   e. *almost completely* = degree; *wonderfully* = manner
   f. *solemnly* = manner; *nightly* = manner

3. Students identify the adverbs in the extract (as underlined below) then rewrite it, removing unnecessary adverbs and replacing some with more precise nouns or verbs.

   The goat, Mildew, ran <u>very quickly</u> along the path, pausing <u>occasionally</u> to sniff <u>curiously</u> at pieces of rubbish. Leaves and twigs were lying <u>haphazardly</u> on the ground. Aaina walked <u>quite slowly</u>. 'I <u>never</u> wanted to come <u>here anyway</u>!' she had shouted <u>crossly</u>, back at the cottage, <u>before</u> she ran down the path <u>angrily</u>. She had opened the window <u>fiercely</u> and breathed in the damp air <u>hungrily</u>. 'I <u>really</u> don't like it <u>here</u>!' she'd said <u>quietly</u> and <u>grumpily</u>. It was better out here walking <u>aimlessly</u> in the forest. She shouldn't have spoken <u>sharply</u> to her brother <u>yesterday</u>. She felt guilty and turned <u>back</u> towards the cottage. The goat, sensing something was up, ran <u>quickly</u> after her

Adverbial phrases

1. Remind students that an adverbial phrase supplies information on where, when, or how something is done.

   Ask students to work on their own, then compare their answers with a partner. They should then check their responses using a dictionary, but circulate to help with queries.

   a. into the forest

   b. down to the beach

   c. Every day; into his rickety shed

   d. with growing unease

   e. In silence; at the huge jellyfish

   f. After the storm; like a small child

2. Students add an adverbial phrase to each sentence. Suggestions are given below, but accept alternative adverbial phrases.

   a. The dog growled *in a menacing way*.

   b. Running, she slipped and fell *onto the ice*.

   c. He shouted to his mum *at the top of his voice*.

   d. The door slammed *shut, loudly*.

   e. The wind blew fiercely *through the open window with a winter chill*.

 ## Using adverbs and adverbials

1. Students complete the adjective and adverb chart on page 60, then insert three other examples.

Adjective	Adverb
rude	**rudely**
thorough	thoroughly
early	**early**
actual	**actually**
lazy	lazily
good	well

2. Students pair sentences with adverbial phrases then write the extended sentences.

Sentence	Adverbial phrase
The old man grabbed the money	with a wicked grin
Mrs Lee made scrumptious cake	for her children
A small mouse scuttled away	as quickly as possible
The parrot flew away	in the street
They decided to check the cellar again	after dinner

The adverb game

Organise students into groups. One person from each group should leave the room, and the rest of the group chooses an adverb. The person then returns and has to guess what the adverb is by asking members of the group to carry out actions 'in the manner of the adverb'.

Extension

Supporting students with adverbs

The colour-coded parts of the speech exercise in the photocopiable material on the accompanying CD give students practice in identifying different types of words and how adverbs describe verbs. Colour coding helps students in many ways, and can also be used very effectively for textual analysis with older students.

And the Mountains Echoed

 Prior knowledge

Remind students of their prior reading in Unit 2 of works by Charles Dickens: they read extracts from *Great Expectations* (of Pip's meeting with Miss Havisham) and *Bleak House* (the description of fog).

Tell students they are going to read an extract from *And the Mountains Echoed* by the Afghan-American author Khaled Hosseini (born 1965). Allow them time to read in silence before reading the extract through with the class. Alternatively or additionally, read it to them as dramatically as possible. Try to ensure students appreciate the harshness of the desert landscape and how this complements Father's mood and appearance.

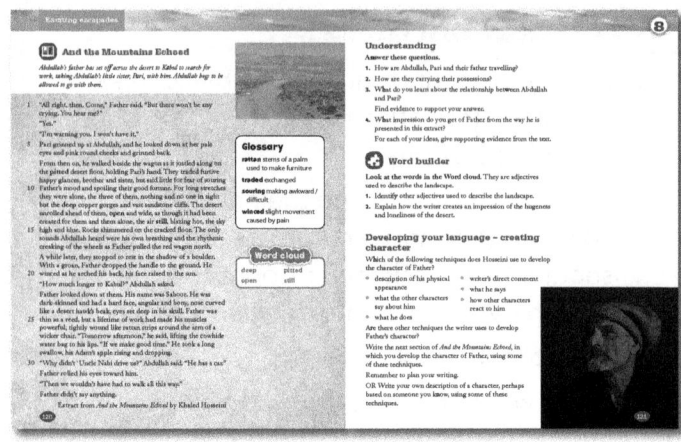

He is determined – 'Tomorrow afternoon ... if we make good time'

He is intimidating/his children are wary of him – 'for fear of souring Father's mood'

The comparison with a hawk makes him sound fierce/dangerous/someone with quick intelligence/a fighter

He doesn't complain – 'He winced.'

Student-book answers

 Understanding

Students may peer mark questions 1–3. Collect in answers for question 4, to check that students understand how to quote from a text correctly, because this is something they will be asked to do in later assessments.

1. They are walking

2. In a wagon

3. Abdullah and Pari are very close/love each other/are very pleased to be together on the journey – they grin at each other, they walk hand in hand, 'They traded (...) happy glances'

4. Students should explain their views in full sentences and quote from the text correctly. If necessary, model how to quote before students answer the questions individually.

   Accept valid alternatives to the following.

   Father is quite stern/strict – 'there won't be any crying'

   He doesn't seem very warm or affectionate towards his children

   He is quiet/doesn't say much – 'Father didn't say anything'

   He is a hard worker/physically strong – 'his muscles powerful'

Vocabulary

1. Other adjectives used to describe the landscape include 'vast', 'wide', 'blazing', 'hot', 'high', 'blue'.

2. Reference to their being 'alone', the phrase 'nothing and no-one'; the adjectives used to describe the desert, 'vast', 'wide', 'high'; the fact it seems as though the desert 'had been created for them and them alone'.

Remind students of the scene they read at the beginning of the unit about a boy in a city being chased and looking for somewhere to hide. Ask students which scene feels more real to them: the extract from *Tribe* by Catherine MacPhail, or the desert scene from *And the Mountains Echoed*. Ask whether their chosen scene feels more real because of character or setting. Establish which character students feel they know the most about. Now look at how Hosseini has created Father as an intimidating, 'hard' figure, as seen through his actions, appearance and how his children react to him.

Creating character

Before students start this task, discuss which techniques writers can use to develop character.

The following techniques are used to present the character of Father:

- description of his physical appearance
- what he says
- what he does
- how other characters react to him

Students should then work individually to develop an impression of Father using some of these techniques. Collect in and mark for content accordingly; credit original use of descriptive detail and use of vocabulary.

Drama

Page 61 of the Workbook asks students to take a scene from a book and rewrite it as a play, TV show, or film script. Remind them to give their sources, title, and author. They may then continue the scene as they wish.

When marking, check to see whether the text has been set out as a script correctly with stage or film directions in brackets, in the present tense.

Stretching students – Introducing empathy

Ask students to suggest memorable books they have read and say why these stories have stayed with them. Then ask what films they especially

remember and why. If students mention actors, ask how these actors made their characters memorable, and if they only remember the film because of the character. Return now to fiction and ask how the authors made these stories so convincing. Students may work in pairs and make notes for one or two books on the following: setting; main characters; secondary characters; how they (the students) connected with or related to a character.

Once students have a sound understanding of why they remember certain stories, explain the concept of empathy. You could describe it as a feeling of sharing the experience being described by a character or the writer. This does not mean the story has to be realistic; it can be fantasy, but the main characters have something about them that we as readers relate to. You could give Hosseini's scene with Father as an example; we as readers react to Father as if he is a real person because we relate to Abdullah and Pari's fear and caution in his presence. If possible, use a scene from a class reader or a story your students know to illustrate this.

Ask students to find a memorable scene from a story (this need only be a page). Arrange groups of four or five and name group leaders. In their groups, students read out their chosen scenes then explain what it is in the writing that affected them, and whether they were conscious at the time of 'living it'. Take feedback from leaders. Try to establish how a good writer draws us into a story, and how empathy does not necessarily mean connecting with a character of our own age or in similar life circumstances.

Exploring more scenes from Dickens

Select another famous Dickens scene such as Miss Havisham in her wedding dress in *Great Expectations*, Oliver asking for more, or Bill Sykes trying to escape in *Oliver Twist*. Ask students to read the scenes and comment on:

- characters – how Dickens describes them and how the reader feels about them
- setting – how Dickens uses setting to create atmosphere.

(Note that Dickens novels are available online. See also: www.online-literature.com/dickens/greatexpectations.)

Relative clauses

Prior knowledge

Write *who, whose,* and *who's* on the board and ask students to put them in sentences orally. Do a quick review of how and why we use *who* and *whose*. If you have a largely bilingual class, ask students to give direct translations.

Read through the explanation of relative clauses on page 122 of the Student Book and clarify any doubts before asking students to answer questions 1 and 2 on their own. Check whether students have previously used or heard the terms defining and non-defining clause rather than restrictive and non-restrictive clauses.

After completing questions 1 and 2 individually, students may then peer mark. For better results, read through the answers when they have finished, with each student marking his/her own work, and troubleshoot as you go.

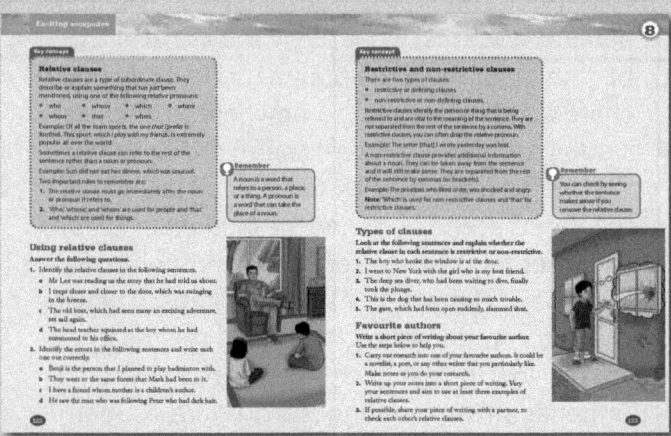

Grammar

Using relative clauses

1. **a.** that he had told us about
    b. which was swinging in the breeze
    c. which had seen many an exciting adventure
    d. whom he had summoned to his office

2. **a.** Benji is the person *with whom* I planned to play badminton.
    b. They went to the same forest that Mark had been to. (No 'it')
    c. I have a friend *whose* mother is a children's author.
    d. He saw the man with dark hair who was following Peter.

Grammar

Restrictive and non-restrictive clauses

To provide extra practice in identifying restrictive and non-restrictive clauses, and using relative pronouns appropriately, model these examples of non-restrictive clauses on the board, showing

the use of commas: *My uncle, who is an engineer, has developed a new type of car. The car, which will run on life-long batteries, is being built in Japan.*

Explain that in each sentence the information about your uncle and his new type of car could be replaced with brackets; instead, we use commas. In both sentences we can leave out the non-restrictive relative clauses that provide extra information without affecting the meaning.

A restrictive clause, on the other hand, only contains essential information. A defining or restrictive clause can be introduced with *that* or *a wh- word: who, whose, which.* We do not put commas in these sentences. For example: *My uncle has designed a car **that** runs on special batteries.*

Give students four small pieces of card and ask them to write the following words on them: *who, whose, which, that.* Then give them a sheet of coloured paper. On each sheet they make up four sentences to match each of the relative pronouns, but they leave out the actual pronouns. So they might have: *I have a pen - never runs out of ink.* Or: *My sister, - plays the trumpet, is in the school band.*

When students have created their four sentences, they should cut them out and pass them to a partner, who places the missing relative pronouns on each. Together, partners then arrange their sentences into categories: restrictive clauses and non-restrictive clauses.

Finally, ask each pair to read out two of their sentences and ask the class to say which category they should be in.

Types of clauses

Remind students that they can test whether a sentence makes sense by removing the relative clause and saying it to themselves.

1. Restrictive or defining
2. Restrictive or defining
3. Non-restrictive or non-defining
4. Restrictive or defining
5. Non-restrictive or non-defining

Favourite authors

Before students begin this task, which is best carried out individually, talk about where they can find the information they need. You may wish to mention the dangers of using Wikipedia, and check they understand how and why to cite sources. Modern authors will have their own dedicated websites. Students can also access 'author bios' on Amazon and Goodreads.

Before they begin their research, it is suggested that you show students two very different ways of accessing information via the Internet. For example, you could first go to www.biography.com and search for Robert Louis Stevenson. Explain to students how they will need to be very selective; in Stevenson's case, they could focus solely on *Treasure Island*. Another angle is to look at an author site, such as www.annefine.co.uk/biography.php. Discuss how to turn first-person autobiographical information into third-person narrative.

Tell students they should aim to write about 300 words. They can check their work with a partner before handing it in and/or reading it to the class. Mark for content and grammatical accuracy.

Relative pronouns

Depending on students' needs, they could do the exercise on page 62 as a quick revision task and peer mark, or it could be set for homework and reviewed with the class the next day. You may wish to remind students with less English or weaker grammar skills of the difference between *whose* and *who's*.

Examples of relative pronouns: *who, whom, whose, that, which, when, where*.

1. The correct relative pronouns.
   a. who
   b. that (can be omitted)
   c. who
   d. whose
   e. that
   f. whose
2. Students write three sentences using different relative pronouns and circle or underline them.

Encouraging reading

Students who find little pleasure in reading fiction often respond better to illustrated non-fiction. Take a group to the library and ask them to choose a non-fiction book. Stay in the library for a silent reading period and, if possible, repeat this activity on a regular basis. Many adolescents have such busy lives nowadays they believe they have no time to sit and read, and/or view reading as a chore. For this reason, avoid setting any tasks; allow them to browse through books and possibly read nothing during the first session at all. Eventually, they will find something to stir their interest. This activity can be done with eReaders in class, but the objective is to show what print books can offer and avoid online distractions.

What makes a good story?

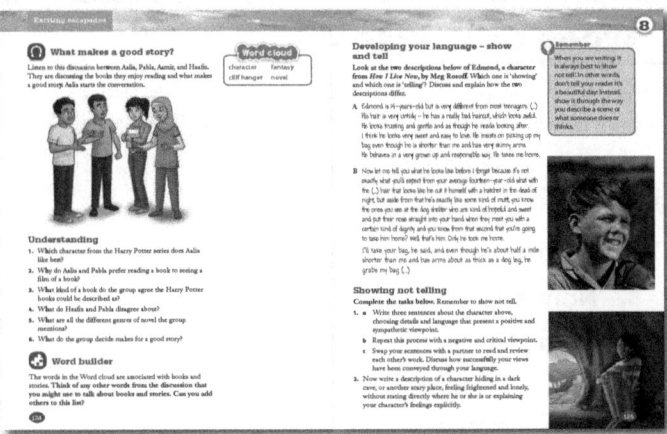

Student-book answers

Understanding

1. Hermione
2. They can imagine characters and setting in their heads.
3. School story/adventure/fantasy.
4. Spooky stories/horror stories.
5. Adventure; fantasy; sci-fi; school stories; animal stories; comedy; horror.
6. Exciting openings, satisfying endings, convincing characters and dialogue, 'baddies you love to hate'.

Vocabulary

Word builder

Other words from the discussion that might be used to talk about books and stories include: setting, blurb, short stories, mini sagas, twist, description. Students may add more words, such as: dialogue, point of view, showing, telling, mysteries and murder stories, crime, romance, and so on.

Student-book answers

Show and tell

Explain that good writers 'show not tell'. Go back to the scene from *And the Mountains Echoed* on page 120 of the Student Book. Students work in pairs, taking turns to tell what happens in the scene from each character's point of view and identifying how and where Hosseini is 'showing', not telling.

Next, direct students' attention to the two descriptions of Edmond from *How I Live Now* by Meg Rosoff. Consider how the first description is 'telling' while the second description is 'showing'. Discuss how the two descriptions differ and which is more appealing to a reader.

Listening

Using the five senses in writing

Read this short extract from the beginning of *Coraline* by Neil Gaiman then answer the questions that follow.

That night, Coraline lay awake in her bed. The rain had stopped and she was almost asleep when something went *t-t-t-t-t-t*. *She sat up in bed.*

Something went *kreee* . . .

. . . *aaaak.*

Coraline got out of bed and looked down the hall, but saw nothing strange. She walked down the hallway. From her parents' room came a low snoring – that was her father – and an occasional sleeping mutter – that was her mother.

Coraline wondered if she had dreamed it, whatever it was.

Something moved.

It was little more than a shadow, and it scuttled down the darkened hall fast, like a little patch of night.

She hoped it wasn't a spider. Spiders made Coraline intensely uncomfortable.

The black shape went into the drawing room and Coraline followed it in, a little nervously.

Questions:

1. Write down which senses you think the author uses in this extract.
2. Which sense do you think the author uses most?
3. From memory, what could you hear in the extract?
4. Write down something that you could see in your mind's eye.

Now ask students to form groups and discuss their responses to the extract.

Answers: The dominant imagery in the extract is aural because of the absence of light.

Showing not telling

1. **a.** Students write three sentences about the character on page 125 of the Student Book, choosing details and language from a positive, sympathetic viewpoint.

    b. They repeat this process with a negative and critical viewpoint.

    c. Students swap sentences with a partner, to read, review, and discuss their choice of language.

2. Students now write a description of a frightened, lonely character hiding in a dark cave or scary place without stating directly where he or she is or explaining the character's feelings explicitly. Allow students to review each other's work as before then ask them to comment on their partner's effective use of language.

Writing

Exciting endings

Use the following rubric to set a writing task. Give students paper and tell them to write as neatly as possible using the five senses.

Use these words to write the ending of a story.

They were still behind. I didn't dare look back to see how near, I but I could hear their feet pounding closer.

You should:

- **include the setting – where you are**
- **help the reader to understand what is happening**
- **show your emotions and feelings.**

Make a plan and spend about 30 minutes writing.

Explain that the words in italics must go at the beginning of their scene. Remind students that they only need to write the closing scene for a story, and they should write in the first person (I). Before they begin, you could discuss the bullet points and briefly review what makes a good ending to a story. Encourage them to write a dramatic closing scene.

This writing exercise is good practice for Checkpoint assessments and later IGCSE First

Language English examinations where the creative writing questions may ask for the opening or close of a story. When marking, look at how students: develop their content; structure their paragraphs; use different types of sentence for effect; use correct spelling and punctuation; and use a wide range of appropriate vocabulary.

Workbook

Show and tell

The exercise on page 63 asks students to explain what techniques the writer uses in each of the extracts to create an impression of character.

In *Thief*, Malorie Blackman uses unusual similes such 'as thin as a noodle' to describe an old man, whose name, 'Old Baldie', also suggests his appearance. The author is telling, but in an entertaining manner. Accept: showing us what a character is like.

In *Street Child*, Berlie Doherty is showing us what Jim is thinking and feeling from a fictitious first-person point of view.

Extension

More work on the 'showing' technique

If you are using a class reader, ask students to work in pairs to find a good example of the 'showing' technique. Get them to read their choices aloud and discuss as a group why it is 'good writing'.

Extended story

Extended story, guided reading

On page 146 of the Student Book, there is an extended extract from *Sky Hawk* by Gill Lewis.

After reading the extract, students are asked to consider what techniques the writer has used to hook the reader with this chapter opener. Students are also asked to consider different text types and settings. Finally, students are asked to write their own exciting ending to the story.

Suggested Student-book answers are given on page 146.

Planning and writing stories

Prior knowledge

Begin by writing the following traditional nursery rhyme on the board (or something similar if students don't know 'Humpty Dumpty'):

Humpty Dumpty sat on a wall.

Humpty Dumpty had a great fall.

All the king's soldiers and all the king's men

Couldn't put Humpty together again.

Ask the class what type of structure the rhyme has (beginning, middle, and end) and ask for examples of other well-known rhymes or fairy tales that use the same structure. For example, Snow White runs away from a cruel stepmother; she goes to live with a family in a forest; a prince comes to rescue her. Then ask what stories they know that do not follow this pattern and encourage the class to discuss ways of adding interest and variety to well-known stories by changing the format — for example, making the ending of *Cinderella*, when the Prince comes to the door with the glass slipper, into a cliffhanger (we are left not knowing whether the shoe will fit).

Arrange the class in small groups and ask them to turn other well-known stories into three sentences. They may change endings if they choose. Alternatively, they make up their own story, with one sentence for the beginning, one for the middle, and one for the end. Set a time limit, then go to page 126 in the Student Book and look at the narrative framework.

Arrange students in new groups to talk about the structure of a novel you are reading in class. Set a time limit and take feedback.

Discuss as a whole class any conflicting ideas or interpretations.

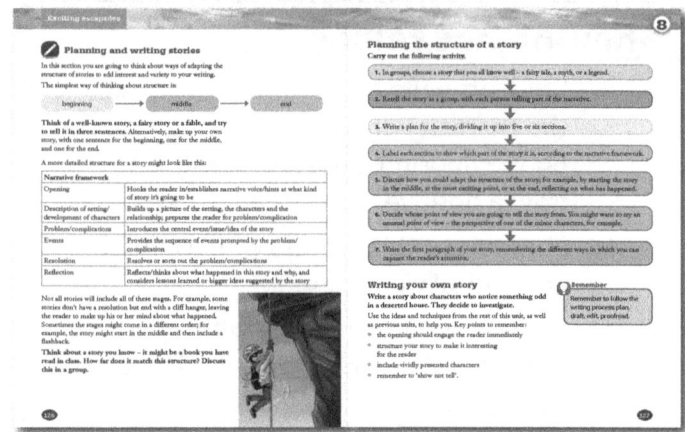

💬 Planning the structure of a story

Arrange groups of four, preferably with students who have not worked together before, and set them the task on page 127 of the Student Book. Before students start step 7, ask them to separate into new groups, where they will discuss their plans. Allow time for the new groups to make suggestions for each member, using this as a peer review exercise for the planning stage. Students then return to their 'home' groups and give feedback in order that the whole group benefits from a range of ideas. Each group then finalises their narrative and tells their story to the class.

Writing your own story

Students should do this activity on their own. Collect in their work and mark for form and content, taking into consideration what the class has been doing in this unit. The story should include convincing characters and an atmospheric setting using the 'show not tell' method.

If your class enjoy writing, set a maximum of 500 words, otherwise ask for around 300 words.

 ## Very short stories

Ask students to do the full exercise on page 64 in silence or for homework. They may then share their stories in groups. Each group selects the best example of a six-word and 140-character story to go on the classroom display board. If you have space, ask all students to copy out their flash fiction, and create a class display.

Acting out a story

Organise students into fairly large groups of 8–10 and assign a group leader as 'director'. Tell them they are going to act out the last book they read in class or tell a story they all know in a maximum of three minutes. Allow time for planning and rehearsal. Each group then performs their story for the class. After they have finished, discuss what the groups chose to leave out and why.

Progress check

This Student Book progress check is designed to help students revisit what they have learned in the unit in a relatively informal manner. Allow students to refer to both their Student Book and Workbook as required. When they have finished, read the answers aloud and let students mark their own or a partner's. Collect their answers in later to see what progress students are making and what areas need repeating or practising.

Take a few minutes after you have gone through the answers to discuss how writing fiction compares to informative and discursive writing. Ask students to think about why the planning stage is important for both, but what different writing techniques they might use for a story and an essay on school uniforms. You can also slip in the trick question: is it more important to have good spelling and grammar in non-fiction or fiction?

This may be a good point to clarify how and why teachers mark essays. Explain that writing is marked according to the task, but the following criteria generally apply: the content, what is in the story, essay or article; the way the content is organised (structure/paragraphing); different types of sentences for different effects; accurate punctuation; a wide vocabulary; good spelling.

You can then ask how reading fiction will help to develop these skills, and if students don't enjoy stories, what they could read instead.

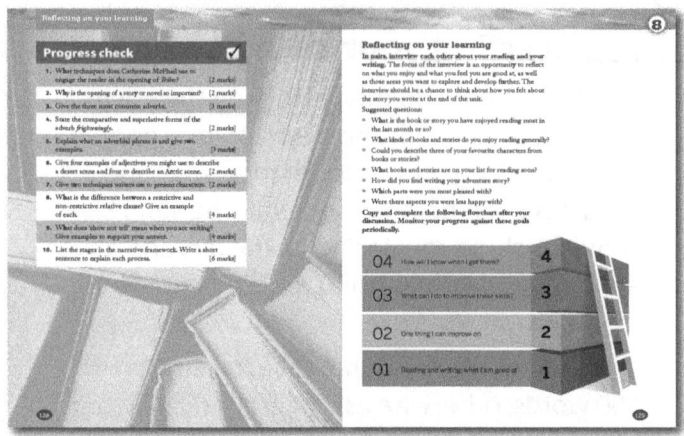

End-of-unit assessment

1. A hook and showing protagonist's point of view. [2]
2. Hooks the readers into story, sets the scene. [2]
3. Not, very, too. [3]
4. More and most frighteningly. [2]
5. An adverbial phrase tells how, where, when, and to what degree. Accept any two examples using two of these. [3]
6. Accept any relevant adjectives. [2]
7. Accept any two relevant techniques. For example:
    - description of physical appearance
    - writer's direct comment
    - what the other characters say about them
    - what they say [2]
8. A restrictive clause identifies the person or thing being referred to; a non-restrictive relative clause provides additional information. Students provide one appropriate example of each. [4]
9. Accept answers that explain 'showing' enables the reader to see or imagine a character or what is happening. Accept any examples that demonstrate this. [4]
10. Students list stages in the narrative framework with a short sentence to explain each process. The stages are:
    i. opening
    ii. description of setting and/or development of characters
    iii. problems/complications
    iv. events
    v. resolution
    vi. reflection. [6]

Exciting escapades quiz

1. 'Hook', and showing an exciting/frightening situation.

2. Add –*ly*.

3. Accept any two examples of adverbs.

4. Accept any three techniques from: description; what a character does (showing); manner of speech; how other characters react.

5. Accept any vocabulary used to discuss fiction and non-fiction, for example, genre, fiction, novels, characters, setting, atmosphere, hook, show and tell, and so on.

6. Students should demonstrate correct usage of who, which, or that in relative clauses, with examples.

7. Extremely short stories or micro-fiction/a story in a very few words/six-word stories. Accept any other suitable definitions.

Reflecting on your own learning

In pairs, students interview each other about their reading and writing, using suggested questions. They should reflect on what they enjoy and feel they are good at, as well as areas to explore and develop further. The interview is also a chance for them to consider the story they wrote at the end of the unit. Set a time limit and take feedback. Interviews can be recorded, to be played back in a few months; this will enable students to consider how they have progressed against their own targets.

Students then copy and complete the flowchart on page 129, to monitor their progress.

Writing a modern version of an old story

Read the following famous words from Lewis Carroll's *Alice in Wonderland* and ask students if they recognise where they come from:

'(...) what is the use of a book,' thought Alice 'without pictures or conversations?'

(...) suddenly a White Rabbit with pink eyes ran close by her.

'Oh dear! Oh dear! I shall be late!'

Now read the opening 2–3 paragraphs to the students (available on the CD) and ask what there was in this story that appealed to both adults and children in Victorian times.

Tell students the book was published in 1865 and encourage them to think how British children lived then: no television or other entertainment apart from books or plays; they were in closer contact with the natural world (rabbits and rabbit holes) and so on. When students have made the connection between the text and the time in which it was written, give them copies of the opening page, which is on the CD. Tell them this is one of the most famous children's stories ever written, but it now seems very old-fashioned. Read the text aloud with the class and ask them to identify what sounds silly or dated to us.

Arrange the class in pairs or small groups. Set the task to rewrite this page for modern readers. Tell students to pay attention to the following: the content (what happens); the main character (Alice); the sentences (over-long by modern standards) and vocabulary.

Students could write with pen and paper or on a computer. When they have finished, one person from each pair or group reads their version aloud. You can then discuss how and why changes have been made.

A printable version of the full transcript for this unit is available on the CD.

Learning objectives

In this unit, students will:

- Give short presentations and answer questions, maintaining effective organisation of talk. **Pages 130–131** *8SL1*

- Comment on how a writer's use of language contributes to the overall effect on the reader, using appropriate terminology. **Pages 132–133** *8Rw1*

- Demonstrate controlled use of a variety of simple and complex sentences to achieve purpose and contribute to overall effect. **Pages 134–135** *8Wp2*

- Explore the range, variety and overall effect of literary, rhetorical and grammatical features used by poets and writers of literary and non-literary texts, considering informal or formal style as well as the choice of words to create character. **Pages 134–135 and 136–137** *8Rw2*

- Develop a consistent viewpoint in non-fiction writing by selecting from techniques and devices used by known writers, and drawing on a range of evidence, opinions, information and purposes. **Pages 134–135** *8Wa3*

- Draw on their knowledge of a variety of sentence lengths and a wide variety of sentence structures, including complex sentences, and apply it to their own writing to make their ideas and intentions clear and create a range of effects. **Pages 134–135** *8Wp1*

- Explore how different audiences choose and respond to texts. **Pages 136–137** *8RO2*

- Explore complex ideas and feelings, both succinctly and at length. **Pages 136–137** *8SL3*

- Develop skills in solo, paired and group assignments, including role-play and drama. **Pages 136–137** *8SL8*

- Confidently use a range of sentence features to clarify or emphasise meaning. **Pages 138–139** *8Wp3*

- Discuss the features of media productions such as news broadcasts, interviews and discussions, analysing meaning and impact of variations in spoken language. **Pages 140–141** *8SL10*

- Develop ideas to suit a specific audience, purpose and task. **Pages 142–143** *8Wa2*

- Draw on knowledge of how and why writers use varying degrees of formality and informality to make appropriate choices of style and register in their own writing. **Pages 142–143** *8Wa5*

Tremendous television

Spend about 5–10 minutes with students, drawing out some of their prior experiences in an informal way. Ask whether they have ever:

- investigated or explored the content of international television programmes

- collaborated in making a video or film and discussed film shots

- created an article for a magazine

- considered the reasons why parents worry about what their children view on television

- reflected on how they select words for a particular purpose and/or audience.

Thinking time

This unit opens by considering television as a 'great time-waster'.

Draw out whether students use television for anything other than pure entertainment. Ask:

- Does reading a book exercise the imagination?

- Is watching television a passive activity?

Ask students to think about their favourite television personalities and characters. Do they seem like 'real people' to them? If so, why?

Ask the class to give reasons why we should applaud TV programme makers.

Tremendous television programmes

Ask students to work in pairs and make a list of television genres (types of television programme). Here is a suggested list with a few subcategories:

Drama – including series and serials

Sports

Situation comedies (sit-coms)

Factual/documentary – including science, nature, politics, travel

Soap operas (soaps)

Children's television – including cartoons and educational programmes

News broadcasts

Cookery

Reality shows

When students have compiled their lists, take feedback and ask them to organise their lists into three categories: drama; factual; entertainment. Take feedback on which genres are hard to define. For example, are cookery programmes and reality shows factual or entertainment? How would they classify travel and holiday programmes?

Students should now work individually. Using their lists, they choose two types of programme that they enjoy and watch on a regular basis, and two they never watch. For each genre or subcategory they should say what they like, or what does not appeal to them. More information on subcategories of genres can be found at: http://www.bbc.co.uk/tv/programmes/genres

Students then share their preferences with a partner. Take feedback and round up the session by demonstrating what a wealth of information and entertainment is available to us daily. Ask what we would do without television in the home, and perhaps ask them to think about what life was like for students their age a hundred years ago.

Speaking and listening

Giving a presentation

In this part of the unit students will learn and practise a range of reading and writing skills related to the media.

Students make a short presentation and respond to questions. They should talk about one or two television programmes they enjoy, but they must plan what to say and write brief notes. Remind them that they are not to read their notes when giving their presentations! They should use their plans to help them, but can develop these as they see fit.

Workbook

Soap-box oratory

Soap plays a curious role in speaking and the media. Soap-box oratory refers to how street vendors sell their goods, and by transference how soap-box orators convey their beliefs and ideas. A 'soap' or 'soap opera' is a series on radio or television about so-called ordinary people. The term derives from the fact that soap companies sponsored the first serial dramas on American radio.

On page 66 of the Workbook, students need to think about how they will use rhetorical and persuasive language. This activity has been designed to get students thinking about language and does not need to be formally assessed.

Television news – an international miracle

Prior knowledge

Before starting the reading, ensure students understand what the Olympic Games are, and how they differ from national sports on television. Ask the class to think about what television was like 50 years ago: black and white images, no live coverage or commentaries, etc. If students are interested in the history of television, you could look at the page on 'John Logie Baird and Television' at www. historylearningsite.co.uk, or 'History of the BBC – 1960s' at www.bbc.co.uk/historyofthebbc.

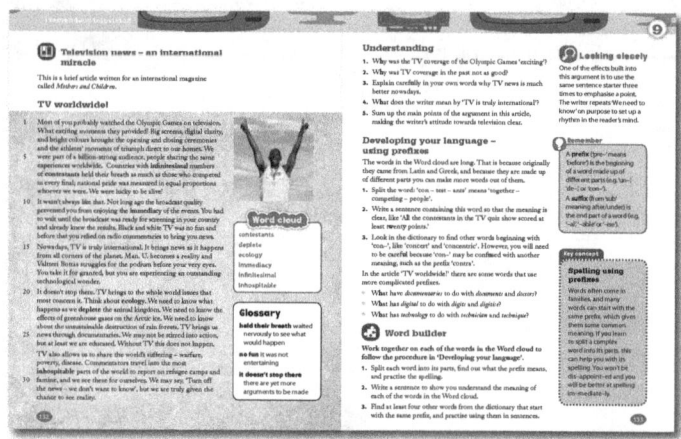

Using prefixes

Remind students of how a prefix works, giving examples of 'un–', 'de–', 'con–'.

Then do the same for the suffix, giving examples with '–al', '–able' or '–ise'.

In questions 1 and 2, students look at the example then write a sentence containing 'contestants' that demonstrates its meaning.

For question 3, students use a dictionary to find other words beginning with 'con–'. Check that they understand the prefix 'contra', to prevent confusion.

The *Oxford English Dictionary for Schools* has a useful section on prefixes and suffixes; see pages 914 and 915.

- The link between 'doctor' and 'document' relates to the word history for 'doctor' being teacher and the 'document' being the lesson.

- Digit and digital relates to the Latin *digitus* (finger or toe) and mathematics. The first nine numbers are called digits from the habit of counting on fingers.

- The Greek words *tekhnikos* and *tekhne* give us words related to technology, skill, and crafts (technician and technique).

📖 Understanding

1. Immediacy and/or live coverage (not knowing who will win).

2. People already knew the results.

3. Students should explain 1 and 2 above in their own words and include reference to digital clarity/colour/spectacle.

4. It has global reach.

5. Students should summarise the twelve main points in their own words, as far as possible:

    i. television is now on big screens with digital clarity

    ii. we can see moments of triumph/ winners winning

    iii. audience of billions

    iv. being part of an audience of billions enables people to share their experiences worldwide

    v. we see equal opportunities for big and small nations

    vi. in the past we had to wait for a broadcast

    vii. television was in black and white

    viii. now it is global/international (we all see the same)

    ix. we are enjoying a technological success

    x. television provides news and information via documentaries

    xi. it is educational

    xii. we can see reality and empathise with those suffering disease, poverty, warfare.

Vocabulary

 Word builder

Working in pairs, students now follow the procedure in Developing your language.

Suggested answers:

- Deplete – de = undo or take away
- Ecology – eco = to do with the environment
- Immediacy – im = not (or opposite of) mediacy (noun meaning without delay)
- Infinitesimal – in = not finite (adjective meaning extremely small)
- Inhospitable – in = not hospitable/welcoming

Students write sentences using each word to demonstrate understanding.

Depending on time and the nature of your class, it may be better to specify which prefix students use.

Workbook

 More interesting prefixes – trans-, cata-, tele-, contra-, hos-, voc-

Encourage students to use a dictionary for this activity, which is suitable for homework or an individual task in class. When students have finished, do a random spot check, to ensure they have not been simply writing down words they don't understand or cannot use. You could have a mini-competition for the longest word and the most difficult word to spell, and/or the most unusual or least useable word.

A good way to consolidate this vocabulary work is for one student to teach another about one or more of their words.

Alternatively, you could turn it into a guessing game. Demonstrate this by giving the class your definition for 'transliterating'. First, they write down what they think it means; they then find the real definition. You could also select a few rarely used words with prefixes and offer three or more definitions for each one, only one of which is correct. The winner is the student or team who guesses correctly.

Note that the prefix 'cata' comes from the Greek word *kata*, meaning 'down'. Suggested words are: catastrophe, cataclysm, catacombs, catapult.

Extension

Speaking and listening – Points of view

Ask students to form groups of three. Two of them take the roles of opposing sports players; the third is the television interviewer. Ask them to find a short extract from a recent sports event of their choice. These can be found on the Internet, or you can set this as homework and students agree to watch the evening sports news ready to do the task in class the following day. A wide selection of press interviews and tennis match coverage can be found on the website for the Spanish tennis player, Rafael Nadal: http://www.nadalnews.com.

Brief the players in the following way: you play on opposite sides; one of you is a winner, the other is the loser. Describe the match from your point of view for a television audience.

Brief the interviewer in the following way: You are the interviewer; try to get the two players to talk about the highlights of their match and how they won or lost. Remind them that this programme will be watched worldwide so they need to be specific and keep a polite tone. Set a time limit of 5 minutes maximum per interview.

Give your groups time to practise their interviews then bring the class together to watch each other. Ask the class to offer constructive criticism – ask them to consider how well each player speaks and how well the interviewer encourages players to describe their thoughts and feelings by framing good questions.

Students may also video their interviews so they can watch their own performances and see how well they speak in public.

Sentence lengths

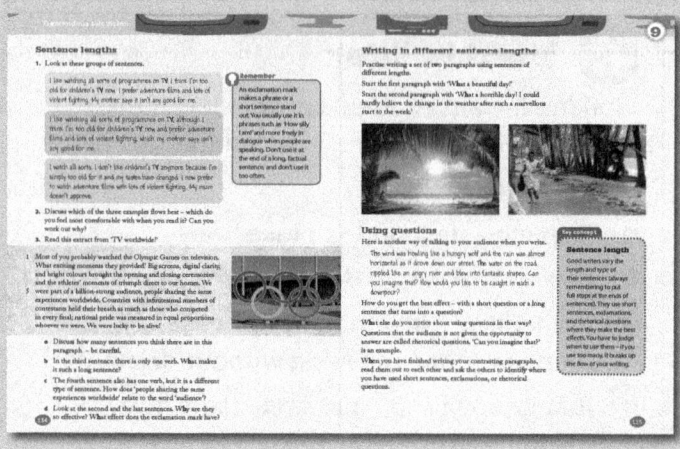

Student-book answers

Sentence lengths

3. **a.** Six sentences.

   b. The third sentence describes/lists the details of the ceremonies that are conveyed to our homes.

   c. '…people sharing the same experiences worldwide' (adjectival phrase) describes the audience.

   d. The second and last sentences are for rhetorical effect.

Grammar

Writing in different sentence lengths

Review sentences of different lengths if students remain unclear. Explain how a simple sentence can be quite long and a complex sentence can actually be quite short. Simple sentences can have long noun phrases, as in: 'Most of the best and brightest students in the class failed that really difficult, confusing grammar test on Tuesday' (simple), or: 'What he told me wasn't true' (complex).

The purpose of this activity is for students to become more aware of how and why they should vary sentence lengths. This is one of the criteria in the Checkpoint writing assessments.

Listening

Sentence length and music

Writing coach Gary Provost gave this advice on using different types of sentence. Read it to the class, demonstrating the first five words on your fingers slowly, then vary the pace of your reading according to the writer's sentence choices. When you have finished, ask how the writer made a paragraph on writing sentences interesting. Then ask students to work on their own and write a paragraph using different lengths of sentence on 'music on the radio', or 'my favourite music'. When they have finished, they should swap papers with a partner and read each other's work. They should mark the different sentence lengths with the following symbols: S = simple and short; C = compound; L/C = long complex. If your students are not familiar with one-word sentences and sentences without a verb, explain that these are called minor sentences; they are not grammatically correct but we sometimes use them for effect, as in 'Music' below. Collect students' paragraphs to check how well they have responded to this exercise.

This sentence has five words. Here are five more words. Five-word sentences are fine. But several together become monotonous. Listen to what is happening. The writing is getting boring. The sound of it drones. It's like a stuck record. The ear demands some variety. Now listen. I vary the sentence length, and I create music. Music. The writing sings. It has a pleasant rhythm, a lilt, a harmony. I use short sentences. And I use sentences of medium length. And sometimes, when I am certain the reader is rested, I will engage him with a sentence of considerable length, a sentence that burns with energy and builds with all the impetus of a crescendo, the roll of the drums, the crash of the cymbals – sounds that say listen to this, it is important.

Grammar

Using questions

Before starting this activity, warn students that while rhetorical questions can be very effective in speeches and creative writing, they should be used sparingly – and they should never be employed in formal writing or an essay. Warn also about using rhetorical questions that may lead to negative answers, such as: 'So what do you think? Are we right?' (The response could be: 'No!')

When students have finished writing their contrasting paragraphs, ask them to read them out to each other in pairs or small groups, so peers can identify where short sentences, exclamations, and rhetorical questions have been employed. This is good practice for later work in IGCSE, where students may be asked to give or write a persuasive speech.

Workbook

 ## The long and the short of it

Students write a story in less than 75 words, using at least one short sentence. It can be an exclamation or a rhetorical question.

When they have finished, ask them to read their stories aloud in class, making them as dramatic as possible.

Then ask how short a story can be. Here are two examples in 5 and 10 words.

- Lost: one ski, never used.
- Lost, new compass, last seen somewhere in desert, whereabouts unknown.

Extension

Travel writing

Ask students to read the two examples of travel writing on the CD for this unit.

The first extract is from Laurie Lee's *As I Walked Out One Midsummer Morning* about his journey through Spain as a young man in the 1930s. You can find episodes on the BBC radio website, go to: http://www.bbc.co.uk/programmes/b047lpgw/episodes/guide.

The second extract is from *Neither Here, Nor There: Travels in Europe* by Bill Bryson. The American Bill Bryson is travelling around Europe with a friend by train during the 1990s.

In these extracts the two authors describe visits to very different places from those with which they are familiar. Read the extracts with the students and review vocabulary as necessary.

Discuss the extracts separately then draw together similar techniques. You can ask the following questions, which students may answer orally or in writing:

Extract 1

1. Find the simile Lee uses to describe the village from a distance. (like cubes of pink sugar)
2. Name two things Lee can smell. (fires and 'the sweet tang of cooking')
3. How does Lee describe the sound of the bell? (jerking gusts of vibration)
4. What is Lee's overall impression of being in the village itself? (a noisy place)
5. Say why he thinks it is so noisy. (he has been sleeping in the countryside/walking on his own)

Extract 2

1. Explain why Bryson feels there is a 'sense of being *inside* a palace'. (town built in an ancient palace, where corridors became streets; palace courtyards now public squares.)
2. Why do you think he says 'the houses look as if they grew magically out of the ruins'? (stairways that go nowhere/columns supporting nothing)
3. Describe the aroma Bryson can smell. (mixture of vanilla, grilled meat and fish)
4. In your opinion, why does Bryson think it is 'entrancing'? (he's from America, which is very different/big and there is a magical quality to Split; everything is on a small scale)

Having established how the authors describe these two places you can now move on to discuss the following:

a. why they wrote about these places
b. how travel writing is to inform and entertain
c. format and use of sentence grammar, which is similar
d. how modern readers might compare these places with what they are like now. (Do students think either has changed very much? Probably not.)

Now move the discussion on to how and why television viewers watch travel and holiday programmes, and if a programme can convey the same sense of being in a place as travel writing.

A mother's complaint

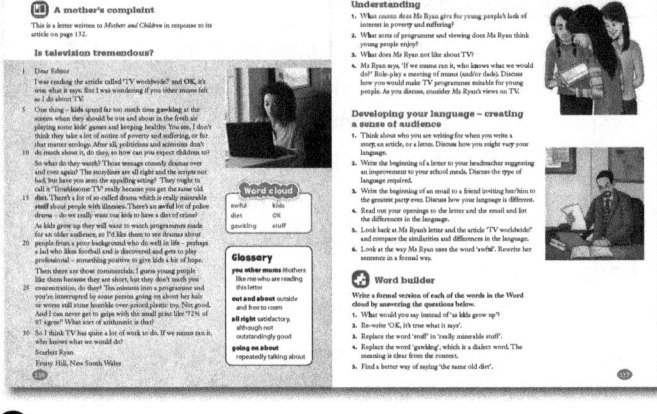

Student-book answers

📖 Understanding

1. Politicians don't care or show interest, so why should young people?
2. Teenage comedy dramas.
3. Repetitive content, too much crime and misery.

Writing

Creating a sense of audience

Before students start this activity, provide support by modelling two very formal and two alternative informal phrases on the board, such as: 'Well, yeah, I think you're sort of right', and: 'I would concede that, given the circumstances, you have a valid point'.

Working together, students should do the following:

1. Discuss how they select language and register for a story, article, or letter according to the reader or recipient.

They then go back to your examples on the board and write a couple of their own.

2. Individually, write the beginning of a letter to their head teacher, to suggest an improvement to school meals. Discuss the type of language they should use beforehand.

3. Still working on their own, students now write the beginning of an email invitation to 'the greatest party ever'. After they have completed the task, discuss how their language is different to that used for part 2 above.

4. Now re-organise the class in small groups. Once they have completed the task, ask groups to choose a spokesperson and ask which of the two styles they found easier to write.

5. Looking back at Ms Ryan's letter and the article 'TV worldwide!', briefly review the differences in language and register.

6. Students now rewrite Ms Ryan's letter as part of the Word builder exercise. They should rewrite the letter formally, for example, by saying: 'There is far too much police drama'.

Workbook

🧩 I don't agree with you

Before students begin their letters, which is best done individually, ask them to review Ms Ryan's letter and identify the points they need to cover. Get them to make a list of points and tick off each point once they have included it in their writing. This is good early practice for summary skills at IGCSE level.

Draw the class's attention to the salutation. Point out that, as they know the name of the person to whom they are writing, the closing should be 'Yours sincerely'. (Remind students that 'Yours faithfully' is for people one does not know, and is used for closing formal letters that begin 'Dear Sir/Madam'.) When marking students' writing, look for consistent and appropriate use of register, variety of sentence lengths, and clarity of argument in sequenced paragraphs.

Situation comedy

Ask students to form groups of four or five and choose one of the situations listed below. Tell them they are going to improvise the situation so there is no need for them to write down their lines, however, they will be asked to repeat the performance so they should plan it carefully in advance.

Situations:

1. A new teacher has come to your school. He or she has been working in a very strict military academy, where students wear uniform and have very strict discipline. Your class has trouble understanding what the teacher wants you to do, but they dare not make fun of him/her because they will get drastic punishments such as running round the football pitch 20 times or doing press-ups in front of the class.

2. One of your friends invites you to stay for the weekend. You go to his or her house only to find that it is actually a castle and his grandparents are members of the royal family. That evening there is a banquet.

3. You and your friends have been invited to hang out with a couple of hip-hop stars in their local area, but when you get there you realise you do not understand the way they speak or behave.

Name one person in each group to be the 'director' who makes final decisions on the scenes and who does what. Set a time limit (10 minutes will be enough). Ask the class to start by improvising the situation, then sit down and plan what they are actually going to do. Groups should do a couple of practices before showing their sit-com to the class.

After the class has seen all the sit-coms, take feedback on what created the comedy, how a clash of ideas/behaviour/expectations can create humour. Remind students of the saying 'there is no drama without conflict'. You can develop this discussion into an analysis of popular comedy shows on television.

Speaking and listening – Formal, neutral, or informal?

This activity gives students further practice in recognising register and selecting appropriate words for different situations.

Ask students to work on their own and, if necessary, hand out sheets of paper. Ask them to turn the page to landscape and draw three columns with the following headings.

In a cafe with friends	Talking to the head of your school	Speaking at a debate at a schools' conference with people of all ages

If necessary, change the heading to suit your environment, but make sure there is a mixture of formal, neutral and informal situations.

Now give students the following words and phrases and ask them to put them into the appropriate columns as shown below. They may choose more than one. Give the first line of each of the columns below as an example.

Hi, good to meet you.	Pleased to meet you.	It is a pleasure to be here.
Put off doing	Put off doing	(postpone/delay)
(Don't stand for it)	We should not tolerate	We should not tolerate
(Numbers have dropped off)	Decrease in number	Decrease in number
It gets on my nerves	It is very irritating	------
(A really big problem)	A considerable problem	A considerable problem
I can't stand that music	I cannot abide/tolerate that music	-----

Students now compare their answers with those of a partner and discuss discrepancies. Write up correct answers on the board and ask students to fill in the gaps with alternative expressions for the situations, here given in brackets. You can extend this activity by asking students to work in pairs; they take turns in giving each other formal and informal phrases to go in the three-column format.

Antecedents and relative pronouns

Prior knowledge

Prior knowledge

Review with the class how we use pronouns and re-introduce antecedents, taking a moment to look at the prefix 'ante–'.

Write on the board *his, hers, its,* and *it's*. Discuss how we use *it's* with an apostrophe and *its* as a pronoun. You can explain that most adults and sign-writers still get this wrong, and you cannot rely on a computer grammar checker to get it right either.

Ask students to identify where to insert the apostrophe and why.

Answers to quiz:

<u>My parents</u> were very proud of <u>their</u> hard-working children.

<u>Mariam, my sister, and I</u> are very fond of <u>our</u> friendly pet snake.

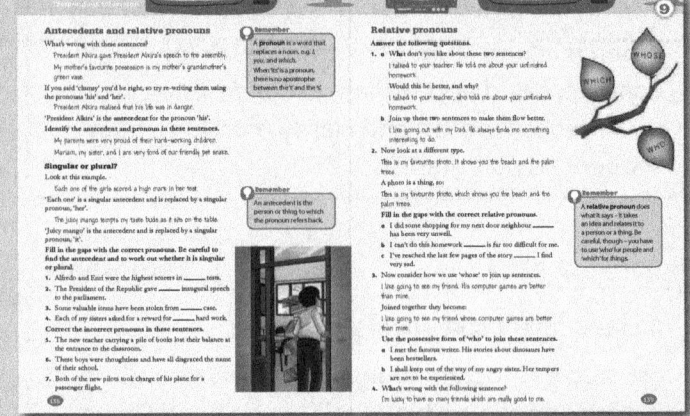

Singular or plural?

Discuss the examples on page 138 of the Student Book and perhaps add a few more examples, such as: 'Every one of us is going on the trip to consolidate.'

Answers:

1. their
2. his
3. their
4. her
5. wrong (correct answer is 'his' or 'her')
6. right
7. right

Grammar

Relative pronouns

Spend a few minutes reviewing 'who' and 'which' if you have students using English as an additional language in the class.

Answers:

2. **a.** who
   b. which
   c. which

After students have finished, discuss how putting a comma after 'story' in sentence c. means the last few pages were sad. If you don't it means the story itself was sad. Ask them to work out why.

Before students move on to question 4, model on the board an incorrect sentence with *who's* and ask students to explain why it is wrong. For example: 'Jose, who's writing is neater than mine, always gets good marks.'

4. **a.** I met the famous writer whose stories about dinosaurs have been bestsellers.
   b. I shall keep out of the way of my angry sister, whose tempers are not to be experienced.
   c. I'm lucky to have so many friends who are really good to me.

Who, which, and whose

Ideally, this activity should be completed alone, perhaps as homework.

1. This is Mr Alioke, <u>who</u> is my uncle.

He is a very rich man and he owns the Alioke estate, <u>which</u> is a major pineapple producing complex.

He is also a very wise man <u>whose</u> opinion (is one) I greatly respect.

Students should finish the next set of sentences using a pronoun then create their own complete sentences for the final task.

Stretching students – Who's who in the news

Read the following information to students and ask them to make notes as you speak on who's who in government. (While the example given below is from the British government, this activity can be modified to suit the political landscape in any country.) Give an example of note-taking before you start and advise students not to try to copy down every word. This is a good way for students to prepare for their classes higher up the school and in further education. When you have finished reading, ask the questions that follow. Students should write down their answers individually. As far as possible, encourage students to work independently in this listening exercise.

Text to read:

Each day you hear about some or all of the people I am going to talk about in news programmes. But do you know who these people are, or what they do? Listen and make notes on some important people in the British news and politics.

The Prime Minister is a Member of Parliament. He or she is the head of the government. The Prime Minister is the leader of the party that wins the most seats in a general election. Once elected, he or she is officially appointed to be Prime Minister by the Queen. The Prime Minister is responsible for choosing the other members of the government, who form the **Cabinet**.

Leader of the Opposition is the leader of the largest party after the ruling party, opposing the

ideas and policies of the political party in power. The Leader of the Opposition chooses Members of Parliament from his or her party to form a 'Shadow Cabinet'.

The Cabinet consists of a maximum of 22 paid government ministers chosen by the Prime Minister. The Cabinet develop government policies and some members head government departments.

Shadow Cabinet

The Shadow Cabinet consists of members from the main opposition party in the House of Commons and the House of Lords. Its role is to examine the work of each government department and develop policies in their specific areas.

Ministers are MPs (Members of Parliament), such as the Minister of Education or the Minister of Transport, who are chosen to run particular parts of the government.

An MP is elected by voters to represent the people who live in a constituency or a local area. MPs deal with problems and help people in their constituencies, whether or not they voted for them.

(Source: http://www.parliament.uk/about/mps-and-lords/principal/government-opposition)

Questions:

a. Is the Prime Minister elected by voters or the Queen? (Elected by voters)

b. Who is the Leader of the Opposition? (Leader of the largest party after the ruling party)

c. Who or what is a Cabinet in politics? (Ministers who develop policies for the government)

d. What does a Shadow Cabinet do? (Makes alternative policies and watches what the Cabinet are doing)

e. What is the job of a Member of Parliament? (To represent/help people in his/her constituency)

When you have finished the reading and gone through the questions to ensure everyone has a sound understanding of who does what in the British Parliament, ask students to form groups and make wall charts on the House of Commons or the House of Lords. Remind them that the purpose is to help their peers understand the daily news (not persuade them to follow a particular political party).

Ask your class to find out the equivalent roles in the political system in their country and make a wall chart.

A choir steps out

Prior knowledge

Before starting this activity, ask students what the words in the Word cloud have in common (they all relate to what and how choirs sing) then discuss their meanings before doing the listening task. The Glossary box contains colloquial phrases, to which you may want to add a roller coaster (amusement park or fairground railway ride) as a way of saying something 'really took off'.

Students could watch the Gumboot dance performed by Waterford School students on 8 March 2013, when King Mswati III of Swaziland visited their school, which is available on YouTube.

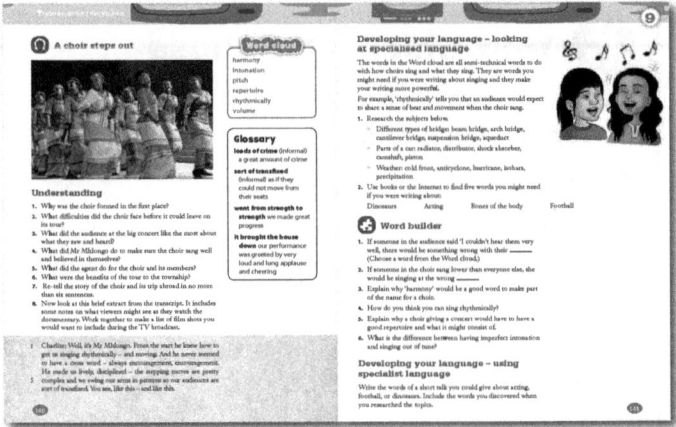

Student-book answers

📖 Understanding

1. As an activity for girls while boys played football.

2. No finance for airfares; parents reluctant to let girls go; Boipelo was very ill.

3. The gumboot (wellington) boot dance.

4. Mr Mhlongo gave constant encouragement.

5. The agent found finance to pay for fares and accommodation, and provided hospital treatment for Boipelo.

6. Brought happiness and some money (and a better self-image).

7. Students retell the story of the choir and its trip abroad in no more than six sentences.

   i. Mr Mhlongo started a choir.

   ii. He recruited 40 girls who wanted to do traditional step-dances.

   iii. They were good right from the very start and received his encouragement.

   iv. The choir appeared at football matches and were spotted by an agent.

   v. The agent provided the means for the choir to go to Europe.

   vi. They were a huge success and able to bring back money into the township.

8. Students make a list of film shots to be used during the TV broadcast.

Vocabulary

Looking at specialised language

1. Remind students of the words they discussed in the Word cloud, which are all semi-technical and related to what and how choirs sing. Tell students they are now going to look at other technical vocabulary for bridges, parts of a car, and the weather.

2. Organise groups and set a time limit for the activity. Students will need to refer to dictionaries. Discourage use of Wikipedia.

   Before starting this activity, ask groups to choose a spokesperson who will report back to the class. Write the headings 'Dinosaurs', 'Bones of the body', 'Acting', and 'Football' in four columns on the board. When students have finished their research, ask the first spokesperson to write their group's words for one column on the board. The next student then fills in the next column, and so on. As you go round the class, group representatives can extend the columns already started with new words. The whole class can then add these words to their own lists, to increase and improve their vocabularies.

Developing your language

Using specialist language

Remind students that, as some words are technical, they may need to explain them while they give their talks. Set a short time limit for the delivery of each talk. Insist students are concise: they must not stray off topic or develop it too far. The task here is focused on the vocabulary, not the world of dinosaurs or football.

Word builder

1. Volume

2. Pitch

3. When combined, the definitions of harmony in the *Oxford English Dictionary for Schools* are ideal for the name for a choir: 'a pleasant combination of musical notes' and 'friendly and peaceful feelings between people'.

4. Singing rhythmically means singing with the regular pattern of beats and stresses in a piece of music.

5. A choir's repertoire consists of numerous and varied songs. It would need to be good to keep the audience interested and so make the concert enjoyable.

6. 'Imperfect intonation' means that the tone and pitch of voice is slightly out, while 'singing out of tune' means the tone and pitch are clearly incorrect.

 ## All about my school

This activity can be done for homework initially then developed into a group activity in class, so that students can role-play interviews. While students are working together, go round the class listening in and drawing their attention to how they are using language: consider whether it is appropriate for the target audience and the person being interviewed.

The father of modern nature programmes

The following information has been taken from: http://www.biography.com/people/david-attenborough. It may help if you can display an image of Attenborough.

Naturalist and television personality David Attenborough is the father of the modern nature documentary.

David Attenborough was born in London, in 1926. After studying the Natural Sciences at the University of Cambridge, he began his career as a producer at the BBC, where he launched the successful *Zoo Quest* series.

He was made controller of BBC2 in 1965 and later, its director of programming. During this time programmes were beginning to be made in colour. Attenborough left the BBC to write and produce various series, including *Life on Earth*, which set new standards for the modern nature documentary. Since then Attenborough has written, produced, hosted and narrated countless award-winning nature-focused programmes. He has devoted his life to celebrating and preserving wildlife.

Attenborough's fascination with the natural world began early. By the age of seven he had assembled a sizable collection of bird eggs and fossils. After leaving school he studied Natural Sciences.

When he started at the BBC he faced two obstacles. First, there were no programmes on nature, and second, his boss thought that his teeth were too big for him to be a TV personality.

Attenborough's greatest success came with *Life on Earth*: 96 episodes that looked at the role of evolution in nature. The show took Attenborough and his crews around the globe. Using cutting-edge filming techniques to bring wildlife into homes worldwide, they gained an estimated viewing audience of more than 500 million. Now in his 80s, Attenborough continues making programmes around the world.

Read the biography of David Attenborough to your class twice. Explain BBC means the British Broadcasting Corporation. Then ask students to answer the following oral questions in writing, from memory.

1. How old was David Attenborough when he had a collection of fossils? (7)

2. What was changing in television when Attenborough became controller of BBC2? (Colour television)

3. Where did David Attenborough study Natural Sciences? (Cambridge)

4. Name one obstacle he faced when he began at the BBC. (No nature programmes/teeth considered to be too big)

5. *Life on Earth* was a documentary series about evolution in nature. What were the estimated viewing figures: 96,000; 80,000; 50 million or 500 million? (500 million)

Writing an article

Prior knowledge

Before students start their writing, spend a few moments discussing the difference between a newspaper report and an article. A report gives facts and details about an event; an article may contain information and conclusions that are not strictly facts. In general, a report is merely informative; an article explains beyond basic facts and may also entertain. Depending where you are, you might like to develop this into a discussion of the content of daily newspapers and what editors include in weekend editions.

Students are asked to write an article, to give information and views on a topic that is of particular interest or concern to them. The article is for publication in a newspaper or magazine, but students need to decide on their target audience. They should re-read 'TV worldwide!' and re-examine its construction and language. Discuss whether it is entirely formal, and review the use of rhetorical language and its target audience.

Depending on how readily you can access British print media, you may like to have a look at how many British newspapers use puns in titles or headlines.

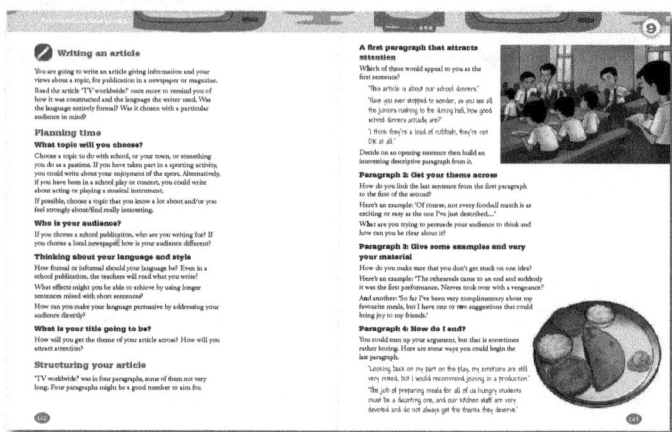

Planning for writing

Writing an article

Put a selection of planning strategies on the board, such as flow chart, concept map, and spidergram. Remind students that they also need to plan the order of paragraphs (four) so their article leads to a satisfactory conclusion. Direct them to the writing frame on page 143. They must consider register and style.

Encourage students to find suitable images for their articles, but remind them of the importance of copyright and why they must not download copyrighted images they do not pay for.

Writing

Marking students' articles

When your students have finished their articles ask them to do the following self-assessment exercise.

1. Using a pencil, divide the article into these sections:
    a. opening paragraph
    b. main body
    c. conclusion.

2. Does the opening paragraph have a strong, original or eye-catching opening? Give yourself a star in the margin if it does.

3. Does the opening paragraph explain what the article is about? Star in the margin if it does.

4. Look at the body of your article: does it contain interesting quotations or data, or details? Star in the margin if it does.

5. Does the middle section supply useful facts or information? Star if it does.

6. Conclusion: Does the conclusion include something from the introduction? Star in the margin if it does.

7. Does the conclusion contain a memorable phrase at the end, or end by restating an important point from the article? Star if it does.

Now ask students to swap their articles with a partner. Partners read the articles and decide whether the stars in the margin are valid or not. Collect the essays in and mark for the following criteria: content; structure of the article (paragraphing leading to a conclusion); use of English, (including register, vocabulary and varied types of sentence); technical accuracy (spelling and punctuation); overall effect.

School Television Network

Tell students that their school is creating a school television network. The purpose of this is to:

- inform students about what is happening in the school on a weekly basis (e.g. sports fixtures, trips, plays, and choir practice, etc.)

- showcase excellent artwork and performing arts work

- demonstrate difficult mathematics and physics questions and how to tackle them, and similar educational material.

Working together, students should decide:

- what other aspects of school life should be included

- how programmes would be presented (for instance, across the whole school or in year groups?)

- what the balance will be between information, education, and entertainment

- what goes in programmes – teachers or students, or both.

Challenge students to create a script for the first news programme, which will inform their audience about what is going to be on the network.

Workbook

 ## Checking your work

The paragraph with corrected spelling, punctuation and grammar is:

> What would the world be like without insects? Suppose they were to disappear tomorrow. Well, for one thing, it would be very quiet; there would be no buzzing. For another thing, we would lose a lot of beauty. We are used to seeing the marvellous colours of butterflies, moths, dragonflies, and beetles. Most serious of all would be the effect on the balance of nature: there would be no bees to collect the pollen and honey they make for us; there would be no aphids for small birds to eat. Nearly every insect has a place in our world. We cannot afford to interfere with this delicate balance; we must not destroy habitats and kill creatures with insecticides.

Punctuation practice

Ask students to find a short news report on the Internet or in a newspaper and copy it out by hand without punctuation. Working in pairs, students read their partner's report and put in the punctuation. Students then check their peer's choice of punctuation against the original.

Warn students that modern journalists and reporters sometimes use punctuation creatively or not at all. If this is the case, students should feel free to improve the writer's English.

Investigative journalism – the history of broadcasting

Tell students that the BBC was founded in 1922 to inform, educate and entertain the general public. Television started in 1925, but not many people had television sets in their homes until the 1950s. Ask students to find out when radio and television programmes were first broadcast in their country.

Students now decide whether they want to investigate the history of radio or television. Their job is to find out what sorts of programmes were broadcast in the early years and, if possible, find clips to demonstrate what it was like to show their class. You can do this as a whole-class activity, assigning specific areas to individuals, such as the first sports broadcasts (radio and television). Alternatively, ask students to form groups and set themselves their own investigative roles. Assign group leaders and set a time limit. As far as possible, allow students to decide how they want to present their findings. The objective is to learn about the history of broadcasting.

When they have finished, students should present their findings to the class and answer questions from their peers.

Progress check

End-of-unit assessment

1. A soap is a serial about everyday lives (1);
   a documentary gives factual information
   about real events (1). [2]

2. Latin (1) and Greek (1). [2]

3. Any phrase after 'How' (1) or after 'What' (1),
   or allow one example of a short, dramatic
   sentence (1), up to a maximum of 2 marks. [2]

4. A question that is not meant to have an
   answer from the reader or listener (1).
   Allow any sensible example for (1). [2]

5. Students should mention adapting how
   you write to the person who will read it (1)
   and any comment about using particular
   language (1). [2]

6. 'Ante' = before (1) and 'ced(e)' = come (1).
   Allow 2 marks for 'come before'. Students then
   explain that an antecedent is the person or
   thing to which the pronoun refers back to
   (1), and write a sentence to give a suitable
   example (1). [4]

7. Four objections to commercials on TV: they
   don't teach concentration (1); they interrupt
   programmes (1); they try to sell over-priced
   toys (1); they use silly statistics, e.g. 72% of
   97 agree (1). [4]

8. Any four words from: cold front, anticyclone,
   hurricane, isobars, and precipitation, plus
   any other similar words, such as warm front,
   occlusion, isotherm, tornado, etc., up to a
   maximum of 4 marks. [4]

9. A relative pronoun relates/joins an idea to
   a person or thing (1); who (1), which (1)
   and whose (1). [4]

10. Any 4 of: in tune/intonation (1); loud enough/
    volume (1); right notes/pitch; (1); sing in
    rhythm/lively (1); in harmony/three
    parts (1). [4]

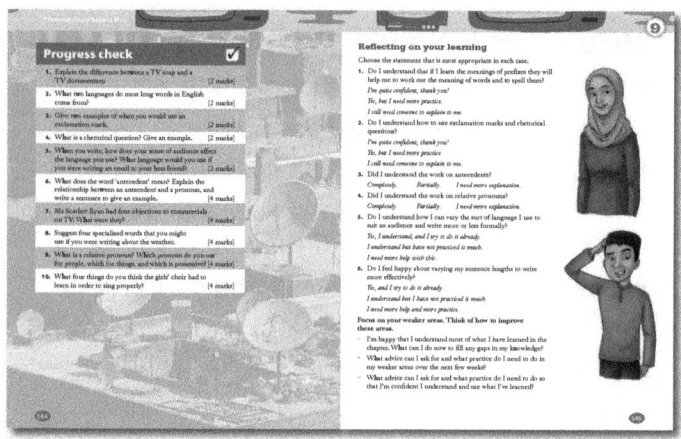

Reflecting on your learning

The informative writing skills and the work on
target readers and audience in this unit impact
on other forms of writing, so it is important that
students are aware of their progress. The grammar
covered informs everything students write.

We recommend you carry out this activity with
students working on their own. A useful activity
after you have finished the reflective piece is to
ask students to write out a sheet with guidelines
for informative writing in articles. They should
then keep this and refer to it in the future.

If you are conducting end-of-term tests, remind
the class that there is a myth that 'you don't have
to revise for English'. It is a myth! The guidelines
for informative writing, which they have just
completed, are testimony to this.

⚙ Tremendous television quiz time

(Answers taken from *Oxford English Dictionary for Schools.*)

1. Speakers used to stand on a soap-box to be heard above the crowd. It is an opportunity for the speaker to make their views public.

2. a. Telescope = to see at a distance.
   b. Cata– (Greek *kata*) means 'down', so both words suggest something brought down.
   c. They have the same word history (*hostal* and the Latin word *hospitale*).

3. The audience would know it was raining, they are standing outdoors; if they cared about getting wet, they wouldn't be standing in the rain listening to the speaker.

4. The response to both (a) and (b) is that students should vary sentence lengths; writing in the same form all the time makes a piece boring and spoils the flow.

5. Students should have remembered to whom they were writing and to be polite. It is important to show courtesy when writing to avoid causing offence and therefore a negative response.

6. 'This is the man *whose* guinea fowl flew into my garden'. Whose = pronoun.

7. Proofreading for spelling and grammar mistakes, but also to check that the chosen writing style is right for the intended audience.

8. Accept answers that include something along the lines of: 'quite' means completely or somewhat/nearly, depending on context, and 'quiet' means not much sound; (possessive) 'their' means belonging to, and 'there' is an adverb/refers to a particular place.

Extension - making a video documentary

Ask students to form groups of four or five and name a group leader. Ask them to choose one of the following topics for a documentary programme to be shown on local television (for viewers of all ages).

1. Make a video documentary of a school activity (sport/extra-curricular activity)

2. Make a documentary on your school (buildings/facilities/school subjects, etc)

3. Make a documentary on a topic of your choice

Explain that the documentary will be shown on local television and it should be a maximum of ten minutes. The documentary will be watched by people who know nothing about your school.

Remind students to think about the following:

- Who the target audience is. This helps them to decide on the content, tone, and style.

- Be careful choosing background music if you do not own the rights. Film makers have to negotiate with record companies for music used in a documentary.

- Create an outline of what is going to be included and how. Think about how they are going to make the video and write the script that goes with it. Think about how to make it original, interesting and entertaining.

If possible, show examples of similar documentaries. Allow students time to plan what they want to do and how, but set a date by which it should all be finished. Once everything is complete, students may show their videos in class. Their peers should offer constructive criticism.

A printable version of the full transcript for this unit is available on the CD.

Sky Hawk

Summary

Sky Hawk is set in a small farming village in the mountains of Scotland. In this extract, Iris (an osprey) divides her time between Scotland and Africa. Iris migrates to Africa with a tracking device and Callum, the 11-year-old narrator of the story, finds a little girl who tries to help him look after the osprey. Iris unites two children from two very different countries.

Understanding

1. This chapter begins with an email which immediately sets the personal tone. The reader is drawn into this private conversation between Callum and Jeneba. This is a dramatic opening and sets the scene for the readers as we learn that Jeneba is in hospital with a broken leg. This email conversation also tells us that we will receive regular news regarding Iris.

   The main story text is narrated by Callum and we see the world though his eyes. With the two text types, we can gather different types of information in order to build a detailed picture.

2. a. The email is vividly different to the narrative of the story. The email contains well-known features, e.g. subject, from, date, etc. The tone and language are both informal and friendly. The email is also in the first person. It contains some personal information about the sender and questions for the recipient.

      The narrative of the story contains all of the features that one would expect to find. It builds up a picture of the setting, the characters and the relationships, as we see the world through the eyes of the narrator. (This is a hook and shows the protagonist's point of view.) We are able to build an idea of the characters by looking at the language that they use, what they say, the way they behave and what they do. Callum also uses lots of adjectives to describe the photos and what he sees.

   b. This email immediately makes the reader feel close to the characters as we are reading a private conversation. It also cleverly sets the scene for the reader. It closes with 'Iris' and we soon realise that this is the main reason for their email correspondence.

      Both text types complement each other as the narrative gives us different information.

   Callum describes the photos and the world around him in great depth as though we are experiencing this all for ourselves. The reader is able to empathise with the characters by reading these two text types.

3. a. The author uses lots of descriptive words and adjectives and this enables the reader to see or imagine these settings and how different they really are.

   b. Africa is described as being very colourful and warm. In contrast, we imagine the mountains in Scotland and the loch. The author is showing us what these settings look like rather than telling us, from a first person point of view. Examples include: 'lots of small round huts and red brick buildings' 'women in brightly patterned clothes.' In contrast, Scotland has 'mountains in the background' and an 'island in the loch'.

4. The children connect through their shared interest for Iris. They are also both curious and interested to hear more about the different life styles that they both have.

5. a. The diary entry starts with the location of the bird (tracking device). The main diary entry is then in italics and in the third person.

   b. The colours are described very vividly so we can picture the scene. We can also feel what the bird is experiencing from the descriptive language and adjectives used: 'Gritty sand', 'The desert sand burned into her back'.

   c. Again, the writer pulls in information from different sources to make the reader feel as though they are experiencing this for themselves. We are able to visualise everything by piecing together all of the different bits of information.

6. Students write an ending using as many of the text types and features as possible.

Language and literacy reference

Active voice versus passive voice – Verbs are active when the subject of the sentence (the agent) does the action. Example: The shark swallowed the fish. Active verbs are used more in informal speech or writing.

Verbs are passive when the subject of the sentence has the action done to it. Example: The fish was swallowed by the shark. Passive verbs are used in more formal writing such as reports. Examples: An eye-witness was interviewed by the police. Results have been analysed by the sales team.

Sometimes turning an active sentence to passive, or vice versa, simply means moving the agent:

- The shark (agent and subject) + verb = active
- The fish (object) + verb = passive

Adjective – An adjective describes a noun or adds to its meaning. They are usually found in front of a noun. Example: Green emeralds and glittering diamonds. Adjectives can also come after a verb. Examples: It was big. They looked hungry. Sometimes you can use two adjectives together. Example: tall and handsome. This is called an adjectival phrase.

Adjectives can be used to describe degrees of intensity. To make a comparative adjective you usually add –er (or use more). Examples: quicker; more beautiful. To make a superlative you add –est (or use most). Examples: quickest; most beautiful.

Adverb – An adverb adds further meaning to a verb. Many are formed by adding -ly to an adjective. Example: slow/slowly. They often come next to the verb in a sentence. Adverbs can tell the reader: how – quickly, stupidly, amazingly; where – there, here, everywhere; when – yesterday, today, now; how often – occasionally, often.

Adverbial phrase – The part of a sentence that tells the reader when, where or how something happens is called an adverbial phrase. It is a group of words that functions as an adverb. Example: I'm going to the dentist **tomorrow morning** (when); The teacher spoke to us **as if he was in a bad mood** (how); Sam ran **all the way home** (where). These adverbials are called adverbials of time, manner and place.

Alliteration – Alliteration occurs when two or more nearby words start with the same sound. Example: A slow, sad, sorrowful song.

Antecedent – An antecedent is the person or thing to which the pronoun refers back. Example: President Alkira realised that his life was in danger. 'President Alkira' is the antecedent here.

Antonym – An antonym is a word or phrase that means the opposite of another word or phrase in the same language. Example: shut is an antonym of open. Synonyms and antonyms can be used to add variation and depth to your writing.

Audience – The readers of a text and/or the people for whom the author is writing; the term can also apply to those who watch a film or to television viewers.

Clause – A clause is a group of words that contains a subject and a verb. Example: I ran. In this clause, I is the subject and ran is the verb.

Cliché – An expression, idiom or phrase that has been repeated so often it has lost its significance.

Colloquial language – Informal, everyday speech as used in conversation; it may include slang expressions. Not appropriate in written reports, essays or exams.

Colon – A colon is a punctuation mark (:) used to indicate an example, explanation or list is being used by the writer within the sentence. Examples: You will need: a notebook, a pencil, a notepad and a ruler. I am quick at running: as fast as a cheetah.

Conjugate – To change the tense or subject of a verb.

Conditional tense – This tense is used to talk about something that might happen. Conditionals are sometimes called 'if' clauses. They can be used to talk imaginary situations or possible real-life scenarios. Examples: If it gets any colder the river will freeze. If I had a million pounds I would buy a zoo.

Conjunction – A conjunction is a word used to link clauses within a sentence such as: and, but, so, until, when, as. Example: He had a book in his hand when he stood up.

Connectives – A connective is a word or a phrase that links clauses or sentences. Connectives can be conjunctions. Example: but, when, because. Connectives can also be connecting adverbs. Example: then, therefore, finally.

Continuous tense – This tense is used to tell you that something is continuing to happen. Example: I am watching football.

Discourse markers – Words and phrases such as on the other hand, to sum up, however, and therefore are called discourse markers because they mark stages along an argument. Using them will make your paragraphs clearer and more orderly.

Exclamation – An exclamation shows someone's feelings about something. Example: What a pity!

Exclamation mark – An exclamation mark makes a phrase or a short sentence stand out. You usually use it in phrases like 'How silly I am!' and more freely in dialogue when people are speaking. Don't use it at the end of a long, factual sentence, and don't use it too often.

Idiom – An idiom is a colourful expression which has become fixed in the language. It is a phrase which has a meaning that cannot be worked out from the meanings of the words in it. Examples: 'in hot water' means 'in trouble'; It's raining cats and dogs.

Imagery – A picture in words, often using a metaphor or simile (figurative language) which describes something in detail: writers use visual, aural (auditory) or tactile imagery to convey how something looks, sounds or feels in all forms of writing, not just fiction or poetry. Imagery helps the reader to feel like they are actually there.

Irregular verb – An irregular verb does not follow the standard grammatical rules. Each has to be learned as it does not follow any pattern. For example, catch becomes caught in the past tense, not catched.

Metaphor – A metaphor is a figure of speech in which one thing is actually said to be the other. Example: This man is a lion in battle.

Non-restrictive clause – A non-restrictive clause provides additional information about a noun. They can be taken away from the sentence and it will still make sense. They are separated from the rest of the sentence by commas (or brackets). Example: The principal, who liked order, was shocked and angry.

Onomatopoeia – Words that imitate sounds, sensations or textures. Example: bang, crash, prickly, squishy.

Paragraph – A group of sentences (minimum of two, except in modern fiction) linked by a single idea or subject. Each paragraph should contain a topic sentence. Paragraphs should be planned, linked and organised to lead up to a conclusion in most forms of writing.

Parenthetical phrase – A parenthetical phrase is a phrase that has been added into a sentence which is already complete, to provide additional information. It is usually separated from other clauses using a pair of commas or a pair of brackets (parentheses). Examples: The leading goal scorer at the 2014 World Cup – James Rodriguez, playing for Columbia – scored five goals. The leading actor in the film, Hollywood great Gene Kelly, is captivating.

Passive voice – See active voice.

Person (first, second or third) – The first person is used to talk about oneself – I/we. The second person is used to address the person who is listening or reading – you. The third person is used to refer to someone else – he, she, it, they.

- I feel like I've been here for days. (first person)
- Look what you get, when you join the club. (second person)
- He says it takes real courage. (third person)

Personification – Personification can work at two levels: it can give an animal the characteristics of a human, and it can give an abstract thing the characteristics of a human or an animal. Example: I was looking Death in the face.

Prefix – A prefix is an element placed at the beginning of a word to modify its meaning. Prefixes include: dis-, un-, im-, in-, il-, ir-. Examples: impossible, inconvenient, irresponsible.

Preposition – A preposition is a word that indicates place (on, in), direction (over, beyond) or time (during, on) among others.

Pronoun – A pronoun is a word that can replace a noun, often to avoid repetition. Example: I put the book on the table. It was next to the plant. 'It' refers back to the book in first sentence.

- Subject pronouns act as the subject of the sentence: I, you, he, she, it.

- Object pronouns act as the object of the sentence: me, you, him, her, it, us, you, them.

- Possessive pronouns how that something belongs to someone: mine, yours, his, hers, its, ours, yours, theirs.

- Demonstrative pronouns refer to things: this, that, those, these.

Questions – There are different types of questions.

- Closed questions – This type of question can be answered with a single-word response, can be answered with 'yes' or 'no', can be answered by choosing from a list of possible answers and identifies a piece of specific information.

- Open questions – This type of question cannot be answered with a single-word response, it requires a more thoughtful answer than just 'yes' or 'no'.

- Leading questions – This type of question suggests what answer should be given. Example: Why are robot servants bad for humans? This suggests to the responder that robots are bad as the question is "why are they bad?" rather than "do you think they are bad?" Also called loaded questions.

- Rhetorical question – Rhetorical questions are questions that do not require an answer but serve to give the speaker an excuse to explain his/her views. Rhetorical questions should be avoided in formal writing and essays. Example: Who wouldn't want to go on holiday?

Register – The appropriate style and tone of language chosen for a specific purpose and/or audience. When speaking to your friends and family you use an informal register whereas you use a more formal tone if talking to someone older, in a position of authority or who you do not know very well. Example: I'm going to do up the new place. (informal) I am planning to decorate my new flat. (more formal)

Regular verb – A regular verb follows the rules when conjugated (e.g. by adding –ed in the past tense, such as walk which becomes walked).

Relative clause – Relative clauses are a type of subordinate clause. They describe or explain something that has just been mentioned using who, whose, which, where, whom, that, or when. Example: The girl who was standing next to the counter was carrying a small dog.

Relative pronoun – A relative pronoun does what it says – it takes an idea and relates it to a person or a thing. Be careful to use 'who' for people and 'which' for things. Example: I talked to your teacher, who told me about your unfinished homework. This is my favourite photo, which shows you the beach and the palm trees.

Restrictive clause – Restrictive clauses identify the person or thing that is being referred to and are vital to the meaning of the sentence. They are not separated from the rest of the sentence by a comma. With restrictive clauses, you can often drop the relative pronoun. Example: The letter [that] I wrote yesterday was lost.

Semi-colon – A semi-colon is a punctuation mark (;) that separates two main clauses. It is stronger than a comma but not as strong as a full stop. Each clause could form a sentence by itself. Example: I like cheese; it is delicious.

Sentence – A sentence is a group of words that expresses a complete thought. All sentences begin with a capital letter and end with a full stop, question mark or exclamation mark.

- Simple sentences are made up of one clause. Example: I am hungry.

- Complex sentence – Complex sentences are made up of one main clause and one, or more, subordinate clauses. A subordinate clause cannot stand on its own and relies on the main clause. Example: When I joined the drama club, I did not know that it was going to be so much fun.

- Compound sentence – Compound sentences are made up of two or more main clauses, usually joined by a conjunction. Example: I am hungry and I am thirsty.

Good writers use sentences of different lengths to vary the pace of their writing. Short sentences can make a strong impact while longer sentences can make text flow.

Simile – A simile is a figure of speech in which two things are compared using the linking words 'like' or 'as'. Example: In battle, he was as brave as a lion.

Simple past tense – This tense us used to tell you that something happened in the past. Only one verb is required. Example: I wore.

Simple present tense – This tense is used to tell you that something is happening now. Only one verb is required. Example: I wear.

Standard English – Standard English is the form of English used in most writing and by educated speakers. It can be spoken with any accent. There are many slight differences between Standard English and local ways of speaking. Example: 'We were robbed' is Standard English but in speech some people say, 'We was robbed.'

Suffix – A suffix is an element placed at the end of a word to modify its meaning. Suffixes include: -ible, -able, -ful, -less. Example: useful, useless, meaningful, meaningless.

Summary – A summary is a record of the main points of something you have read, seen or heard. Keep to the point and keep it short. Use your own words to make everything clear.

Synonym – A synonym is a word or phrase that means nearly the same as another word or phrase in the same language. Example: shut is a synonym of close. Synonyms and antonyms can be used to add variation and depth to your writing.

Syntax – The study of how words are organised in a sentence.

Tense – A tense is a verb form that shows whether events happen in the past, present or the future.

- The Pyramids are on the west bank of the River Nile. (present tense)
- They were built as enormous tombs. (past tense)
- They will stand for centuries to come. (future tense)

Most verbs change their spelling by adding –ed to form the past tense. Example: walk/walked. Some have irregular spellings. Example: catch/caught.

Topic sentence – The key sentence of a paragraph that contains the principal idea or subject being discussed.

Word cloud dictionary

24/7 *adverb*
Twenty-four hours a day, seven days a week; all the time.

Accept *verb*
To take a thing that is offered or presented to you; to say yes to an invitation or offer.

Account *noun*
A description or story about something that happened.

Ambush *verb*
To lie in wait for someone in order to attack them.

Ancient *adjective*
Belonging to the distant past; very old.

Apocalypse *noun*
The complete final destruction of the world, as described in the biblical book of Revelation.

Are you dissing…?
An expression that means are you speaking disrespectfully or criticising…?

Assess *verb*
To decide or estimate the value or quality of a person or thing.

Atom *noun*
The smallest particle of a chemical element.

Awful *adjective*
Very bad.

Biodiversity *noun*
The variety of plant and animal life in a particular area.

Biotechnology *noun*
The use of living micro-organisms and biological processes in industrial and commercial production.

Blow *verb*
To be moved or carried by air or the wind.

Brittle *adjective*
Hard but easy to break or snap.

Calamity *noun*
An event that causes great damage or distress.

Calcium *noun*
A chemical substance found in teeth, bones, and lime.

Carbohydrate *noun*
A compound of carbon, oxygen, and hydrogen (e.g. sugar or starch) found in food and a source of energy.

Cataclysm *noun*
A violent upheaval or disaster.

Catastrophe *noun*
A sudden great disaster.

Cavernous *adjective*
A cavernous room or space is a huge empty one.

Cereal *noun*
A grass producing seeds which are used as food, e.g. wheat, barley, or rice; a breakfast food made from these seeds.

Character *noun*
A person appearing in a story, film, or play.

Classical *adjective*
To do with ancient Greek or Roman literature or art; classical art or music is serious or conventional in style, and is often associated with the 18th century in Europe.

Cliff hanger *noun*
A tense and exciting ending to an episode of a story.

Clump *noun*
A cluster or mass of things or people.

Collide *verb*
To crash into something.

Colossal *adjective*
Extremely large; enormous.

Cool crystal blue *adjective*
Of a colour intermediate between green and violet, as of the sky or sea on a sunny day, as of frozen ice.

Concerned *adjective*
Worried or anxious about something; involved in or affected by something.

Confusedly heaped *adverb/verb*
Lying in a disorganized pile.

Conservation tillage *noun*
A method of farming that leaves the residue of the previous year's crops on fields before and after planting the next crop.

Contestant *noun*
A person taking part in a contest; a competitor.

Creative *adjective*
Showing imagination and thought as well as skill.

Crescent *noun*
A narrow curved shape coming to a point at each end.

Cultivation *noun*
The action of using land to grow crops; the process of growing or developing things by looking after them.

Debacle *noun*
A complete failure or disaster.

Deep *adjective*
Going a long way down or back or in.

Deliver *verb*
To take letters or goods to the person or place they are addressed to.

Deplete *verb*
To reduce the supply of something by using up large amounts.

Destroy *verb*
To damage something so badly that it is completely spoiled.

Diet *noun*
The sort of foods usually eaten by a person or animal; special meals that a person eats in order to be healthy or to reduce weight.

Discontented *adjective*
Noun discontent, lack of contentment; dissatisfaction.

Drapery *noun*
Cloth arranged in loose folds.

Dude *noun*
A person; a man.

Dull thud *noun*
A muffled, heavy sound, such as that made by an object falling to the ground.

Ecology *noun*
The study of living things in relation to each other and to where they live.

Elliptical *adjective*
Shaped like an ellipse.

Enduring *adjective*
Verb to endure, to suffer or put up with difficulty or pain; to continue to exist, to last.

Engage *verb*
To engage someone's interest or attention is to attract and retain their attention.

Extraordinary *adjective*
Very unusual or strange.

Fantasy *noun*
An imaginative piece of music or writing.

Fat *noun*
A white greasy substance found in animal bodies and certain seeds; oil or grease used in cooking.

Fiasco *noun*
A humiliating or embarrassing failure.

Frightening *adjective*
Verb to frighten, to make someone afraid; to become afraid; to be frightened of someone or something is to fear them.

Fringe *noun*
A decorative edging with many threads hanging down loosely.

Gallop *verb*
To go at the pace of a gallop; to run fast; to proceed at great speed.

Gateway *noun*
An opening containing a gate; a frame or arch built over a gate.

Gawk *verb*
To stare openly and stupidly.

Glance *verb*
To look at something briefly.

Glare *verb*
To stare angrily or fiercely; to shine with a bright or dazzling light.

Glassy *adjective*
Noun glass, a hard brittle substance that is usually transparent or translucent; a container for drinking from, made of glass; a mirror; a lens or optical instrument.

Grind *verb*
To crush something into tiny pieces or powder; to sharpen or smooth something by rubbing it on a rough surface.

Grip *noun*
A firm hold.

Harmony *noun*
A pleasant combination of musical notes.

Haul *verb*
To pull or drag something with great effort.

Hem *verb*
To hem someone in is to surround them and prevent them from leaving.

Herbicide *noun*
A substance for killing plants.

Hesitate *verb*
To be slow or uncertain in doing or saying something.

Hold your horses
An expression that means wait a moment.

Hollow *adjective*
Having an empty space inside, not solid.

Iconic *adjective*
Very famous or popular; widely recognized and well-established.

Imagination *noun*
The ability to imagine things; the ability to be creative or inventive.

Immediacy *noun*
The quality of bringing one into direct and instant involvement with something, giving rise to a sense of urgency or excitement.

Incredible *adjective*
Impossible to believe; extremely good.

Indecision *noun*
The inability to make decisions; hesitation.

Independent *adjective*
Not dependent on any person or thing for help, money, or support; not connected or involved with something.

Infinitesimal *adjective*
Extremely small.

Inhospitable *adjective*
Unfriendly to visitors; giving no shelter or good weather.

Insecticide *noun*
A substance for killing insects.

Insecure *adjective*
Not secure or safe; lacking confidence about yourself.

Inspiration *noun*
A sudden brilliant idea; a person or thing that fills you with ideas or enthusiasm.

Intimidate *verb*
To frighten someone with threats into doing something.

Intonation *noun*
The tone or pitch of the voice in speaking; intoning.

Kid *noun*
A child.

Layer *noun*
A single thickness or coating.

Legend *noun*
An old story handed down from the past, which may or may not be true.

Limp *verb*
To walk with difficulty because of an injury to your leg or foot.

Malevolent *adjective*
Wishing to harm people.

Multifarious *adjective*
Of many kinds, very varied.

Myth *noun*
An old story containing ideas about ancient times or about supernatural beings.

Nightmare *noun*
A frightening dream; an unpleasant experience.

Not necessarily *phrase*
(As a response) what has been said or suggested may not be true or unavoidable.

Novel *noun*
A story of fiction that fills a whole book.

Nudge *verb*
To poke a person gently with your elbow.

Nutrient *noun*
A nourishing substance.

Nutritious *adjective*
Giving good nourishment.

Oil *verb*
To put oil on something.

OK *adverb, adjective*
All right.

Old-fashioned *adjective*
Of the kind that was usual a long time ago, no longer fashionable.

Open *adjective*
Allowing access, passage, or a view through an empty space; not closed or blocked.

Opportunity *noun*
A good chance to do a particular thing.

Oval-shaped *adjective*
Having a rounded and slightly elongated outline or shape like that of an egg.

Overawe *verb*
To overcome or inhibit someone with awe.

Paralyse *verb*
To cause paralysis in a person or a part of the body; to be paralysed with fear or emotion is to be so affected by it that you cannot act.

Participate *verb*
To take part in something or have a share in it.

Perfect *verb*
To make a thing completely free from faults or defects; make as good as possible.

Perfection *noun*
A perfect state or achievement.

Perpetual *adjective*
Lasting for a long time, occurring repeatedly, continual.

Pesticide *noun*
A substance for killing harmful insects and other pests.

Pitch *noun*
The highness or lowness of a voice or a musical note.

Pitted *adjective*
Having a hollow or indentation on the surface.

Poison *noun*
A substance that can harm or kill a living thing if swallowed or absorbed into the body.

Pound *verb*
To run or go heavily.

Preen *verb*
A bird preens its feathers when it smooths them with its beak.

Prestigious *adjective*
Inspiring respect and admiration; having high status.

Primitive *adjective*
At an early stage of civilization; at an early stage of development, not complicated or sophisticated.

Prod *verb*
To poke something or someone; to stimulate someone into action.

Protein *noun*
A substance that is found in all living things and is an essential part of the food of animals.

Race *noun*
A competition to be the first to reach a particular place or to do something.

Rap sheet *noun*
A report, school file; a criminal record.

Redundant *adjective*
No longer needed or useful; superfluous.

Renowned *adjective*
Famous or celebrated.

Repertoire *noun*
A stock of songs, plays, jokes etc. that a person or company knows and can perform.

Rhythm *noun*
The regular pattern of beats or stresses in a piece of speech or music; a regularly recurring sequence of movements or events; adverb rhythmically.

Rough-work *verb*
To create a first draft of something.

Run *verb*
To move with quick steps so that both or all feet leave the ground at each stride.

Rush *verb*
To go or move quickly.

Satisfy *italic*
To give someone what they need or want.

Scant *adjective*
Barely enough or adequate.

Scatter *verb*
To throw or send things in all directions; to run or leave quickly in all directions.

Senility *noun*
The condition of being senile: weak or confused and forgetful because of old age.

Sever *verb*
To cut or break something off.

Shadow *noun*
The dark shape that falls on a surface when something is between the surface and a light; an area of shade.

Shrink *verb*
To become smaller, or to make something smaller.

Signify *verb*
To mean something.

Sitch *noun* Situation

Slack *adjective*
Not pulled or held tight, loose; not busy, not working hard.

Sleep *noun*
The condition or time of rest in which the eyes are closed, the body relaxed, and the mind unconscious.

Snow-slip *noun*
A mass of snow falling rapidly downhill.

Squirm *verb*
To wriggle about when you feel embarrassed or awkward.

Stagger *verb*
To walk unsteadily.

Still *adjective*
Not moving; not disturbed by wind or sounds.

Stout *adjective*
Thick and strong.

Strand *noun*
Each of the threads or wires twisted together to form a rope, yarn or cable.

Strap *verb*
To fasten or bind something with a strap or straps.

Strike *verb*
To hit someone or something.

Stuff *noun*
Miscellaneous things.

Sunken *adjective*
Sunk deeply into a surface.

Sustainability *noun*
Verb to sustain, to keep someone alive; to keep something happening; to undergo or suffer something harmful or unpleasant; to support or uphold something.

The price of fame *noun*
The result of being well-known.

Threat *noun*
A warning that you will punish, hurt, or harm a person or thing; a sign of something undesirable; a person or thing causing danger.

Throw *verb*
To put something in a place carelessly or hastily.

Time-honoured *adjective*
Respected or valued because it has existed for a long time.

Torrent *noun*
A rushing stream, a great flow; a heavy downpour of rain.

Totally awesome man
An expression that means really impressive you know.

Tradition *noun*
A belief or custom passed down from one generation to another.

Traumatise *verb*
To shock or distress someone in a way that produces a lasting effect on their mind.

Trudge *verb*
To walk slowly and wearily.

Unearthly *adjective*
Unnaturally strange and frightening; very awkward or inconvenient.

Unique *adjective*
Being the only one of its kind; unlike any other.

Unprecedented *adjective*
That has never happened or been done before.

Unrequited *adjective*
Unrequited love is not returned or rewarded.

Variety *noun*
A quantity of different kinds of things.

Veer *verb*
To change direction, to swerve.

Vicious *adjective*
Cruel and aggressive; severe or violent.

Vitamin *noun*
Any of a number of substances that are present in various foods and are essential to keep people and animals healthy.

Volume *noun*
The strength or power of sound produced by a radio, television, or other equipment.

Wall *noun*
Something that serves as a block or barrier.

Wither *verb*
To become dried up and shrivelled; to fade away or fall into decline.

Worse *adjective*
More bad; less good.

Wrench *verb*
To twist or pull something violently.

Yell *verb*
To give a loud cry, to shout.

Yield *verb*
To produce as a natural product or profit.